face2face

Advanced Student's Book

Gillie Cunningham, Jan Bell & Theresa Clementson
with Chris Redston

CAMBRIDGE
UNIVERSITY PRESS

Contents

VIDEO See Teacher's DVD

VIDEO See Teacher's DVD

1A Make a good impression

Vocabulary communicating
Grammar time expressions with the Past Simple and Present Perfect

Review Past Simple and Present Perfect

1 **a** Use these prompts to make questions with *you*. Use the Past Simple or Present Perfect.

1 / learn / English for a long time?
Have you been learning English for a long time?
2 How old / be / when / have / first English lesson?
3 When / be / the last time / speak / English outside class?
4 / have to / write anything in English last month?
5 / ever / read / a novel that was written in English?
6 / see / any films in English recently?
7 How long / come / this school?

b Check in GRAMMAR 1.1 p135.

c Work in pairs. Ask and answer the questions in **1a**. Ask follow-up questions.

Have you been learning English for a long time?

I first learned it at school, actually … but I forgot most of it, so I decided to do this course.

Vocabulary Communicating

2 **a** Tick the words in bold you know. Check new words/phrases in VOCABULARY 1.1 p134.

1 It's essential to **make eye contact** when you're speaking to someone.
2 On average, I **come into contact with** about 20 people a day.
3 On the whole, women **gossip** more than men.
4 In general, men **butt in** more than women, which women find very annoying.
5 If you **overhear** people **having a row** in public, you should **intervene**.
6 Politicians generally **witter on** without ever answering the interviewers' questions.
7 Elderly people have good reasons to **grumble about** the youth of today.
8 It's rude to **eavesdrop on** other people's conversations.
9 Couples who constantly **bicker** should split up.
10 Women **chat up** men as often as men chat up women.

b Tick the sentences you agree with. Change the other sentences to make them true for you.
Perhaps it's not essential to make eye contact, but it might seem rude if you don't.

c Work in pairs. Compare ideas. Do you agree with each other?

Speaking and Listening

3 **a** Think of someone (not in the class) who is popular. Why is he/she popular? Write five reasons.

b Work in pairs. Tell your partner about the person you chose. Are any of the reasons for their popularity the same?

c Agree on three important communication skills that help to make someone popular. Tell the class.

4 **a** Look at the introduction and the book cover. What did the author and his publishers initially think about the book?

How to Win Friends and Influence People, written by Dale Carnegie in 1937, has become an all-time international best seller. The first print run was limited to 5,000 copies, which was an indication of how small a readership the author and the publishers were expecting. However, from the very beginning, the book's runaway success meant the publishers had difficulty keeping up with demand.

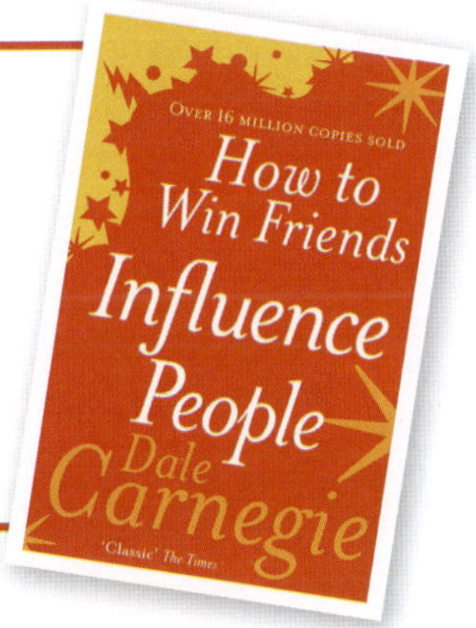

b CD1 1 Listen to Sy, Amy, Ann and Dean at their book club. Which of Carnegie's suggestions do they mention?

c Listen again. Answer these questions.

1 a Why did Ann suggest the book to the group?
  b Why wasn't she very impressed with it at first?
2 a Does Sy usually read books like this?
  b Which of Carnegie's points does he strongly agree with?
3 a Did Dean expect to enjoy the book?
  b Why does he talk about his friend, John?
4 a Which of Carnegie's suggestions did Amy try out?
  b How did the man in the ticket office react?

d Work in pairs. Which of Carnegie's suggestions do you think is the most important and why?

HELP WITH PRONUNCIATION
Attitude words/phrases

5 **a** CD1 2 Listen to three extracts from the book club conversation. Notice the intonation of the attitude words/phrases in bold and the pause that follows.

1 **Apparently**, // it's sold over 16 million copies …
(*apparently* = to say you have read or heard that something is true)

2 **Actually**, // I think people are getting fed up with me talking about it!
(*actually* = to emphasise a previous statement, and add new information)

3 **To be honest**, // it's the first time I've read a book like this …
(*to be honest* = to give an opinion, often unexpected or negative)

b Listen again and practise saying the sentences.

c Practise saying the extracts in **5a** with these words/phrases. Which can be continued with *because*? Think of a suitable ending.

Frankly Presumably In fact

d Work in pairs. Ask each other about the books you read.

Have you read any self-help books recently?

No. Actually, I've never read a self-help book in my life!

HELP WITH GRAMMAR

Time expressions with the Past Simple and Present Perfect

6 **a** Look at these sentences. Are they talking about a definite time in the past, or time up to and including now? Which verb form is used?

1 I've bought quite a few self-help books over the past few months.
2 I've read about 150 pages so far.
3 During the last couple of weeks I've actually been trying out some of Carnegie's suggestions.
4 Until now, I've never really had any contact with the guy in the ticket office.

b Underline the time expression in each sentence in **6a**.

c Sometimes we can use the Present Perfect or Past Simple with the same time expression. Compare these sentences. Why did Speaker A use the Past Simple? Why did Speaker B use the Present Perfect?

1 A I **told** at least ten people about it at work this week.
the speaker considers the working week finished
B I**'ve told** at least ten people about it at work this week.
the speaker considers the working week unfinished
2 A I **read** it during the summer holidays.
B I**'ve read** a lot of books during the last month.
3 A Since Ann **suggested** this one, I've read a couple of his other books.
B I've read lots of his books since I**'ve been** unemployed.
4 A As soon as I **finished** reading it, I gave it to my brother.
B As soon as I**'ve finished** reading it, I'm going to give it to my brother.

d Check in GRAMMAR 1.2 p135.

7 **a** Write sentences about things you have read or done recently. Use the Past Simple or Present Perfect with these time expressions.

1 as soon as
2 during
3 since
4 this week
5 over the past few weeks/months
6 so far

As soon as I finished my exams, I read Anna Karenina*.*

b Work in pairs. Discuss your sentences. Ask follow-up questions.

Reading

8 **a** Work in pairs. Give examples of what you consider to be good and bad service in shops, restaurants, etc.

b Read the article. Why do very friendly shop assistants annoy the writer?

c Read the article again. Tick the true sentences. Correct the false ones.

1 The writer was in a hurry when she went into the shop.
2 She wondered why the shop assistant's behaviour had upset her.
3 She enjoyed the food she had at the restaurant.
4 She told the waitress what she thought of the food.
5 No psychological study has the same view as hers.
6 She wouldn't object to assistants who were naturally friendly.
7 The second time she met the shop assistant, she felt the same way.
8 She was persuaded to buy something without realising it.

Fake nice

TEN DAYS AGO, on the way to a meeting, I remembered that I was running low on face cream. There was a chemist's across the road so I ran in, grabbed a jar at random and headed over to the counter.

"Having a good day?" asked the girl at the till, beaming blissfully.

"Yes thanks," I replied.

"That's great." She ran the scanner over the jar, and made purposeful eye contact.

"Been shopping all morning?"

Not having the time to take her through my diary, I made a vaguely affirmative noise.

"Yeah? Lucky you!" She told me the price and said, "So, got anything planned for this afternoon?"

"Oh, you know," I said, aware of time ticking by. "This and that. Stuff."

As I hurried on my way I found myself thinking about the girl and the **barrage of niceness** I had just experienced. Why did it make me feel so bad? Was it **churlish** not to chat back? Or was this sort of **pushy friendliness**, in its way, every bit as rude? I was reminded of this when I met a friend for lunch. I had the fishcakes. They were perfectly disgusting.

"Everything all right with your meal?" asked the waitress, interrupting our conversation with a happily expectant grin.

"Fine," I said. What else could I have said even if I'd wanted to? I didn't have time and, anyway, it might have made my friend uncomfortable.

Later, I thought about manners. As a society, we do not take manners (by which I mean how we behave towards strangers) very seriously. If you are approaching a bank or shop, the person just ahead of you is sure to let the doors swing back in your face. Middle-aged men park in disabled spaces, teenagers slump in their seats on the bus, pretending not to notice the pregnant woman standing in front of them.

Yet it's obvious on the High Street that 'fake nice', as practised by my cashier and the waitress, is on the increase. It has become a highly overused marketing weapon and you can't go into any shop without some perky person rushing up and saying, "Hi! Need any help?" You smile back through gritted teeth, "Just looking, thanks." Queuing at the supermarket is a matter of answering the cashier's "Still raining?" without betraying the fact that you heard them ask someone else this very question two minutes earlier. Call me miserable, but I'm not stupid. I know what these people want. They don't want to be my friend. They want my money.

Apparently, research has shown that if an assistant treats you as a friend, there's a psychological effect: the customer feels wanted and needed, and will return. Or will they? Other studies suggest that this sales technique is a turn-off. Perhaps the solution is to appoint people who are genuinely interested in people, not those who are trained to be insincere robots.

Recently, I found myself back at the chemist's where it all started. I have to get a present for a friend, and in any case, I'm interested to see whether Scary Friendly Girl is there. Ah, yes she is, at the till, giving it lots of oomph and sparkle. I select some almond hand cream and put it on the counter in front of her. She looks up and beams at me. I submit to the overwhelming power of her spurious affection. I'm not in a hurry this time and the experience is not unpleasant.

When I get home, I check my receipt. There's one item that doesn't ring any bells. I go through the carrier bag and find nothing to explain it, so I pick up the phone and call the chemist's. I'm told that I purchased something called a 'Take Care of Your Skin' card that entitles me to all sorts of extra perks and beautifying treats. However, no one asked me if I wanted to buy it. "Are you absolutely sure?" the manager asks.

I think about it. I remember the soporific feeling of being buried under a soft wave of niceness. I recall zoning out a little. No, actually, I'm not sure, after all.

9 **a** Look at the words/phrases in blue in the article. Who are they referring to?

b Try to guess the meaning of the words/phrases in blue. What do they suggest about the writer's attitude?

10 Work in pairs. Look at the short conversations in the article and answer these questions.

1 What words are missing from the questions?
2 What types of word can we miss out in informal written and spoken English?

11 Work in groups and discuss these questions.

1 How would you have responded to the shop assistant and the waitress? Why?
2 How would you describe the service in shops and cafés in your country? Has it changed over the years?

Get ready ... Get it right!

12 Choose three topics you would like to talk about.

- films/TV/music
- sport
- clothes
- pets
- work/studies
- other

13 **a** Work in pairs. Look at your partner's topics and write six questions about them.

How many films have you seen during the last six months?

b Take turns to ask and answer the questions. Tell the class something about your partner.

Actually, Lisa hasn't watched any films recently because she hasn't had time.

1B Friends – the new family?

Vocabulary prepositions and phrases
Grammar cleft sentences: *what* and *it* clauses

QUICK REVIEW Time expressions
Write three sentences about yourself using: *so far*; *this week*; *during the last few days*; *up until now*; *as soon as*; *in the past few months*. Two sentences should be true and one should be false. Work in pairs and say your sentences. Guess which of your partner's sentences is false.

Speaking and Listening

1 Check the meaning of the phrases in bold below. Then work in pairs and discuss the questions.

1 As a rule, do you tend to **unburden yourself** to friends or to members of your family?
2 By and large, is it men or women who find it easier to **unload** their worries **on to** other people?
3 Broadly speaking, do adults in your country **bottle up** their feelings or let them out?
4 Do you think, in the main, that teenagers would rather **confide in** their parents or their friends?

TIP • The underlined expressions are used to make generalisations.

2 **a** Work in pairs. Who would you expect men, women and teenagers like the ones in the photos to confide in?

- their friends
- both friends and family
- someone else
- no one

b CD1 3 Listen and check.

c Listen again. Tick the true sentences. Correct the false ones.

1 Dave and his friends tend to talk about only serious issues.
2 Dave thinks men make friends with people who enjoy the same things.
3 Helen sees her friends every day.
4 Helen's friends are very patient with her.
5 Andrea trusts her hairdresser to be discreet.
6 Andrea enjoys listening to her hairdresser's problems.
7 Most of Alex's conversations are about everyday events.
8 Alex confides in people of his own age.

d Work in pairs and discuss these questions.

1 Which things that the speakers talked about do you identify with?
2 Do you think people confide in each other about different things at different ages?

HELP WITH GRAMMAR
Cleft sentences: *what* and *it* clauses

Cleft sentences divide a message into two parts, using *what* or *it* clauses. They can focus attention on new, more important or contradictory information.

(I can get a bit stressed by work.) ***What*** *I do if I get stressed* ***is*** *talk to my friends.* (new information)

(I get on well with my parents.) However, ***it's*** *my friends* ***that*** *I talk to if I have a problem.* (contradiction)

WHAT CLAUSES

3 **a** We use *what* clauses to emphasise the new information in a conversation. Look at these examples and answer the questions.

What we talk about	*isn't*	*deep and meaningful, though.*
What I do if I get stressed	*is*	*talk to my friends.*
What happens	*is*	*we bottle things up.*

1 Which words give new information in the sentences?
2 What is the main verb in each sentence?
3 What is the subject of the main verb?

TIPS • When we use *who*, *why*, *whose*, *when*, *where*, etc. instead of *what*, we usually use an expression such as *a person*, *the reason*, etc., with or without the *wh-* word.
A person (who) I tend to confide in is my hairdresser.
• To give a reason, we can follow *be* with *to* + infinitive.
The reason (why) Lucy came early was to help me out.

IT CLAUSES

b Look at these cleft sentences with *it*. Answer the questions.

- *It'd probably be my parents who I'd talk to first.*
- *It wasn't until he broke up with his girlfriend that my hairdresser started to confide in me.*

1 Does the speaker emphasise the information in the *it* clause or in the *who/that* clause?
2 What verb follows *it*?

c Check in GRAMMAR 1.3 p136.

4 **a** Complete these sentences about yourself.

1 What I do if I get stressed is …
2 The reason I'm here is …
3 It wasn't until …
4 A person I tend to confide in …
5 What amuses me …
6 A place I really love …

b Work in groups. Say your sentences. Ask follow-up questions.

IS TRUE FRIENDSHIP A THING OF THE PAST?

To anyone paying attention these days, it's clear that social media — the modern-day water coolers — are changing the way we live.

Indeed, we might feel as if we are suddenly awash with friends. Yet right before our eyes, we're also changing the way we conduct relationships. Face-to-face chat is giving way to texts and messaging; people even prefer these electronic exchanges to, for instance, simply talking on a phone. It appears that, increasingly, we prefer to keep people at arm's length. Smaller circles of friends are being partially eclipsed by social-networking acquaintances routinely numbered in the hundreds. Amid these smaller trends, growing research suggests we could be entering a period of crisis for the entire concept of friendship. Where is all this leading our society? Perhaps to a dark place, one where electronic stimuli slowly replace the joys of human contact.

A recent report notes that one in three British people would like to live closer to their families, though social trends are forcing them to live farther apart. Typically, the pressures of urban life are blamed: in London, a poll had two-fifths of respondents reporting that they face a prevailing drift away from their closest friends. Witness crowded bars and restaurants after work: we have plenty of acquaintances, though perhaps few individuals we can turn to and share deep intimacies with. American sociologists have tracked related trends on a broader scale, well beyond the urban jungle. According to work published in the *American Sociological Review*, an American has only two close friends on average, and a quarter don't have any.

It should be noted that other social scientists contest these conclusions. Hua Wang and Barry Wellman, of the universities of Southern California and Toronto respectively, refer to "some panic in the United States about a possible decline in social connectivity". But notice their language: "social connectivity". That is not the same as intimate friendship. While social-networking sites have grown exponentially, the element that is crucial, and harder to investigate, is the quality of the connections they nurture.

Yet we know that less is more when it comes to deeper relationships. It is lonely in the crowd. A connection may only be a click away, but cultivating a good friendship takes more. It is simply not that easy to find people with whom we are on the same wavelength. It seems common sense to conclude that 'friending' online nurtures shallow relationships – as the neologism 'friending' itself implies.

No single factor or person is at fault, of course. The pressures on friendship today are broad. They arise from the demands of work, say, or a general busyness that means we have less quality time for others. But it is 'fallow' time which is vital for deeper friendships. It is when we are at a loose end that we simply 'hang out', with no tasks, no deadlines and no pressures. It is in those moments that people get to know others for who they really are.

Close friends, Aristotle observed, "share salt together". It's not just that they sit together, passing the salt across a meal table. It's that they sit with one another across the course of their lives, sharing its savour – its moments, bitter and sweet. "The desire for friendship comes quickly; friendship does not," Aristotle also remarked. It's a key insight for an age of instant social connectivity, an age in which we paradoxically have an apparently growing need to be more deeply connected.

Reading and Vocabulary

5 Work in groups. Discuss these questions.

1 Do you think the quality of friendship has changed in recent years? If so, can you think of some reasons for this change?

2 Which of these ideas do you agree with? Give reasons.

- a People are not able to communicate as well as they used to.
- b People know more people but have fewer real friends than they used to.
- c Social media are responsible for the decline in close friendships.

6 **a** Read the title and introduction of the article. Which of the ideas mentioned a–c in **5** do you think the writer is making?

b Read the whole article to check your ideas. Has your answer changed?

c What does the writer think about these topics?

1 face-to-face contact
2 social connectivity
3 friending
4 the pressures on friendship today
5 sharing salt together

d Work in pairs. Use your own words to compare your answers to **6c**. Which of the opinions in the article do you agree or disagree with? Give reasons.

HELP WITH VOCABULARY
Prepositions and phrases

TIP • Make a note of words/phrases together with their prepositions and try to learn them as 'chunks' of meaning.

7 **a** Look at the phrases from the article in the word map below. Match them to definitions 1–6.

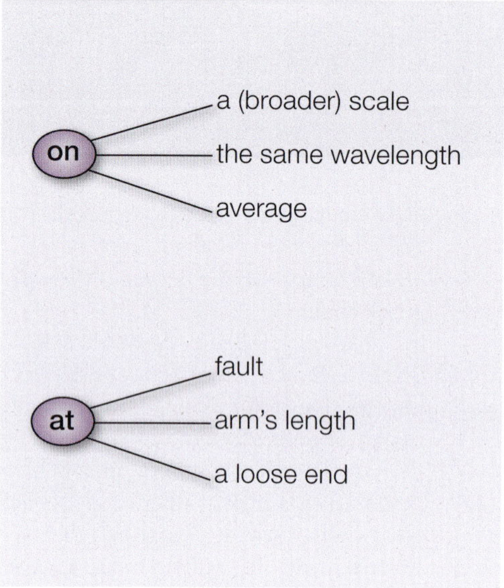

1 responsible for a problem
2 with similar views/opinions
3 with nothing to do
4 typically
5 a distance
6 relating to the size or level of something

b Match these words/phrases with the prepositions in the word map.

purpose	glance	times	good terms
a regular basis	hand	demand	
the increase	random	short notice	

c Work in pairs. What do you think the prepositions and phrases in **7b** mean?

d Check in VOCABULARY 1.2 p134.

8 **a** Complete these sentences with a preposition.

1 Who do you meet __________ a regular basis?
2 How often do you cancel arrangements __________ short notice?
3 Are you __________ good terms with your colleagues?
4 What do you do when you're __________ a loose end?
5 How much can you usually find out about someone __________ a glance?
6 Have you ever broken something __________ purpose?
7 What social phenomena are __________ the increase in your country?
8 Do you always have your phone __________ hand?

b Work in pairs. Ask and answer the questions in **8a**. Ask follow-up questions.

Get ready ... Get it right!

9 Tick the sentences you agree with. Change the other sentences to make them true for you. Then complete sentences 7 and 8 with your own ideas.

1 It's social networking that is changing the nature of society today.
2 What you're looking for in a friend is someone who is on the same wavelength.
3 Friends are people who will always stick up for you, whatever happens.
4 You can't really be 'just friends' with someone of the opposite sex.
5 A real friend is someone who will tell you the truth even if it's something you don't want to hear.
6 Women form closer friendships than men.
7 It ...
8 What ...

10 **a** Work in groups. Discuss what you have written and give reasons.

b Tell the class three things that you agreed on.

We agreed that what we tend to look for in a friend is someone who is loyal and ...

1 Writing

Spelling homophones
Connecting words addition
Writing task an online profile; sharing personal information

1 Work in pairs and discuss these questions.

1 Are blogs a good way to share information?
2 What information would/do you provide in a blog?

2 Work in pairs. A new group of students studying abroad are sharing information on a blog. Read the blog profile. Ignore any mistakes for now. Then cover it and try to remember seven things about Kanokchon.

3 **a** Fill in the gaps with these connecting words/phrases. Sometimes there is more than one possible answer. WRITING 1.1 p136.

also	as well	what's more
besides	too	not only

1 She's been running the company since November. She's got three children to look after, ________ .
2 Chinese food is very tasty. It's quite cheap ________ .
3 The traffic is really heavy at this time of day. The roads are ________ extremely icy, so be careful.
4 The village is ________ remote, but totally inaccessible by road.
5 I haven't got any change on me. ________ , you already owe me money from last time.
6 The problem we were set was extremely difficult to solve. ________ , we didn't have much time to do it.

b Look at the blog again. Correct the underlined mistakes using the same connecting words of addition. There is more than one possible answer.

4 **a** Choose the correct spelling. WRITING 1.2 p136.

1 I think it's her brother *whose/who's* the difficult one in that family.
2 I'm not entirely convinced *there/they're* up for the challenge, are you?
3 He might *of/'ve* forgotten my mobile number.
4 It's not unusual for you to forget *you're/your* own telephone number!
5 We must make sure that they check in *they're/their* luggage on time.

b Find and correct five common spelling mistakes in the blog profile.

BLOG POST

KANOKCHON WRITES …

I'm from Bangkok in Thailand but I'm here for a year doing my Master's degree in Business. I'm finding it quite hard, to be honest. It's <u>besides</u> the business course that's difficult, but also the language. <u>As well</u>, I really miss seeing all my friends and family, but it's Sathimanee, whose my girlfriend, that I miss the most. We've been together for years, but I keep worrying that she might of met someone else!

On the other hand, they're lots of things that I'm really enjoying. Yesterday, I saw snow for the first time, which was absolutely amazing! I went ice skating for the first time <u>what's more</u>. I fell over constantly and got extremely wet (and nearly froze to death), but I'm definitely going again so I can learn to ice skate properly. <u>Also</u> learning to do new things, I'm enjoying the social life. Their really are people here from all over the world! Tonight, my friend Ahmed is cooking Saudi food for a group of us. Next week it will be my turn! Do get in touch if you want to share you're cooking skills!

3 COMMENTS

5 **a** You decide to create a blog to share information with other students. Make notes for your profile.

b Work in pairs and compare your notes. Should you add or delete any information?

c Choose one or two points you want to emphasise. Use cleft sentences with *what* and *it*.

6 **a** Write your profile.

b Check your writing for the correct use of these features.

- spelling
- connecting words
- cleft sentences

7 **a** Read other students' profiles. Write some questions about any interesting information you find.

b Ask and answer your questions to find out more information.

For more Writing practice: Portfolio 1, Workbook p54.

Favourite sayings

Vocabulary sayings; idioms
Real World explaining and paraphrasing

QUICK REVIEW Prepositions and phrases
Think of three phrases which use *at* and *on*. Work in pairs. Take turns to say one of your phrases but don't say the preposition. Your partner says the phrase with the correct preposition: **A** ... *arm's length* **B** *at arm's length*.

1 **a** Match the first half of sayings 1–8 to endings a–h.

1 Rome wasn't	a before mouth.
2 Don't make a mountain	b built in a day.
3 Once bitten,	c nothing gained.
4 Actions speak	d louder than words.
5 One man's meat	e is another man's poison.
6 Engage brain	f out of a molehill.
7 Nothing ventured,	g than never.
8 Better late	h twice shy.

b Work in pairs. Compare answers. What do the sayings mean? Check in VOCABULARY 1.3 ▸ p134.

c Choose a saying from your country. How can you explain what it means in English?

2 **a** CD1 ▸ 4 Listen to five people talking about sayings that they like. Put the sayings in pictures A–E in the order they are talked about.

b Work in pairs. Match the sayings to these meanings.

1 You shouldn't worry about things that might or might not happen in the future.
2 It's important to choose the right person for the right activity.
3 It's pointless doing something yourself if you know someone who can do it for you.
4 If you mix with a bad crowd, you'll be judged the same way as the crowd.
5 If you don't offer people enough money to do a job, you won't get the best person.

c Listen again. Check your answers.

d Work in pairs. Which of the sayings in **1a** and **2a** do you like best and why? Tell the class.

A

Horses for courses.

B

Why have a dog and bark yourself?

C

If you pay peanuts, you get monkeys.

D

If you fly with the crows, you get shot with the crows.

E

Let's cross that bridge when we come to it.

REAL WORLD Explaining and paraphrasing

3 **a** Complete these phrases with *what* or *which*.

1 __________ simply/just/basically means …
2 And __________ it/this/that means is …
3 __________ I mean by that is …
4 By __________ I mean …
5 __________ I'm trying to say is …
6 __________ is to say …

b Complete these phrases.

that simply other way

1 To put it __________ , …
2 __________ is to say, …
3 Or to put it another __________ , …
4 In __________ words, …

c Check in **REAL WORLD 1.1** **p136**.

4 **a** Complete sentence beginnings 1–6 with one or two words. Then match them with endings a–f.

1 __________ I'm trying to say is we should
2 She's quite a closed person. What I mean __________ that is you can never tell
3 There are roadworks on the way, __________ basically means
4 This is a difficult situation, by __________ I mean we need
5 We urgently need to reduce our costs. In other __________ ,
6 It's a hard-drive back-up system, or to put it __________ ,

a what she's thinking.
b you have to allow an extra hour for the journey.
c it ensures that you won't lose what's on your computer.
d cross that bridge when we come to it.
e to think about it more carefully.
f we have to make some people redundant.

b Work in pairs. Take turns to say a complete sentence from **4a**. Do you have the same answers?

5 **a** **CD1 5** You are going to play a game called *Bluff*. Listen to two teams taking part in the game. Then answer the questions.

1 What is the game about?
2 What does each person on the first team have to do?
3 What does the second team have to do?

b Work in pairs. Which do you think is the real definition of the Australian expression 'She'll be apples'?

c **CD1 6** Listen and check.

6 Work in two groups. Group A, try to guess the meaning of idioms 1–3. Group B, try to guess the meaning of idioms a–c.

Group A
1 rave about something
2 hit the roof
3 call it a day

Group B
a be up for something
b talk shop
c lose your bottle

7 Group A p105. Group B p108.

She'll be apples

continue2learn

Vocabulary, Grammar and Real World
- **Extra Practice and Progress Portfolio 1** p114
- **Video (*Let's talk*)** p124
- **Language Summary 1** p134
- **Workbook 1** p4

Reading and Writing
- **Portfolio 1** Topic sentences Workbook p54
  Reading an article about a modern problem
  Writing topic and supporting sentences

2A Exceptional people

Vocabulary intensifying adverbs
Grammar relative clauses with prepositions

QUICK REVIEW Sayings
Work in pairs. Give the beginning of four English sayings. Your partner completes and explains them. **A** *We'll cross that bridge …* **B** *We'll cross that bridge when we come to it. What this means is … .*

Reading

1 **a** Look at the book cover and the definition of *savant*. What do you think Daniel Tammet's unusual abilities are?

b Read the article. Name two things Daniel can do exceptionally well and two things he finds difficult.

c Read the article again and choose the best ending for these sentences.

1 Daniel didn't speak much as a child because he …
 a was shy.
 b was more interested in the numbers in his head.
 c found it difficult to learn to talk.
2 Daniel finds mental arithmetic easy because he …
 a enjoys working out the answers.
 b doesn't have to write anything down.
 c can see the answers in his head.
3 Regarding savants, scientists are not able to tell us …
 a the reasons for their skills.
 b the type of skills they often have.
 c how many savants exist.
4 Daniel is unusual for a savant because …
 a he has a range of abilities.
 b his abilities are exceptional.
 c he can offer insights into his abilities.
5 Working independently is important for Daniel because …
 a flexibility is a priority for him.
 b it enables him to do things in his own way.
 c he prefers working directly with his clients.
6 Nowadays, Daniel finds it …
 a easier to appreciate his individuality.
 b harder to deal with painful experiences.
 c harder to cope with life's ups and downs.

d Work in pairs. Discuss these questions.

1 Why do you think Daniel finds *Pi* as beautiful as the Mona Lisa or a Mozart symphony?
2 Daniel says: "I would have traded everything for normality. But I've since learned that being different isn't necessarily a bad thing." Why do you think his attitude has changed?
3 Which do you think is more important in life: academic brilliance or emotional intelligence? Give reasons.

A GENIUS EXPLAINS

Daniel Tammet is an autistic* savant with an extraordinary gift for numbers and languages. Unlike other savants, Daniel has described how he does it in a book, *Born on a Blue Day*, in which he writes about his life.

"I've got a quiet voice," he says, in his gentle monotone. "I think it's because as a child I didn't speak very much. It was hard for me to find my voice, because I was absorbed in my own world." Daniel's world is a rich and strange one, in which every number up to 10,000 has colour, texture and emotional resonance. "The number one is a brilliant, bright white, like somebody shining a torch in my eyes … Four is shy and quiet, like me. Eighty-nine is like falling snow."

Daniel's condition allows him to achieve extraordinary mathematical feats, all of which he finds simple; he holds the European record for recalling Pi – the mathematical constant – to the furthest decimal place. It took him five hours and nine minutes.

"Pi is for me an extremely beautiful thing," he says, "like the Mona Lisa or a Mozart symphony." For Daniel, mental arithmetic is a gorgeous kaleidoscopic process. "When I divide one number by another, say, 13 divided by 97, I see a spiral rotating downwards in larger and larger loops that seem to warp and curve. The shapes coalesce into the right number. I never write anything down."

Savants constitute less than 1% of the population, and about 10% of the autistic population, yet their abilities are shrouded in mystery. Savant skills tend to occur in five areas: music, art, calendar calculating, mathematics and mechanical or spatial skills (for instance, the capacity to measure distances without instruments). Generally, a single special skill exists but, in some instances, multiple skills can occur. One skill for which all savants are known is an extraordinary memory.

savant /ˈsævənt/ someone who has unusual, often exceptional, abilities or knowledge

Daniel Tammet

While many savants have a restricted vocabulary and are not able to explain their abilities, this is clearly not the case with Daniel. Not only can he describe how his mind works, but he can also speak ten languages, including Lithuanian and Welsh. He is even creating his own language: Mänti, meaning a type of tree.

However, Daniel's condition also has its limitations. "I had to teach myself to look into people's eyes," he explains. "Before that, I used to look at their mouth, because it was the part of their face that was moving." He would find it impossible to fit a 9–5 job around his daily tasks, all of which he does in the same order every day. For instance, he drinks his five cups of tea at exactly the same time each day and feels upset and anxious if his routine is interrupted. In order for work to fit in with his particular needs, he set up his own business, writing internet courses for private clients in language learning, numeracy and literacy, which he does at home. This has the advantage of being in his control and allowing him to work autonomously.

Daniel's condition was not diagnosed until he was 25. Growing up as an undiagnosed savant was not easy and he was often lonely. It was difficult being at school surrounded by children, none of whom understood his condition. "I was desperate for a friend. My brothers and sisters had friends and I used to watch them playing, to try to work out what they did and how friendship worked. I would have traded everything for normality. But I've since learned that being different isn't necessarily a bad thing."

Daniel feels he is progressing towards 'outgrowing' his autism. He cried for the first time in his adult life a few years ago, when his cat died. He is getting better at social interaction.

"Every experience I have I add to my mental library, and hopefully life should then get easier." In this, he seems to sum up the progress we all hope for.

**autistic* = having a mental condition that makes people unable to communicate well

HELP WITH GRAMMAR
Relative clauses with prepositions

2 **a** Match the sentences to these styles of English.

- more formal, usually written English
- less formal, usually spoken English

1 a Daniel has described how he does it in a book **in which** he writes about his life.
  b Daniel has described how he does it in a book **that** he writes about his life **in**.

2 a One skill **for which** all savants are known is an extraordinary memory.
  b One skill **that** all savants are known **for** is an extraordinary memory.

b Complete these rules.

In more formal, usually written English …

1 *that* changes to ______ after a preposition.
2 the preposition comes ______ the relative pronoun.

c Look at the phrases in bold in sentences a and b and answer the questions.

a *Daniel's condition allows him to achieve extraordinary mathematical feats,* ***all of which*** *he finds simple.*

b *It was difficult being at school, surrounded by children,* ***none of whom*** *understood his condition.*

1 What does *who* change to when it comes after a preposition?
2 Which ideas do the phrases in bold refer to?
3 Which phrase in bold is the subject of the clause that follows?
4 Which phrase in bold is the object of the clause that follows?
5 What additional determiners (*all*, *none*, etc.) can combine with *of which* or *of whom* in non-defining relative clauses?

TIP • When we are speaking informally, we can use *none of them*, *all of them*, etc. Notice the change in word order.

He would find it impossible to fit a 9–5 job around his daily tasks. ***He does all of them*** *in the same order every day.*

He would find it impossible to fit a 9–5 job around his daily tasks, ***all of which he does*** *in the same order every day.*

d Check in GRAMMAR 2.1 p138.

3 **a** Complete each gap in the article with a preposition, and *which* or *whom*.

b Work in pairs. Change the gapped sentences to a more informal spoken style.

KIM PEEK, who died in 2009, was known as a 'megasavant' due to his exceptional memory. At the age of four, although no school would accept him, he sought out encyclopaedias, atlases and telephone directories, all [1] ______ he memorised. As a result of his motor deficiencies, Kim was looked after by his father, [2] ______ he totally depended. It was Kim's life [3] ______ the Oscar-winning film, *Rain Man*, was based. Following the film's success, Kim was invited to take part in public appearances. On some of these occasions, screenwriter Barry Morrow, [4] ______ Kim had collaborated, gave him the Oscar statuette to carry. These appearances increased Kim's self-confidence. He thoroughly enjoyed meeting people and had a marked sense of humour. He also loved showing strangers his remarkable ability for calendar calculations, by telling them [5] ______ day of the week they were born.

Listening

4 **a** Look at the photo of Tommy McHugh, a builder who became a painter. What do you think of his work?

b CD1 7 Listen to the radio programme. Why did Tommy become a painter?

c Listen again and complete these sentences.

1 Tommy hadn't done any painting at all until he reached his ______ .
2 He compares his mind to a ______ , which generates bubbles full of creative ideas.
3 After hospital, Tommy and his wife received no ______ .
4 Tommy's life changed when Marion Kalmus told him that he was an ______ .
5 Changes to the temporal lobe increase people's ______ .
6 As well as painting, many people with Tommy's condition tend to ______ a lot.
7 Being very productive can result in work of variable ______ .
8 Although Tommy's lifespan is uncertain, he regards his life as an ______ .

5 **a** Work in pairs. Try to summarise Tommy's story.

b Discuss these questions.

1 Do you think what happened to Tommy was good or bad?
2 How do you think Tommy feels? What about his ex-wife?

HELP WITH PRONUNCIATION
Speech units

6 **a** CD1 8 Listen and notice how the presenter organises what he is saying into speech units. The speech units are marked with //.

The transformation in Tommy has been quite // remarkable. // So // what happened six years ago // to bring it about? // The extraordinary answer // is // a brain haemorrhage. // One day Tommy was in the bathroom // when he remembers something // popping in his head.

TIP • Speech units help us to organise what we say by dividing it into groups of words. Speech units can vary in length in order to emphasise particular words.
// popping in his head //

b Listen again and practise.

c Work in pairs. How do you think the extract below can be organised into speech units? (There are many possible answers.)

A few days later, he was sent home with a bag full of tablets. I didn't know what to do – he couldn't walk, or feed himself, or do anything really. Sometimes he didn't even know where he was. It was awful. He was totally frustrated, angry, and in pain.

d CD1 9 Listen to Jan. Practise saying the extract in **6c**, paying attention to speech units.

Vocabulary Intensifying adverbs

7 **a** Which adverb does not go with these adjectives or verbs? Check in VOCABULARY 2.1 p137.

1 I ~~*utterly*~~*/thoroughly/really* enjoy …
2 I'd be *deeply/strongly/totally* frustrated if …
3 It's *highly/completely/extremely* (un)likely that …
4 I *strongly/firmly/highly* believe that …
5 I *bitterly/deeply/perfectly* regret …
6 I was *bitterly/utterly/extremely* disappointed when …
7 I *completely/entirely/highly* agree …
8 I *vividly/distinctly/perfectly* remember …

b Use five of the adverbs and adjectives/verbs to make true or false sentences about you. Think about how to organise your sentences into speech units.

c Work in pairs. Take turns to say your sentences. Guess which of your partner's sentences are false.

Get ready … Get it right!

8 Think of someone who should win an award for being exceptional (someone famous or someone you know). Write five reasons.

9 **a** Work in groups. Take turns to tell each other about the person you chose.

I firmly believe my cousin Julia should win the award. She was ill for a while and made redundant, neither of which put her off starting her own business.

b Vote for the person you think should win the award. Then tell the class.

2B Memorable places

Vocabulary adjective word order
Grammar participle clauses

QUICK REVIEW Relative clauses with prepositions; intensifying adverbs Think of two famous places you have visited. Prepare to describe them. Work in pairs. Your partner tries to guess the place you're describing. **A** *I thoroughly enjoyed visiting this Spanish city, in which you can find Gaudí's famous cathedral.* **B** *Is it Barcelona?*

Speaking and Reading

1 Work in pairs. Which three reasons are most important to you when choosing a holiday, and why?

- the climate
- the tourist facilities
- the landscape
- the local culture
- the accommodation
- the cost of the holiday
- the nightlife

2 **a** Look at the photo of Kerala on p21. What do you think the writer loved about this place?

b Read the article on p21 and check your ideas.

c Read the article again. Answer these questions.

1 Why did the writer choose January to visit Kerala?
2 What did the writer find surprising about Kerala?
3 What does the writer predict will happen to Kerala soon?
4 Which is the best way to travel if you want to see the 'real' Kerala?
5 What is unusual about the way people fish in Cochin?
6 Why are some famous people attracted to Kerala?

d Work in pairs. In which place, if any, have you 'lost your heart'? What made it so wonderful? How would you spend a perfect day there?

HELP WITH GRAMMAR Participle clauses

- Participle clauses can be used to give more information about things, events or ideas in a sentence. They are often used to make a piece of writing more varied and sophisticated.

3 **a** Look at participle clauses 1–5 in the article. Which ones use the forms below?

- a present participle
- a past participle
- a perfect participle

b Compare examples a–e below with clauses 1–5 in the article. What changes occur when we use participle clauses?

a … **so** they act as a vital means of communication between remote villages and crowded towns.
b **While** you glide silently along in a canoe, you get to see a rural Kerala preserved through the ages.
c **Because** it's caught locally every day, it's always wonderfully fresh.
d **After** I'd had an indulgent lunch, I'd lie in a hammock.
e **If** it's poured very slowly across your forehead, the oil feels like a cow is licking you.

TIP • When we use *not* in a participle clause, it usually comes before the participle.

Not knowing much about Kerala, we bought a guidebook.
not ~~*Knowing not*~~ *much about Kerala, …*

c Match the words in bold in a–e in **3b** to meanings 1–4.

1 cause
2 result
3 condition
4 time

d Complete the rule.

Past participles are used in *passive/active* clauses, and present participles are used in *passive/active* clauses.

e Check in GRAMMAR 2.2 p139.

4 Rewrite these sentences, starting with a participle clause.

1 Because I didn't know my way round Kerala, I headed straight for the Tourist Information office.
2 The rain was very heavy at that time of year, so it caused flooding everywhere.
3 If it is visited out of season, Kerala is not full of tourists.
4 As we drove through the Periyar Wildlife Sanctuary, I was lucky enough to spot wild elephants.
5 After walking in the Wildlife Sanctuary, I took a boat trip on Periyar Lake.
6 After I'd had breakfast, I went swimming in the lake.

5 **a** Think of an interesting experience you have had. Write a short paragraph, using participle clauses, to describe the ideas, events and things that happened.

b Work in groups. Read about each other's experiences and ask questions to find out more.

I lost my heart in ... KERALA

WHY?

It's incredibly beautiful and hypnotic, with lush vegetation, white beaches and vividly green countryside. Entire communities live along the canals and lagoons, which stretch over 1,900 km, [1]**acting as a vital means of communication** between remote villages and crowded towns. In order to avoid the monsoon season, I went in January. At that time of year, the weather is great and you are normally guaranteed warm days and cooler, comfortable nights.

I didn't expect to find it still so unspoilt, given that it's relatively close to Goa. People don't seem to have worked out yet that Kerala is a lot nicer and much less touristy. So you feel as if you're discovering somewhere entirely new, like you're on a totally different planet. However, since it's been nominated one of National Geographic's '50 must-see destinations of a lifetime', it's only a matter of time before all this now changes.

WHAT SHOULDN'T I MISS?

Take a trip along the backwaters. [2]**Gliding silently along in a canoe**, you get to see a rural Kerala preserved through the ages and completely hidden from the road. You'll pass locals doing their laundry in the river, schoolteachers taking classes on the banks and so on, which is an enchanting experience. Make sure you take a camera.

A stopover in the fascinating capital, Cochin, is also a must. A cluster of islands surrounded by a network of rivers and lakes, Cochin is home to a unique culture. There's extraordinary fishing on the coast there; people hang from their boats into the water and pick up fish with their teeth, before chucking them into enormous nets. In the evenings, go to a restaurant and try the wide variety of fish Kerala is so famous for. [3]**Caught locally every day**, it's always wonderfully fresh.

A PERFECT DAY

I would probably wake up around 10 a.m. and tuck into a delicious Indian breakfast of pancakes with lots of curry powder. Then I'd take to the backwaters for three or four hours. Later on, [4]**having had an indulgent lunch**, I'd lie in a hammock, sipping fresh coconut milk through a straw and reading a good book. I might follow in the footsteps of the Hollywood stars, who come to Kerala in search of Ayurveda, the natural Indian healthcare which dates back more than 3,000 years. The treatments use herbal oils made from the exotic spices that are so plentiful here. [5]**Poured very slowly across your forehead**, the oil feels like a cow is licking you; this may sound revolting but is actually very enjoyable and is supposed to be good for people suffering from the stresses and strains of modern life.

After supper, totally relaxed, I'd head for bed, not forgetting to put on an eye mask in order to avoid seeing any of the local spiders!

Listening

6 **a** CD1 10 CD1 11 Look at the photos and captions. Listen to two conversations. Did Bruce and Melissa enjoy their holidays?

b CD1 10 Listen to Bruce again. Answer these questions about his comments.

1 "**They** were quite grey." (What were? Give more information.)
2 "**It**'s brilliant for **that**." (What is *it*? What is it brilliant for?)
3 "**They**'re great." (What are *they*? What do they do?)
4 "You can walk right up to **them**." (Up to what? Why can you do this?)

c Look at these words/phrases Melissa uses. Which describe her expectations and which describe her actual experiences?

1 a beautiful lodge
2 driving, pounding rain
3 a log cabin
4 a sandy beach
5 gravel
6 a very small dinghy
7 choppy seas

d CD1 11 Listen to Melissa again and check. Add details about her actual experiences.

e Which of these places would you prefer to go to? Why?

HELP WITH VOCABULARY Adjective word order

- When describing a noun, there is an order that adjectives usually follow. Notice that opinions come before facts, the general before the specific.

opinion	size	age	colour	origin	material	
beautiful			white		sandy	beaches
stark		modern			log*	cabins
	massive	100-year-old				tortoises
charming				rustic	stone*	cottages

*These are nouns used as adjectives.

7 **a** Look at these adjectives in bold. Do they describe opinion, size, age, colour, origin or material?

1 **breath-taking high snow-capped** peaks
2 **delicious Thai fish and coconut** curries
3 **extravagant white marble** buildings
4 **picture-book medieval Italian** villages

b Look at these examples. When speaking, we try not to put too many adjectives in front of the noun. How do we avoid doing this?

- *rather stupid-looking clumsy birds,* ***with*** *blue feet* ***and*** *long necks*
- *charming rustic* ***cottages*** *in stone*
- *delicious Thai curries,* ***(which were) made of*** *fish and coconut*

c Check in VOCABULARY 2.2 p137.

8 Add the extra information in brackets. Use a relative clause and/or *with*, *and* or *in*.

1 a delightful Victorian cottage (six bedrooms, quiet area)
2 a spacious, modern flat (well-decorated, inexpensive)
3 a classic round-necked sweater (blue, cotton)
4 a funny, well-written contemporary drama (original, superbly acted)
5 a scruffy young writer (dark hair, beard)
6 an Italian sports model (metallic grey, sun-roof)

Come face to face with blue-footed boobies in the Galápagos Islands.

Spend summer in Ireland
Stay in charming rustic stone cottages and sunbathe on its beautiful white sandy beaches.

Get ready ... Get it right!

9 Think about a place that you have been to that you either love or hate. Use adjectives to describe it.

10 **a** Work in groups. Describe your place. Ask follow-up questions.

> The first time I visited this city I really disliked it because it was so noisy and chaotic, with a lot of traffic and pollution. But ...

b Tell the class about the best or worst place you heard about.

2 Writing

Punctuation apostrophes
Connecting words time (1)
Writing task a travel review: describing and recommending places

1 Work in pairs. What do you know about Venice?

2 **a** Read extract A, from a review of Venice. Find and correct eight mistakes with apostrophes. WRITING 2.1 p140.

A

Venice is one of Europes most romantic cities. I vividly remember the first time I saw it because its so beautiful and theres nowhere else like it anywhere in the world. [1]As soon as you come out of the station you see all the boat's going up and down the Grand Canal, which contributes to its' fairytale atmosphere.

I [2]first went there with my parents when I was ten, and I've been going there [3]regularly, for the last 20 years. [4]When I arrive, I usually take the river bus and I'm still impressed by the stunning building's which line the canals. In fact, the building's unique architecture makes Venice a real open-air museum. [5]Then, I like to go for a wander around the citys colourful, narrow streets and drop in to the local people's bars for the best coffee in the world. [6]While I sit drinking, life bustles on around me. Pure bliss.

b Read extract B, from another review. Add one apostrophe to sentences 1–6.

B

[1]Venice is a historic city of small islands, carved up by canals which have proved central to the citys development and economy. [2]Today, the canals boats still provide the means for transport of goods and people within the city. [3]The city is often threatened by the Adriatic Seas tides, which cause floods between autumn and early spring. [4]During the 20th century, many wells were constructed to satisfy the local industries requirements and as a result, Venice began to subside. The sinking has slowed markedly since these wells were banned in the 1960s. [5]However, the city is still threatened by low-level floods that have made many of Venices old houses uninhabitable. [6]Some recent studies have suggested that the citys no longer sinking, but this is not yet certain.

3 **a** Read extract A again. Replace the underlined connecting words/phrases with phrases in the box (not all of which are necessary).

while	as soon as	originally	the moment
afterwards	ever since	meanwhile	

b Fill in the gaps with words/phrases from **3a**. Sometimes there is more than one possible answer. WRITING 2.2 p140.

1 __________ I arrived there, I wanted to make it my home.
2 Tourism improved __________ they renovated the centre.
3 __________ the canals were built, the city has suffered from flooding.
4 The town was __________ inhabited by farm workers.
5 I visited some old friends __________ I was staying there.
6 I decided to stay in a cheap hotel. __________, I regretted it.
7 I sat anxiously waiting for the call. __________, I tried to get on with some work but kept looking at the clock.

4 **a** Choose a place you know well that you would recommend to tourists. Make notes on these topics.

- what the place is known for
- a description of the place
- your personal experience of being there
- when to visit and what to see

b Work in pairs. Discuss your notes. Would you like to visit your partner's place? Why/Why not?

5 **a** Write a review of the place you discussed in **4b**, which would be suitable for a travel website.

b Check your writing for the correct use of these features.

- apostrophes
- connecting words/phrases
- adjective word order
- intensifying adverbs

6 Read other students' reviews. Choose two places you would prefer to visit.

7 **a** Work in groups. Discuss the places you chose.

b Which place is the most popular? Why?

For more Writing practice: Portfolio 2, Workbook p57.

Spoilt for choice

Vocabulary describing places
Skills Reading: tourist information; Listening: interview about tourism
Real World making recommendations

QUICK REVIEW Adjective order **Work in groups. One person describes something, using one adjective. The next person adds an adjective in the correct order. A** *an old man* **B** *a nice old man* **C** *a nice old British man*

1 **a** List places in China that you have heard of or been to. How much do you know about these places?

b Look at the photos and read the website extracts. Which areas or cities would you like to visit? Put them in order.

2 Underline the words/phrases that you think the writer uses to make the areas sound interesting and attractive. Check in VOCABULARY 2.3 p137.

3 CD1 12 Listen to Cheng, a tourism specialist. What does he say about the two most popular tourist destinations?

4 **a** CD1 13 Listen to Cheng talking about the diversity that China has to offer as a holiday destination.

1 Make notes on additional information about the places on the map.
2 Find Guilin on the map.
3 Why does Cheng recommend it?

b Work in pairs. Compare notes. Then listen again to check.

5 CD1 14 Work in pairs. Listen to the next part then discuss the questions.

1 Which city offers the best nightlife?
2 Why is food in China so diverse?
3 Which place sounds the most interesting? Why?

6 **a** Think of three places a visitor should see to appreciate your country. Make notes on how you can describe them in an interesting way. Use these Real World phrases.

REAL WORLD Making recommendations

- In (Shanghai), you must try the …
- If you enjoy (culture), there are …
- You can visit (Guilin), which is definitely worth seeing.
- If it's (history) you're after/into, …
- You can't beat/do better than …

b Work in groups. Tell each other about your places. Say why you chose them and who would enjoy them. If you are from the same country, did you choose the same places? Why?

Chengdu, south-west China

Chengdu is a modern city, full of traffic and high-rise department stores. So why visit? In Chengdu's teahouse culture, you can enjoy tea while people-watching and playing mahjong. It is the best place in the world to see the Giant Panda, with 85% of the world's remaining pandas living in reserves in Sichuan. Beyond the city, you can experience the spectacular Huanglong Valley (Yellow Dragon Valley). Bordered by snow-clad peaks and glaciers, the valley's numerous ponds are strewn with gold-coloured limestone deposits; this means that in sunlight, a golden dragon seems to surge forth from the forest, giving rise to the valley's name.

Hainan Island, south coast

While northern China is snowy and icebound, in Hainan it is possible to swim in the sea and enjoy warm sunshine all year round. Hainan is a tropical paradise, and is known as the 'Eastern Hawaii'. In addition to stunning golden beaches, it boasts such tropical scenery as the Dongjiao Coconut Plantation. In fact, Hainan Island is also called 'Coconut Island' for its production of this fruit. Each year in late March or early April, the islanders hold the Coconut Festival. Hainan is especially popular in winter and with newly married couples.

Xi'an, north-west China

Were China a tree, Beijing would be the crown, while Xi'an would be its deep roots. As the saying goes, "Go to Shanghai and you will find a 100-year-old China; go to Beijing and you will find a 1000-year-old China; go to Xi'an and then you will find a 3000-year-old China". Xi'an records the great changes of the country just like a living history book. Home to the Terracotta Army, the city has a historical heritage second to none. Today, despite the searing summer heat and the freezing winters, Xi'an is a joy to visit.

Beijing, north China

Many people say that the real culture of Beijing, China's capital city, lies in the winding lanes known as *hutong* (meaning 'water well') and the courtyards. The *hutong* originated during the Yuan Dynasty (1271–1368) when people settled around the water wells, leaving a passageway between two courtyards to make entering them more convenient. There are tens of thousands of hutong surrounding the Forbidden City, once home to the emperors. Shut away from the hustle and bustle of the city outside, the *hutong* dwellers enjoy a peaceful existence. Come and wander round these lanes, and you'll get a true taste of Beijing.

continue2learn

- **Vocabulary, Grammar and Real World**
  - **Extra Practice and Progress Portfolio 2** p115
  - **Video (*Remarkable!*)** p125
  - **Language Summary 2** p137
  - **Workbook 2** p9
- **Reading and Writing**
  - **Portfolio 2** Competition entries Workbook p57
    Reading a competition about inspirational people
    Writing using monolingual dictionaries

Vocabulary connotation: positive and negative character adjectives
Grammar patterns with *it*

QUICK REVIEW Intensifying adverbs
Work in pairs. Take turns to complete one of these sentences about yourself: ***I vividly remember ... ; I strongly believe that ... ; I was bitterly disappointed when ... ; I'm extremely unlikely to ... .*** **Ask follow-up questions.**

Vocabulary
Positive character adjectives

1 **a** Write the names of people you know who can be described using these words. Check new words in VOCABULARY 3.1 p141.

courageous	decisive	
deferential	innocent	
meticulous	modest	outgoing
spontaneous	thrifty	

b Work in pairs. Swap lists. Ask about the people on your partner's list.

Speaking and Reading

2 Work in pairs. Answer the questions.

1 What is your idea of a successful person?
2 Which characteristics from **1a** do you think are necessary to be successful? Why?
3 Do you think everyone would like to be successful? Why?/Why not?

3 **a** Look at the title of the article and the picture. What do you think the article is going to suggest?

b Read the article and check your ideas. Match headings a–g with paragraphs 1–7.

a In the spotlight
b An unexpected result
c Male and female priorities
d What most people believe
e What happens next?
f Know yourself
g A lack of self-awareness

Born to lose?

WE ALL WANT TO WIN – OR DO WE?

1 There are certain things in life that are beyond question and it's clear that one of these 'unquestionables' is that everyone wants to win. At the enjoyable end of the victory spectrum is the sheer exhilaration of crossing the finishing line first, coming top of the class or spraying champagne from the podium. At the other lies that depressing, kicked-in-the-guts ache of being the loser. So surely, we all hate it when we lose – or do we?

2 Professor Schultheiss from the University of Michigan carried out various laboratory experiments on 108 college students, and it surprised him to discover that some people became stressed after winning in the laboratory task. This research challenges the widely held belief that the will to win is a universal human desire. Schultheiss concludes that people can be split into wolves (who are utterly driven to win and find it difficult to cope with losing) and sheep (whose triumphs over others bring distress).

3 Dr Michelle Wirth says it's difficult to know whether sheep consciously feel stressed because, when asked if they prefer to win or lose, most people say they'd rather win. Similarly, people are not always conscious of where they sit on the power-motivation spectrum. According to Dr Wirth, if you ask people if they like being in a position of power, they usually say no. It's just not an aspect of their personality that most people are conscious of.

4 Dr Wirth believes that knowing which category you fall into – wolf or sheep – can bring benefits. "If you can figure out which one you are, you can tailor your working environment to suit you. There are some people who get pleasure and satisfaction from being in positions of power, and there are those who are less comfortable dominating others."

5 Dr Adrian Atkinson, a business psychologist, believes power motivation is linked with personality. Wolves are likely to be highly competitive and driven by a need to achieve. Sheep are relatively uncompetitive and do not feel the compulsion to achieve. For Dr Atkinson, "The explanation could be more to do with the perceived consequences of winning than winning itself. Winning increases uncertainty, because people think, 'So, what now? What will be expected of me?' Competitive people with a high need for achievement like this uncertainty. More deferential people may find this uncertainty stressful."

6 Dr Wirth believes that it might be the attention generated by winning that triggers the stress response. "People with high power motivation like to be the centre of attention, so it follows that not winning is stressful." Apparently, these people find it hard to accept that someone else is getting the accolade that they feel should have been theirs, whereas for low-power individuals, public recognition is equally stressful and they would do anything to avoid it.

7 Professor Cary Cooper, of Lancaster University, says that there is likely to be a strong gender split between sheep and wolves, with more women than men being sheep. "It's not that women hate winning, but they don't mind losing. They are usually focused on more important things, such as the health and well-being of their family, and are able to contextualise losing. Men are more work-focused and achievement-orientated. Men are conditioned by society to win – it's a vestigial part of their behaviour that they haven't let go, which is rather sad. If men were rational, which they are not, they'd realise that they don't need to compete all the time."

4 **a** Put these sentences in order according to the article.

a Most people aren't aware of which group they belong to.
b Some people feel stressed when their success is made public.
c The desire to win is a shared behaviour trait influenced by environmental factors.
d Dr Schultheiss expected that everyone in the experiments would find losing stressful.
e Job satisfaction isn't necessarily determined by how much power you have over others.
f The writer finds it hard to believe anyone would prefer to lose. *1*
g Some personality types thrive in situations where future expectations may change.

b Work in pairs. Compare your answers. Find evidence in the article to support each statement in **4a**.

5 Work in groups. Discuss these questions.

1 Are there people who really don't mind losing, for example when doing sport?
2 Is it possible to be both a sheep and a wolf? Why?/Why not?
3 How do you feel when faced with uncertainty about the future?
4 Do you agree that there is a gender division between sheep and wolves?
5 Do you think you are a sheep or a wolf? Why?

HELP WITH GRAMMAR
Patterns with *it*

6 Which of these extracts (1–7) use *it* as subject? Which use *it* as object? Read the explanations below to check.

1 It is clear that one of these 'unquestionables' is that everyone wants to win.
2 … it's just not an aspect of their personality that they are conscious of.
3 … it's difficult to know whether sheep consciously feel stressed …
4 … so it follows that not winning is stressful.
5 … it surprised him to discover that …
6 So surely we all hate it when we lose …
7 … people can be split into wolves, who find it difficult to cope with losing …

IT AS SUBJECT

- If the subject of the verb is a long and grammatically complex structure, we often put it at the end of the clause/sentence. We use *it* as the subject of the verb at the beginning of the clause/sentence.
  Whether sheep consciously feel stressed is difficult to know.
  → ***It's** difficult to know whether sheep consciously feel stressed.*

IT AS OBJECT

- We often use *it* as the object of a verb where it refers to a clause later in the sentence.
  *So surely, we all hate **it** when we lose.*
  not ~~*So surely, we all hate when we lose.*~~

7 **a** Match the five examples of *it* as subject in **6a** to these structures.

***it* + verb …**
1 + adjective + (*that*) *It's clear that …*
2 + (*not*) + noun + (*that*)
3 + adjective + infinitive with *to*
4 + *that* clause
5 + object + infinitive with *to*

b Match the two examples of *it* as object in **6a** to these structures.

verb + *it* …
1 + *when*
2 + adjective + infinitive with *to*

TIP • There are many common expressions with *it* as subject: *It's no good …*; *It's no use …*; *It's no wonder that …*; *It's no coincidence that …* .

c Check in GRAMMAR 3.1 p142.

8 **a** Use these prompts to make sentences about yourself or people you know.

1 It's obvious …	5 … prefer(s) it when …
2 It's difficult to …	6 … can't bear it when …
3 It's no wonder …	7 … consider it impolite …
4 It's surprising …	8 … would love it if …

b Work in pairs. Tell each other your sentences. Ask follow-up questions.

Listening and Vocabulary

9 **a** CD1 ▸ 15 Listen to the preview of a radio programme. What is 'impostor syndrome'?

b CD1 ▸ 16 Listen to Valerie, Richard and Miranda. Complete these sentences with their names.

1 ________ knew about impostor syndrome before the interview.
2 ________ has never experienced impostor syndrome.
3 ________ works in TV.
4 ________ is a garden designer.
5 ________ is doing a postgraduate degree.

c Listen again. Choose the correct answers.

1 a Valerie *thinks/doesn't think* her clients realise she lacks confidence.
  b She *experienced/didn't experience* impostor syndrome when she was a teacher.
2 a Richard *makes/doesn't make* mistakes in his work.
  b He says there *are/aren't any* people in the media who experience self-doubt.
3 a Miranda *feels/doesn't feel* she's been very lucky.
  b She *is/isn't* paying for her studies herself.

10 Work in groups. Discuss these questions.

1 Do you think that many people experience 'impostor syndrome'?
2 What advice would you give to someone who suffered from it?
3 Do you think impostor syndrome exists more among qualified people?
4 Do you think that everyone in very responsible positions feels this way sometimes? Why?/Why not?

HELP WITH PRONUNCIATION
Speech units and stress (1)

11 **a** CD1 15 Listen to the definition of 'impostor syndrome' again and write down exactly what you hear.

b Look at Audio Script CD1 15 p166 and check what you wrote. What problems did you have (for example, not hearing some words)?

12 **a** Listen again. Divide the text on p166 into speech units (//) and mark the word which is stressed most in each speech unit.

TIP • We stress certain words because they carry important information or because they are ideas that we wish to focus on.

Have you heard of // impostor syndrome? //

b Practise saying the definition.

HELP WITH VOCABULARY
Connotation: positive and negative character adjectives

- Sometimes two character adjectives can describe similar traits, but one may have a positive and one may have a negative connotation.

13 **a** Compare these extracts and answer the questions.

RICHARD I don't want to sound <u>arrogant</u>.
INTERVIEWER And you're generally quite <u>confident</u> that you can deliver what they want?

1 Do both of the underlined adjectives refer to someone who is very sure of himself?
2 Which adjective means the person thinks he is better than other people?
3 Which adjective has a positive connotation? Which has a negative connotation?

b Match these negative character adjectives to the positive character adjectives in **1a** on p26.

reckless	tight-fisted	fussy	forceful	submissive
reserved	impetuous	loud	naïve	

c Work in pairs. Compare answers.

d Match cartoons A–D with character adjectives from **13b**. Try to define the adjectives.

e Check in VOCABULARY 3.2 p141.

14 **a** Choose three adjectives from **1a** and **13b** to describe yourself.

b Work in pairs. Tell your partner which adjectives you chose and why.

A

B

C

D

Get ready ... Get it right!

15 Look at these sentences. Make notes on what you could say for and against each one.

- It's impossible to be rich, powerful and nice.
- Every employee in a company should have a turn at being a manager.
- It's essential to listen to other people's opinions before making decisions.
- Schools should teach students to be meticulous when presenting work.
- Self-confidence is necessary for success.

16 **a** Work in groups. Discuss the sentences in **15**.

It's ridiculous to say ...

b Tell the class which sentences your group agreed with.

A happy, healthy life

Vocabulary phrasal verbs: health
Grammar inversion

QUICK REVIEW introductory *it* Think about things that are happening in the world at the moment using three of these sentence stems: *It amazes me that ... ; I find it difficult to see how ... ; It was good to hear that ... ; I think it's terrible that ... ; I love it when ...* . Work in pairs and compare your ideas.

Vocabulary Phrasal verbs: health

1 **a** Guess the meanings of the phrasal verbs in bold. Check in VOCABULARY 3.3 p141.

1 What do you do if you feel a cold **coming on**?
2 When you are bitten by an insect, does the area around the bite usually **swell up**?
3 Have you ever **picked up** a stomach bug when travelling somewhere new?
4 Have you ever tried using steam when your nose **is blocked up**?
5 If you **go down with** flu, do you usually still go to work?
6 Do you usually catch bugs that **are going around**?
7 Does your doctor usually **put** people **on** antibiotics if they have a cold?
8 Have you ever **come out in** a rash because you were allergic to something you'd eaten?
9 Have you ever **come off** antibiotics before you were supposed to?
10 Have you ever suffered from a condition that **flares up** from time to time?

b Work in pairs. Ask and answer the questions.

Reading and Speaking

2 Work in groups of four. Look at the photos and the article headline. Predict the suggestions that the article might give.

3 Student A p105. Student B p109. Student C p111. Student D p112.

4 **a** Work in the same groups of four. Discuss these questions. Give examples.

1 Which suggestions are common knowledge in your country?
2 Which research findings, if any, surprised you?
3 Would you disagree with any of the suggestions? If so, which one(s)?
4 Would you consider following any of the suggestions? If so, which one(s) and why?

b Tell the class your conclusions.

GREAT WAYS TO WELL-BEING

You don't have to follow a punishing diet or spend hours on the treadmill. The path to a healthier way of life may be easier than you think.

HELP WITH GRAMMAR Inversion

5 **a** Look at these examples. What changes are made when we begin a sentence with a limiting adverbial (e.g. *seldom*) or a negative adverbial (e.g. *under no circumstances*)?

1 a People seldom associate being married with being healthy.
  b **Seldom** do people associate being married with being healthy.

2 a You should not exercise immediately after eating a heavy meal.
  b **Under no circumstances** should you exercise immediately after eating a heavy meal.

b Look at the limiting and negative adverbials in bold in these sentences. Then underline the inversion.

1 **Not only** does dental hygiene save painful and expensive visits to the dentist, it may also prevent strokes.
2 **Not until** last week did he agree to stop smoking.
3 Very **rarely** do you hear anything negative about eating fish.
4 **Only recently** have experts come to appreciate the health benefits of eating curry.

c Look at sentences 1–3 in **5b**. What auxiliaries are used when we invert Present Simple and Past Simple?

d Look at these clauses in pink and blue. Which clause has the inversion?

1 Not until she learns to relax will things get better.
2 Only when we got the dog did we start going for long walks.

TIPS • Inversion *can* occur after another complete clause beginning with *not until*, *only when*, *only if*, *only after*.

• Although inversion is usually found in literary and formal texts, we also use it in less formal spoken and written English when we want to add emphasis or dramatic effect.

e Check in GRAMMAR 3.2 p142.

6 **a** Read two more ways to stay healthy. Find and correct five mistakes with inversion.

1

Only recently experts have suggested that there are many health benefits from being exposed to sunlight. Not only it helps reduce depression and pain, it also reduces high blood pressure.

2

Seldom we hear anything positive about drinking wine. However, research suggests that not only drinking a moderate amount of red wine reduces the risk of heart attacks, it can also help protect elderly people from mental decline. But of course, under no circumstances people should drink and drive.

b Work in pairs. Student A, read out your corrected version of paragraph 1. Student B, read out your corrected version of paragraph 2. Do you agree with each other's corrections?

Listening

7 **a** Work in pairs. You are going to listen to six people talking about what they do to cheer themselves up. Look at the photos and guess some of the things they might talk about.

b CD1 17 Listen to three conversations. Were any of your predictions correct?

c Fill in each gap with a name (Naomi, Rachael, Helen, Alex, Ian and Fran).

1 __________ needs exercise.
2 __________ makes arrangements to see friends.
3 __________ likes to be on their own.
4 __________ and __________ think about happy memories.
5 __________ has done the same thing since childhood.

d Listen again. Answer the questions.

1 a RACHAEL I'll open one of those. (Open what?)
  b NAOMI It really does take you out of your down moment. (What does?)
2 a ALEX I can do it any time I like. (Do what?)
  b HELEN It's impossible to feel stressed when you're zipping around like that. (On what?)
3 a IAN … because it's great fun and colourful. (What is?)
  b IAN I'll try to be cynical about it. (About what?)

8 **a** CD1 18 In spoken English, the speaker often uses fillers (*you know*, *kind of* etc) or makes false starts (*I've got … I've kept all the letters*). This allows the speaker more thinking time. Look at this extract. Underline different examples of redundancy.

FRAN Well, generally if I, um, if I'm not feeling, erm, too happy then, erm, I need something to work towards, so, erm, I try and make contact with friends that I don't really see very often and, erm, and I find that if I'm, I'm with them then I kind of forget about what's going on at the time and just remember the things I, you know, used to do with them, and, erm, they just kind of, er, accept my personality so I don't have to, you know, that, that trivial thing that's usually making me not very happy. Doesn't really mean very much to them so …

b Work in pairs. Compare answers.

c Look at Audio Script CD1 18 on p167. Check your answers.

Get ready … Get it right!

9 Make a list of things that you do to cheer yourself up when you're feeling a bit low. Think about all the positive effects associated with each activity.

→ *go for a run and listen to music on an MP3 player*
→ *gets you out of the house, healthy, takes your mind off your problems*

10 **a** Work in groups. Take turns to try to persuade other students to try your ideas.

> Try it. Not only does it get you out of the house, but it's also very good for you physically.

b Tell the class about your group's most unusual and most popular ideas.

3 Writing

Connecting words contrast (1)
Spelling one word, two words or hyphenated
Writing task a semi-formal email; cancelling an arrangement

1 Work in pairs and discuss these questions.

1 Do you feel you have a good work–life balance? If not, how could you improve it?
2 How often do you cancel social or business commitments?
3 How would you tell the people concerned? What kind of language would you use?

2 Read the situation below. What should Sofia say to her boss?

> Sofia is a freelance journalist who writes a popular weekly column for a newspaper. She was going to write next year's columns but very recently decided to take a year off to travel and research a new book. She writes an email to her boss, Celia, at the newspaper, explaining why she cannot continue writing the column.

3 Read Sofia's draft email. Ignore any spelling mistakes for now. How do you think Sofia's boss will feel when she reads it? Why?

4 **a** Choose the correct spelling. WRITING 3.1 p143.

1 This isn't an *every day / everyday* occurrence.
2 I take *everyone / every one* of my jobs seriously.
3 It's a *twelve-hour-a-day / twelve hours a day* job.
4 Is there *anyone / any one* you know who can help?
5 Is there *anyway / any way* I can make it up to you?
6 He *maybe / may be* tired.

b Find and correct five spelling mistakes in the draft email. (A missing hyphen counts as a spelling mistake.)

5 Look at the underlined connecting words in the email and notice the punctuation. Complete sentences 1–5 using the same connecting words. Sometimes there is more than one possible answer. WRITING 3.2 p143.

1 I've decided to give up my job, __________ I love my work.
2 __________ I was planning to say no at first, I've changed my mind.
3 I very much enjoy writing the column, __________ I've always wanted to travel.
4 Travelling gives you time to think, __________ working full-time doesn't.
5 I know this is not ideal. __________ , I hope we will work together again.

Dear Celia,

It was good to see you at the planning meeting a few weeks ago. However, since then, I have decided that I cannot continue writing the column for you.

Quite unexpectedly, I have been asked to write a book, which involves a year's research and travel. My first response was to say no, but after some thought, I've changed my mind. Not until I thought about it, did I realise that I desperately need a break from every thing. Doing a fulltime, five-days-a-week job for years, I have only had time to think about every day concerns, whereas travelling will give me a new perspective on life. Although I very much enjoy writing the column, I've always wanted to write a book, so this is a great opportunity.

Many apologies, Celia, and even though this situation is not ideal, I hope that we maybe able to work together again in the future.

Best wishes,

Sofia

6 Work in pairs. Read the task and discuss the questions.

You have agreed to do something for a work contact. However, your plans have changed and you have to cancel the arrangement. Write an email, explaining why you have to cancel.

1 What have you agreed to do and what has made you change your plans? (e.g. give a presentation, go on a business trip, etc.)
2 How many points are you going to make?
3 How many paragraphs do you need to cover your points?
4 Which connecting words can you use to link your points?
5 What language from lessons **3A** and **3B** can you use?

7 **a** Work alone. Write your email.

b Check your email for these features.

- connecting words/phrases
- spelling
- language from lessons **3A** or **3B**.

8 Read another student's email. How does it make you feel? Underline words/phrases that explain your answer. Then discuss ways to improve your email.

For more Writing practice: Portfolio 3, Workbook p60.

It's the way you say it

Vocabulary euphemisms
Real World being tactful

QUICK REVIEW Inversion

Complete these sentences for yourself: *Rarely ...* ; *Not only ...* ; *Under no circumstances ...* . Work in pairs. Swap papers. Say your partner's sentences without inversion: *Rarely do I have time to relax these days. I rarely have time to relax these days.*

1 **a** How would you say the phrases in bold in a more direct way? Check in VOCABULARY 3.4 p141.

1 I think you were being **economical with the truth** on that occasion.
I think you were telling a lie on that occasion.
2 You get a discount on public transport if you're **a senior citizen**.
3 My dad's somewhat **behind the times** when it comes to technology. He still watches videos.
4 Rosie's car **has seen better days**. She could really do with a new one.
5 You'll have to speak up – she's **getting on a bit** and is **hard of hearing**.
6 I was feeling a little **under the weather** yesterday, so I stayed in bed.
7 Your son can be **a bit of a handful** at times and finds the work we're doing **challenging**.
8 It's **a bit on the chilly side** in this room. Can we turn the heating up?

b Work in pairs. Take turns to test each other on the euphemisms in **1a**.

economical with the truth

That means 'telling a lie'.

2 **a** Look at the cartoons on p35 and read situations A–D. In which of these situations might you complain, refuse an invitation, disagree or give your opinion?

A Your partner has taken you to the cinema as a birthday treat. You didn't like it but your partner did.
B Your boss asks you round for a meal but you don't want to go.
C The waiter asks you if you liked your very expensive meal. You are not happy with it.
D A friend is trying on some new trousers. You really don't like them on him/her.

b For each situation, think of ways in which you could respond in a direct way and in a less direct way. Why might you prefer to be more tactful?

3 **a** CD1 19 Listen to four conversations in which two people respond in different ways. Match each conversation to situations A–D in **2a**.

b Listen again. Which response do you think is more tactful, a or b? Why?

c Work in pairs. Look at Audio Script CD1 19 p167 and practise the tactful conversations in **3a**. Take turns to respond tactfully.

REAL WORLD Being tactful

4 **a** Write these headings in the correct places (1–5).

~~using past forms~~ using adverbs of attitude
using modals using vague language
not sounding negative

1 *using past forms*
We **were planning** to go to the cinema tomorrow.

2 ______
They **could** do with being (a bit looser).
It **could have** been a bit hotter.
I'**d** go for black instead if I were you.

3 ______
We must all get together **some time**.
(They could do with being) **a bit** looser.
It was **sort of** interesting in parts.
The steak was **on the tough side**.

4 ______
I think darker colours **suit you better**.
I've seen better performances.

5 ______
Quite honestly, I've seen better performances.
Unfortunately, the steak was ... .

b Check in REAL WORLD 3.1 p143.

5 CD1 20 Listen to five sentences and practise saying them in a tactful way.

6 **a** Match pairs of sentences 1–4 to situations A–D in **2a**.

1 a Tomorrow's not ideal for me, I'm afraid.
  b We'd hoped to go and visit Lisa's parents then.
2 a Frankly, it wasn't quite up to your usual standard.
  b Well, I would have to say we've had better here.
3 a It wasn't very gripping at times.
  b I wouldn't see it again but it had its moments!
4 a I think I might choose something a bit less fussy.
  b I'm not over the moon about the style, personally.

b Work in pairs. Can you think of anything else you might say in the situations?

A

B

C

D

7 **a** Work in pairs. Read conversations 1–4. Rewrite B's responses to make them more tactful.

1 **A** Rick and I were hoping you and Harry could spend next weekend with us. Our kids would love you to.
  B No, sorry, we've made other arrangements.

2 **A** So, did you like the film? I really enjoyed it.
  B Did you? I didn't.

3 **A** So, what do you think of my new hairstyle?
  B It looks ridiculous!

4 **A** I hope you're satisfied with your accommodation.
  B Well, we're not. The room is too small.

b Work with another pair. Read your conversations and suggest improvements to make them tactful.

8 **a** Work in pairs. Choose a situation and write a conversation for one of the situations, of at least four lines.

1 Your elderly cousin invites your family to a party, but your teenage children really don't want to go.

2 Your friend is enthusing about a CD she's just bought, which you really dislike. Give your reaction.

3 Your brother has just moved into a new house, which you think is horrible. Give your opinion.

b Swap papers with another pair. Try to extend the other pair's conversation.

continue2learn

Vocabulary, Grammar and Real World

- **Extra Practice and Progress Portfolio 3** p116
- **Video (*Well-being*)** p126
- **Language Summary 3** p141
- **Workbook 3** p14

Reading and Writing

- **Portfolio 1** A proposal Workbook p60
  Reading a proposal for gym membership
  Writing putting forward ideas in a proposal

4A Society and the media

Vocabulary news collocations
Grammar phrases referring to the future

QUICK REVIEW Euphemisms
Work in pairs. Make euphemisms from these words: *economical*; *behind*; *weather*; *chilly*; *handful*; *better*. Take turns to make sentences with the euphemisms.

Vocabulary
News collocations

1 **a** Match the verbs in A to the words/phrases in B. Check in VOCABULARY 4.1 p144.

A	B
follow	publicity
seek	a press conference
hold	the front page
go	to press
make	the news
sue	the headlines
hit	a press release
receive	a story
run	for libel
issue	a lot of coverage

b Fill in the gaps with a word from **1a**.

1 How do you __________ the news? Do you: read a newspaper; read the news online; watch it on TV; or listen to the radio?
2 What's the latest story to __________ the headlines in your country?
3 What type of news regularly receives a lot of __________ in your country?
4 Do newspapers in your country often __________ stories about politicians' private lives?
5 Which people in your country actually __________ publicity?
6 Do you know of any famous people who have __________ a newspaper for libel?

c Work in pairs. Ask and answer the questions in **1b**. Ask follow-up questions.

1

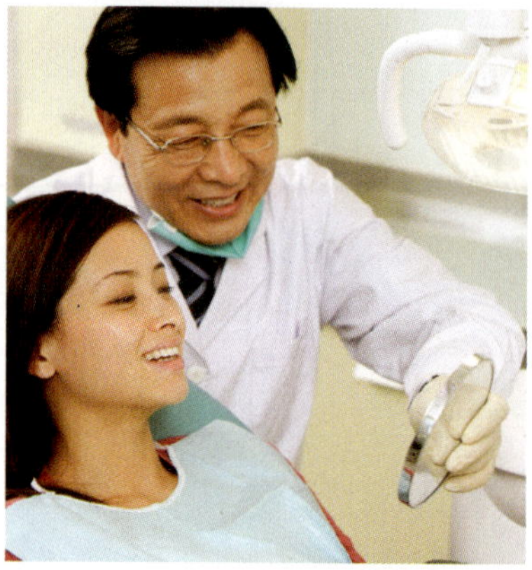

An innovative dentist hopes to ease his patients' fears after creating a musical drill to help keep their minds off the intrusive instrument. Dhanni Gustiana has tested out his unique song-playing equipment at his Indonesian dental surgery in Purworejo, Central Java. He replaced the usual buzzing sound on a conventional dentist's drill with music via an MP3 player.

The modified drill is sure to prove popular with his younger patients, who can even request their own music to make their visit to the dentist a bit more pleasant. In addition to playing music, the drill comes with its very own disco lights.

Read more ...

2

Young novice drivers should spend at least a year as learners before being allowed to take their test, insurers proposed today. Graduated driver licensing was also put forward. This would include restrictions in the first six months after passing the driving test, including limiting the number of young passengers in a car, a zero alcohol limit, and no driving at night. Newly qualified young drivers are already subject to similar restrictions in Australia, New Zealand and in parts of the US; and Northern Ireland is about to introduce reforms.

The insurers said that an 18-year-old driver was more than three times as likely to be involved in a crash as a 48-year-old driver.

Read more ...

3

A report has claimed a four-day week "has huge benefits for employers". Its author, Andrew Simms, said, "Studies show lower absentee rates and a more motivated workforce, and the business saves money by shutting down for a day." A trial in Utah, US, slashed absentee rates by 14%, saving millions of dollars, while the practice is common in Germany and the Netherlands, with more big companies due to introduce the scheme. Simms believes the scheme has obvious benefits for workers, with reduced stress and more free time, but others believe it is unlikely to appeal to employees, who may fear loss of pay and greater pressure to complete work in a shorter time scale.

Read more ...

4

Have you noticed the fish on your plate getting smaller? According to experts, sea fish could lose a quarter of their current size by 2050 because of global warming. Using computer models to study the effect of expected climate change on fish across the world, scientists have concluded that the maximum body weight of fish is likely to shrink by 14% by 2050.

Fish size is largely dependent on seawater oxygen levels, which reduce as temperatures rise. Researchers from the University of British Columbia say they are surprised at the extent of the change. Pollution is bound to 'further exacerbate' the effects, they added. **Read more ...**

5

The space around Earth is packed with nearly 22,000 spent rocket stages and countless dead or dying satellites and other man-made fragments. So how dangerous is space debris? 'Extremely' is the answer. And the problem is certain to get worse.

Fortunately for us, most debris burns up when it re-enters the Earth's atmosphere. However, as space becomes more crowded, it will get harder for satellites to dodge collisions. Fragments as small as a single centimetre have the potential to destroy whole satellites because of the speed at which they are travelling. Space agencies around the world are working urgently to find a way to avert future disasters which are bound to be caused by space debris. **Read more ...**

Reading

2 **a** Work in pairs. Read news headlines a–f below. What do you think the stories are about? Which sounds the most interesting?

a Driving age **about to** rise
b Crowded space **on the verge of** catastrophe
c Patients **to** be entertained by musical drill
d Restrictions **set to** improve safety on the road
e Shorter week **due to** be introduced
f Size of fish **to** shrink as sea temperatures rise

b Match headlines a–f to news items 1–5. Which headline does not belong to any of the stories?

3 **a** Read news items 1–5 again. Then complete these sentences in your own words.

1 a The dentist has created a musical drill because …
  b Younger patients will like the drill because …
2 a Insurers want young drivers to learn for a year before taking their test because …
  b Graduated driver licensing has already been introduced …
3 a Andrew Simms believes a four-day week will benefit employers because …
  b He believes employees will favour the scheme because …
4 a Fish are getting smaller as a result of …
  b Scientists are surprised by …
5 a The problem of space debris is getting worse because …
  b Space agencies need to solve this problem quickly because …

b Work in pairs and compare answers.

4 **a** Look again at stories 2 and 3 and discuss these questions.

1 What is the situation in your country?
2 Do you agree with the proposed course of action?

b Present your ideas to the class.

HELP WITH GRAMMAR
Phrases referring to the future

5 **a** Look again at headlines a–f below. Change them into sentences by adding the correct form of *be*, and an article where necessary.

- a Driving age about to rise
- b Crowded space on the verge of catastrophe
- c Restrictions set to improve safety on the road
- d Size of fish to shrink as sea temperatures rise
- e Patients to be entertained by musical drill
- f Shorter week due to be introduced

TIP • News headlines are not usually written as complete sentences.

b Look at the words/phrases in blue in headlines a–f and in pink in extracts 1–5 below. Match the words/phrases to these meanings.

- something will happen, probably in the near future
- the speaker or writer is saying how certain this is

1. The modified drill is sure to prove popular with his younger patients.
2. Others believe it is unlikely to appeal to employees who may fear loss of pay.
3. The maximum body weight of fish is likely to shrink.
4. Pollution is bound to 'further exacerbate' the effects.
5. The problem is certain to get worse.

c Look again at the words/phrases in pink and blue. Which is followed by a noun? What verb form follows the other phrases?

TIP • *due to* is often used when we are talking about a particular time: *She is due to arrive later today.*

d Check in GRAMMAR 4.1 p144.

6 **a** Make sentences with these prompts and the names of countries, people, etc.

1. likely / win / match
   Brazil is likely to win their next match against England.
2. sure / do / well
3. likely / get married
4. verge / make / decision
5. bound / spend / time
6. about / sell
7. due / retire
8. certain / become successful

b Work in pairs. Tell each other five of your sentences. Ask follow-up questions.

Listening and Speaking

7 **a** Make a list of the most popular TV programmes in your country. Tick the ones you watch.

b Work in pairs and compare lists.

8 **a** Read the news item below. What types of TV programme are likely to replace current reality TV shows on Channel 13, and why?

b Do you think this reflects viewers' opinions in your country? Why?/Why not?

NEW TV BOSS ON THE VERGE OF AXING REALITY TV SHOWS

THE NEW HEAD of Channel 13, Millicent Davies, is about to make major changes to programming schedules. "We believe people are ready for a change – a move away from the tired formulas of reality TV. Our research shows that viewers would like to see a return to more fact-based programmes – documentaries or wildlife films, for example. They would also like more drama and more comedy and this is what we intend to offer."

9 **a** CD1 21 Listen to Sue and Dan discussing television. Answer these questions.

1 What programmes does Sue like and why?
2 Why doesn't Dan like the same programmes?
3 What programmes does Dan like?

b Work in pairs. Who said the following, Sue or Dan?

1 Sometimes you just want to **put your feet up** and **let it wash over you**.
2 It's **intellectually bankrupt** and it's just rubbish.
3 It's a **sad indictment on** society.
4 That's a bit **heavy**.
5 It's to see the worst in people. It's **poking fun at people**.
6 They know **what they're letting themselves in for**.
7 There's enough sport on TV **as it is**, it's on all the time.
8 What I want is some good comedy for me to relax.
9 Well, **each to their own**.

c Listen again and check.

10 Match the words/phrases in bold in **9b** to meanings a–i.

a making people seem ridiculous
b not intelligent in any way
c watch or listen without concentrating
d everyone likes different things
e relax in a comfortable environment
f what kind of unpleasant situation they're getting involved in
g a sign that a system is wrong
h too serious or difficult to enjoy
i the way it is now

11 Work in pairs and discuss these questions. Give reasons.

1 Whose opinions do you agree with more: Sue's or Dan's?
2 What do you think are the worst types of TV programme?
3 What are the best?

HELP WITH PRONUNCIATION

A series of items

12 **a** CD1 22 Listen again and notice how Dan uses rising intonation to indicate a series of similar items.

It's // er // it's a tired template // that's been ↗**used** //
that's pro↗**vo**cative // it's there to create ↗**con**flict //
it's to see the ↗**worst** in people. //
It's actually // it's poking ↘**fun** at people //
at their ↘misery.

b Listen and practise saying the extract.

TIP • The last item often has a falling tone, to signal the end of the series.

c Work in pairs. Look at Audio Script CD1 21 on p167. Practise the end of the conversation in bold.

Get ready ... Get it right!

13 **a** Look at these statements. Do you agree or disagree?

1 The internet will replace television as the main form of home entertainment.
2 People won't go to the cinema to watch films but will simply download films onto their mobile phones or computers.
3 User-generated content (videos, photos, blogs, etc. that anyone can publish online) will continue to increase.
4 CDs and DVDs will continue to exist.
5 Live performances by singers, bands, orchestras, etc. will remain popular.
6 People will continue to buy books and libraries will still exist.

b Work in groups. Discuss each statement.

c Tell the class your conclusions.

4B Cities and technology

Vocabulary near synonyms
Grammar future in the past

QUICK REVIEW Phrases referring to the future Work in groups. Talk about stories that are in the news. Try to use phrases like *set to*, *due to*, *about to*, *on the verge of*, etc. Tell the class about the most interesting news item you discussed.

Reading and Vocabulary

1 Work in pairs. Tell each other about a big city you know or have lived in. How has it changed over the years?

2 **a** Look at sentences 1–6 and try and predict the missing information about the development of cities.

1 Originally humans didn't stay in one place because …
2 Trade and education began to develop once people …
3 Some cities didn't survive because of …
4 In the 1800s, many people from the countryside came to cities because …
5 People in the country and in cities lived longer due to …
6 People continue to move to cities today because …

b Read the article about how and why cities developed. Were your predictions correct?

3 **a** Read the article again. What is the link between these numbers?

a 11,000 and 120,000
b 3% and 50%
c 13%, 50% and 75%

b Work in pairs. Use the sentences in **2a** and your own ideas to summarise the article.

4 **a** Work in pairs. Make a list of possible benefits and problems of having most of the world's population living in cities.

b Work in groups. Compare your lists. Are there more benefits or problems?

The world goes to town

The majority of people live in cities. Human history will increasingly become urban history, says **John Grimmond.**

WHEREVER YOU THINK THE HUMAN STORY BEGAN, it is clear that ***homo sapiens*** did not start life as urban creatures. Man's habitat at the outset was dominated by the need to find food; hunting and foraging were rural pursuits. Not until the end of the last ice age – about 11,000 years ago – did humans start building anything that might be called a village, and by that time man had been around for about 120,000 years. It took another six millennia for the population of cities to grow to more than 100,000. Even in the 1800s, only 3% of the world's population lived in cities. That figure has now risen to over 50%. So, wisely or not, human beings have become *homo urbanus*.

The development of cities is synonymous with human development. The first **villages** came with the emergence of agriculture and the domestication of animals: people no longer had to wander as they hunted and gathered but could instead draw together in settlements. Around 4,000 years ago, metal tokens – the forerunners of coins – were produced as receipts for grain; not coincidentally, cities began to take shape at about the same time.

The city soon became the centre of exchange, learning, innovation and sophistication. It was life in the city that made it possible for man to acquire skills, learn from other people, study, teach and develop social arts that made **country folk** seem very uneducated.

Of course, not all cities were the same. As they developed, some were known as the hub of an empire (Constantinople), of learning (Bologna), or

commerce (Hamburg). Some flourished, some died, their longevity depending on factors as varied as war, disease, misgovernment or economic collapse.

Whatever the particular circumstances of a city, though, its success was likely to be governed by technological change. For example, improvements in transport made the growth of trade possible. Then in the 19th century, the invention of engines and manufacturing machinery provided factory work which attracted multitudes of rural inhabitants to leave the land for the city.

The latest leap, from 13% to over 50% (in just over 100 years), also owed something to science and technology. **Improvements** in medicine meant that more and more people could live together without succumbing to disease. These same developments in medicine similarly lengthened lives in the countryside, leading to a huge **rise** in the rural population. However, this increase has not been matched with commensurate growth in rural prosperity. As a result, more and more villagers have been upping sticks to seek a better life in cities. The sheer scale and speed of the current urban expansion, particularly in China and India, is unlike any other big change in history to date; by 2050, an expected 75% of all human beings are likely to live in cities.

HELP WITH VOCABULARY

Near synonyms

- We often avoid repeating the same words so that what we say or write is less repetitive and more interesting.

It is clear that __homo sapiens__ did not start life as urban creatures. __Man's__ habitat at the outset …

5 **a** Find synonyms or near synonyms for these words in the article.

1 homo sapiens: *man*; ______________; ______________
2 villages: ______________
3 country folk: ______________; ______________
4 improvements: ______________
5 rise: ______________; ______________

TIPS • Synonyms are not always interchangeable.

1 **formality**: *kid* and *child* are similar but *kid* is more informal. *How are the kids?* (informal) *There are 14.8 million children in the UK.* (more formal)
2 **collocations**: *huge* and *large* are similar but do not always collocate with the same words. *I've got a huge ~~large~~ problem.*
3 **grammatical agreement**: *I like/enjoy travelling. I ~~enjoy~~ like to travel.*
4 **connotation**: *determined* and *obstinate* describe similar characteristics, but *determined* has a more positive connotation. *I admire her because she's so ~~obstinate~~ determined.*

b Check in VOCABULARY 4.2 p144.

6 Make the blog below less repetitive by replacing the words in bold with the correct form of synonyms in the box.

~~enjoy~~	be forced to	urban	passers-by
vehicles	suddenly	come to a standstill
exasperating	allow	gaze at

enjoy
Personally, I like living in a city. I [1]~~**like**~~ the bustle and sounds of [2]**city** life and I love people-watching. In fact, I often sit in cafes just [3]**watching** [4]**people** in the street. I don't even mind all the cars. I know it's infuriating when you're driving along and [5]**cars** unexpectedly [6]**stop** for no apparent reason. Then you [7]**have to** wait for ages before anything moves. But let's face it, it can be equally [8]**infuriating** when you're driving in the country and you [9]**unexpectedly** have to stop to let a herd of sheep pass by. Then ten minutes later you have to stop again to [10]**let** a herd of cows past!

Listening

7 **a** Look at photos 1–4 of props from the *Star Trek* TV series. What is today's equivalent of the technology?

b CD1 23 Listen and check your answers.

8 Listen again. Choose the correct answer.

1. The first cell phones were roughly *10/50* times as heavy as modern phones.
2. Dr Raymon is *an astronaut/a scientist* involved in the exploration of space.
3. Voyager 1 is about to *leave the solar system/return to Earth*.
4. Surgery before the 1970s *was/wasn't* safe.
5. Dr Adler *is working on/has produced* equipment that can destroy cancerous cells without surgery.
6. Steve Perlman *worked for/took his idea* to Apple.
7. QuickTime *followed/preceded* the iPod.

9 CD1 24 Look at speech bubbles A–D. Listen and fill in the gaps with three, four or five words.

A We didn't know our ideas [1]__________ successful. In the original series nothing was based on scientific research. We just made it all up. Little did we know these gadgets were going to inspire a generation of young earthlings. And some of these young fans [2]__________ to spend their lives trying to turn *Star Trek* fantasy into reality.

B Years later, we [3]__________ that many of the inventors in Silicon Valley had been *Star Trek* fans as kids. All these geeks in the 1960s decided they were actually going to make personal computers like those that Spock used, and that included pocket or tablet computers. But it wouldn't happen overnight.

C We didn't realise that these bits of cardboard and plastic being used on set [4]__________ transformed into everyday modern technology.

D And we thought that *Star Trek* [5]__________ entertainment.

HELP WITH GRAMMAR Future in the past

10 **a** Look at these sentences and answer the questions.

1. In which one are we predicting the result?
2. In which one do we know the result?

a *We didn't know our ideas were going to be successful.*
b *We believe our ideas are going to be successful.*

b Match the sentences in **10a** to these meanings.

1. talking about the future seen from now
2. talking about the future seen from a point in the past

c Complete the table with verb forms 1–5 in speech bubbles A–D.

the future seen from now	the future seen from the past
am/is/are going to + infinitive	*was/were going to + infinitive*
will + infinitive	
am/is/are supposed to + infinitive	
am/is/are about to + infinitive	
am/is/are to + infinitive	

d Check in GRAMMAR 4.2 p145.

11 **a** Complete these sentences. At least two sentences should be false.

1. Yesterday, I was about to …
2. Last summer, I was going to … , but …
3. This time last year, I had no idea I'd …
4. When I was little, I always knew I was going to …
5. Once, I made a promise to (myself, etc.) that I'd always …

b Work in pairs and say your sentences. Your partner guesses which ones are true. Ask follow-up questions about the true sentences.

Get ready … Get it right!

12 Work in groups. Group A p106. Group B p109. Group C p111.

Writing

Connecting words contrast (2)
Punctuation capital letters and full stops
Writing task a proposal

1 What types of programme should there be more of on TV? What programmes should there be fewer of? Why?

2 Read the writing task below. Then read the extract from a student's answer. Ignore any mistakes for now. Do you agree with their ideas? Why?/Why not?

> Following changes to TV programming at Channel 13, TV6 is also keen to review its schedule. The editor has asked viewers to write proposals, suggesting what types of programme should be shown less, and what should replace them. Give an example of the types of programme you mention, briefly describing the content, and justifying your suggestions.

There is not enough variety on TV, for instance, there are two series currently showing on the topic of designing or improving houses and a third is due to start. an example is Great Designs, in which the presenter dr Paul Boyer visits people's dream houses and interviews the owners. Although the houses are unusual and sometimes amazing, the topic of Architecture has limited appeal. In the real world, few people have the money to spend on great house designs, nonetheless, these people seem to have unlimited funds to pour into their dream homes.

It would be better to replace these programmes with something about the Arts; For instance, a series which reviews new films and interviews the actors. Despite the interest in Celebrities, there are no interesting programmes which look seriously at films. I understand a new chat show interviewing famous people is about to start, Nevertheless, ...

3 **a** There are a number of mistakes with punctuation in the extract. Replace three commas with full stops.

b Find and correct eight mistakes with capital letters. WRITING 4.1 p145.

4 Choose the correct connecting words. Sometimes both answers are possible. WRITING 4.2 p145.

1 Viewing figures are down *despite/but* the programme has not been cancelled.
2 *In spite of/Although* she has been contacted, we have had no reply.
3 I dislike reality TV. *Nevertheless/However*, Callow's new series is worth watching.
4 Few people have the money to spend on great house design. *Nonetheless/Even though*, these people seem to have unlimited funds.
5 He only got 50% in his exam *nevertheless/however*, it's better than last year.
6 *Despite/In spite of* all their hard work, they failed to make the deadline.
7 The film was finally completed *in spite of/although* the budget issues.
8 *Despite/Although* being late, their proposal will be considered.

5 **a** Read the extract again. Match the underlined words with these patterns.

a + noun phrase or verb + *ing*
b + clause (subject + verb)

b Replace the underlined words with another word/phrase which has the same grammar pattern and meaning.

c Continue the final sentence. Then compare your sentences in groups.

6 **a** Plan an answer to the writing task in **2**.

- Make notes about the ideas you want to include (e.g. the types of programme, an example, reasons for what you propose, etc.).
- Organise your notes into two or three paragraphs.
- Think about an introduction and conclusion.

b Work in pairs and compare notes. Do you have similar or different ideas?

7 **a** Write your proposal.

b Check your writing for these features.

- punctuation
- connecting words
- repetition (if you have repeated words, replace them with synonyms)

8 **a** Work in pairs. Read your partner's proposal, using the checklist in **7b**.

b Discuss possible problems together. Improve your writing if you can.

For more Writing practice: Portfolio 4, Workbook p63.

Making a splash

Vocabulary newspaper language
Skills Reading: two news stories; Listening: interview with a sub-editor
Real World persuading

QUICK REVIEW Near synonyms Make a list of as many near synonyms as you can for these words: *enormous*; *let*; *infuriating*; *enjoy*; *clever*; *unexpectedly*. Work in pairs. Tell each other your synonyms.

1 a Look at the images and headlines from two different news sources on the same day. Then work in pairs and answer these questions.

1 In what ways are the two news sources different? Think about the way they look and what the main stories are.
2 Which is a 'tabloid' and which is the 'quality press'?
3 Which one do you think is more popular? Why?
4 What kind of readership do you think each one might appeal to?

b CD1 25 Listen to part of an interview with Andrew Cook, a sub-editor on a national tabloid newspaper. Compare your answers in **1a** with what he says.

2 a Listen again. Complete this information with one or two words.

1 Although the way news is delivered has changed, the __________ of the different news sources hasn't changed.
2 In the quality press, the language is more __________ and the presentation of the news is more __________.
3 Tabloids control how you __________ and __________ .
4 The tabloids attract __________ of readers.
5 The more __________ news sources are less popular with readers.
6 The quality press often lead with __________ stories.
7 'Downmarket' tabloids prefer stories about film stars, royals and __________ stories.
8 Andrew says that a 'splash' is a story that appears on the __________ .
9 The people who buy Andrew's paper tend to be __________ families.

b Read these extracts from the interview. What do the words/phrases in bold mean?

1 … they still present the news in a more **sober kind of fashion** …
2 … the tabloid papers tend to **shout at you** …
3 … something with a much, sort of **brasher, instant appeal** …
4 … so-called **red-top** tabloids …
5 … the **heart of our audience** …

A

HERO PILOT SAVES FLIGHT BA038

Give him a medal as big as a frying pan

By MARTIN FRICKER & REBECCA EVANS

A HEROIC British Airways pilot averted catastrophe yesterday by gliding his jet into Heathrow after its engines failed.

Capt Peter Burkill kept Flight BA038 airborne over houses and schools before crash-landing in a field. Only 19 of the 136 people on board were hurt.

A witness said: "He deserves a medal as big as a frying pan."

The jet swooped in a few feet above cars heading for the airport.

B

Heathrow escape for 150 passengers and crew as BA jet crash-lands before runway

More than 150 passengers and crew escaped disaster yesterday after a British Airways jet crash-landed short of the runway at Heathrow airport, just missing a nearby road. The Boeing 777, arriving from Beijing, struck the ground at 12.43pm on the grassy approach to the airport's south runway, crushing its undercarriage, which became detached, and skidding on its belly for several hundred metres.

The 16-strong crew and 135 passengers were evacuated via the emergency slides. Thirteen people including four crew were treated in hospital for minor injuries.

3 Read news stories A and B. What are the main differences in the language used? Think about the length of sentences and paragraphs and the choice of vocabulary.

4 **a** CD1 26 Listen to Andrew. Are these statements true or false, according to him?

1 Sentences in the quality press are usually shorter and clearer.
2 The language of tabloids tends to have a dramatic feel.
3 Paragraphs are deliberately kept very short in tabloids.

b Andrew uses these phrases to describe the language of tabloid news. What do you think they mean?

1 snappier language
2 crisp sentences
3 a crash, bang, wallop style
4 in tune with the audience

c CD1 27 Listen to Andrew explaining how a story gets chosen as headline news. Answer these questions.

1 Who do the reporters have to convince to choose their story?
2 How should the story be written?

5 Work in pairs and discuss these questions.

1 Were you surprised by anything Andrew said?
2 Does your country have 'quality' and 'downmarket' press?
3 What kind of news sources are popular in your country?

6 Work in groups. Student A p106. Student B p108. Student C p112.

REAL WORLD
Persuading

- You've got to admit …
- I'd have thought this story would make a better splash.
- Don't you think more people are interested in … ?
- This is just the kind of story people want to read.

continue2learn

Vocabulary, Grammar and Real World

- **Extra Practice and Progress Portfolio 4** p117
- **Video (*TV addicts*)** p127
- **Language Summary 4** p114
- **Workbook 4** p19

Reading and Writing

- **Portfolio 4** A website post Workbook p63
  Reading a website post
  Writing ways to organise discussion writing

5A Behind the glamour

Vocabulary word building (1): prefixes with multiple meanings
Grammar reflexive pronouns

QUICK REVIEW News collocations Write as many news collocations as you can. Work in pairs. Take turns to say the noun in the collocation. Your partner says the verb. A *publicity*. B *seek publicity*.

Speaking and Reading

1 **a** Work in pairs. Discuss these questions.

1 Why do you think so many people are interested in the lives of celebrities?
2 Why do you think some people want to work with celebrities?
3 What are the possible advantages and disadvantages of being a celebrity personal assistant?

b Read the article and check your ideas.

2 Choose the correct answers. Find evidence in the article.

1 The writer's interviews with two celebrity personal assistants aim to …
  a encourage people to look favourably on the job.
  b give a detailed picture of how celebrities live.
  c illustrate their attitudes to the job.
2 The writer suggests that celebrity assistants are motivated by …
  a the possibility of becoming famous themselves.
  b the close connection with famous people.
  c the fact that the work itself is not too demanding.
3 Dean Johnson said that …
  a film stars have a higher profile than politicians.
  b celebrity assistants are just as powerful as their employers.
  c he is motivated by his love for the world of entertainment.
4 The seminar speaker …
  a encouraged everyone to join the profession.
  b stressed that commitments can be a problem.
  c said that the job suits strong, independent people.
5 Annie Brentwell said the job required her to …
  a be continually aware of what role she should play.
  b be a true and loyal friend to her employer.
  c share her emotions with her employer.
6 Brentwell enjoyed …
  a being able to attend events frequently with her employer.
  b being treated like a celebrity on special occasions.
  c achieving her routine tasks on a daily basis.
7 Despite occasional worries about her chosen profession, Brentwell …
  a did not believe the job could affect her well-being.
  b was never interested in looking for a different job.
  c was pleased with her reputation in her field.

3 Work in pairs and discuss these questions.

1 What is the writer's attitude to the job?
2 What do you think about the job? Give reasons.
3 Dean Johnson says "entertainment is what captivates the world today". What does he mean and do you agree?
4 If you could work for any celebrity, who would you choose and why?

A celebrity lifestyle?

The personal assistants to film stars are overworked, underpaid and invisible. Why would anyone want the job? **Jake Halpern** went to investigate.

The Romans had personal assistants – or 'courtiers' as they were known then – and Napoleon Bonaparte allegedly employed an assistant with the same-sized feet, whose primary job it was to break in the emperor's new shoes. It stands to reason that a city like Los Angeles, home to so many of the famous and the **semi**-famous, is also home to the Association of Celebrity Personal Assistants (CPAs).

CPAs make up a unique niche among Hollywood professionals. Unlike lawyers and agents, who rub shoulders with Hollywood stars and often make millions of dollars, assistants are not paid particularly well, especially given their round-the-clock obligations. Proximity to the stars appears to be the only perk their job offers. The bulk of their work is drudgery: doing laundry; fetching groceries; paying bills. Nevertheless, most consider their line of work as a lifelong profession. It is not the means to an end, but an end in itself.

I spoke to a personal assistant, Dean Johnson, about why he does it. "I don't consider myself vain or superficial, but we all like to be close to something that's powerful and entertainment is what captivates the world today. These celebrities are known around the world. We assistants are the gatekeepers, and that's a powerful position to be in." Why not go and work for the people running the country, then, I asked him. "Most people can't name

the secretary of state, but they can name Hollywood actors," he said. "It's sad but true."

Dean invited me along to a seminar entitled 'Becoming a CPA'. The first speaker began by laying down some hard truths.

"You must be in good health at all times. If you get recurrent colds or are generally stressed, this job is not for you. You also need to be flexible, which means it's probably better if you don't have a spouse, kids, pets or even plants. You have to have a 'can-do' attitude. If there's one word that celebrities don't want to hear, that word is 'no'."

A participant at the seminar, Annie Brentwell, agreed. "The most important thing is not to express or even think about your own needs. If my employer has to think about me, it detracts from what they are doing."

Brentwell was constantly adjusting her psyche to become the perfect complement or **counter**balance: she could play the humble servant, the trusted confidante, the admirer, or the supportive family member. Yet, even when she emulated a friend, it wasn't realistic because, on principle, she was refusing to talk about herself or to recognise her own emotions. The result was a **pseudo**-friendship, in which one person did all the talking and feeling, while the other deftly manoeuvred to stay out of the way. There was never any real **inter**action. When I asked her how she took care of her own mental well-being, she laughed.

"This job can really burn you out. I imagine that psychologists wouldn't approve of what personal assistants do, because we're consciously choosing not to feel certain emotions when we are on the job."

As hard as her job was, however, Brentwell said she did enjoy being a personal assistant at times. The first – and rarest – came on those occasions when she could play 'dress up' and go to a glamorous event with her employer. The most dramatic example was when she accompanied her previous employer, actress Sharon Stone, to a movie premiere. As a treat, Stone allowed Brentwell to wear her jewellery and shoes.

"Best of all, there's the limo ride and the whole experience of walking along the red carpet, seeing the flashing lights and having that very special feeling for one night."

Another, more common, joy came on the days when she worked herself into a stupor. "If you have a demanding day, when you work from early morning until late at night and you've done all the things they throw at you – both important and trivial – you feel like a **super**woman. I'm proud of my ability to lose myself and do whatever I have to do, even at the risk of health or sanity."

Brentwell also felt proud of how many people wanted her to work for them but she was occasionally assailed by doubts about her future.

"I wish I had travelled more. And I do wish that I had kids." There were times when these thoughts made her consider quitting this line of work. She insisted, however, that there was still time.

HELP WITH VOCABULARY

Word building (1): prefixes with multiple meanings

- If we don't know the meaning of a noun, adjective or verb, we can often guess from its prefix.

4 **a** Match these prefixes from the article to meanings a–g.

counter inter super pseudo semi under over

a between (two things, people, etc.)
b in opposition to
c better/more than usual
d too much
e partly
f not enough
g not real

b The same prefix can sometimes have more than one meaning. Match the prefixes in bold in sentences 1–6 to meanings a–f.

1 The wires were tightly **inter**locked.
2 There has been a **counter**-attack by the rebels.
3 I've heard that man is **super**-rich.
4 Lightning flashed **over**head as we walked.
5 Next, you have to draw a **semi**circle.
6 The ground was very wet **under**foot.

a from above/on top/across
b joined together
c as a reaction to
d half
e below
f extremely

c Check in VOCABULARY 5.1 p146.

5 **a** What prefixes from **4a** and **4b** can you add to these words to describe people or actions?

1 achiever *overachiever, underachiever*
2 motivated
3 professional
4 national
5 paid
6 intellectual
7 productive
8 human

b Work in pairs. Describe a word from **5a** and guess which word is described.

When someone gets more money than they deserve.

Overpaid?

Listening and Speaking

6 **a** Work in pairs and look at the photo of extras on a film set. What do you think their job is like? Think about these topics.

1 their working hours
2 their pay
3 the kind of roles they get

b CD2 1 Listen to an interview with two extras and make notes under headings 1–3 in **6a**. Then work in pairs and compare notes.

7 **a** CD2 2 Listen again to Daniel. What does he say about these things?

1 why he became an extra
2 what he does while he's waiting
3 seeing himself act
4 getting a slightly better part
5 becoming an actor himself

b CD2 3 Listen again to Kate. What does she say about these things?

1 why she became an extra
2 the people who become extras
3 what the stars are like
4 the negative things about the job
5 the positive things about the job

c Work in pairs. Give reasons why you would or wouldn't like to be an extra. If you would, which films or television series would you most like to appear in?

HELP WITH PRONUNCIATION

Speech units and stress (2)

8 **a** CD2 4 Listen and notice the different stress patterns in these sentences. Match sentences 1–3 to meanings a–c.

Daniel, what makes people like yourself want to be an extra?

1 Well // I guess I've always been keen on // amateur dramatics.
2 Well // I guess I've always been keen on // amateur dramatics.
3 Well // I guess I've always been keen on // amateur dramatics.

The speaker is focusing on …

a the person (perhaps in contrast to another person).
b the length of time.
c the particular interest.

TIP • We place the main stress on a key word in each speech unit in order to emphasise a particular message (for example, new information in response to a question).

b Read the questions and answers from Kate's interview. Underline the words you think are most likely to be stressed in Kate's replies.

1 INTERVIEWER You do mostly TV work, don't you?
KATE Yes // you know // lots of soap operas // period dramas // that sort of thing.
2 INTERVIEWER And what kind of people become extras?
KATE Oh all sorts // from young drama students to // solicitors on their day off // bored housewives // whoever.
3 INTERVIEWER Do you ever get the chance to meet the principal actors?
KATE Well // we're actually actively encouraged // not to interact with them.
4 INTERVIEWER And do you enjoy it?
KATE I like the job itself.

c Work in pairs. Compare your answers. Can you explain your choices?

d CD2 3 Listen and check. Did you have the same answers?

HELP WITH GRAMMAR

Reflexive pronouns

9 **a** Match examples a–c to uses 1–3 of reflexive pronouns.

a Daniel, what makes people like **yourself** want to be an extra?
b She read the script to **herself**.
c I like the job **itself**, but …

1 after *as well as*, *as (for)*, *like*, etc. instead of object pronouns, although these are possible. This use of the reflexive can show politeness.
2 to emphasise a noun, pronoun or noun phrase
3 to make it clear that the object (after a preposition) refers to the same person/thing as the subject of the verb

b Check in GRAMMAR 5.1 p147.

10 **a** Choose the correct answer.

1 I find it difficult to study unless I really *concentrate/concentrate myself*.
2 My family and I regularly *meet/meet ourselves* and go out together.
3 It's important to have a job where you can work and *enjoy/enjoy yourself* at the same time.
4 If I find something difficult, I try to *help/help myself* first before asking someone else.
5 When I speak English, there are times when I *feel/feel myself* very tired.
6 If I went on holiday *by myself/myself*, I would have a good time and wouldn't feel lonely.

b Work in pairs. Discuss which sentences in **10a** are true for you. Give reasons.

Get ready … Get it right!

11 Work in pairs. Student A p106. Student B p110.

The young ones

Vocabulary verb + infinitive with *to* or verb+*ing*; verb–noun collocations

QUICK REVIEW Prefixes with multiple meanings Work in pairs. Take turns to say sentences that are true for you, using words with these prefixes: *over-*; *under-*; *inter-*; *semi-*; *counter-*; *super-*. Ask follow-up questions. **A** *I overspent again last month.* **B** *Why?*

Reading and Vocabulary

1 **a** How many very successful young people do you know/have you heard of? What have they done?

b Read the title and introduction to the article on p51, and look at the photos and captions. What factors do you think make some people very successful at a young age?

2 Work in groups. Read an extract from an article called *Young achievers*.

Group A p107.
Group B p110.
Group C p112.
Group D p113.

Make notes on these questions for your person.

1 When did he/she take up his/her interest? Was there a reason for it?
2 What exceptional personal qualities do you think he/she has?

3 **a** Discuss the questions in **2** in your groups.

b Work in groups of four, with one student from each group, A, B, C and D. Tell each other about the people you read about and discuss your answers to the questions in **2**.

4 **a** Read these sentences. Which of the four people do you think they apply to? Why?

1 Without this focus to my life, I probably wouldn't have a job.
2 I used to be quite difficult to live with at times.
3 Sometimes I feel like an impostor.
4 I'd do this even if I wasn't being paid for it; it's just what I do.
5 This work has helped me to cope with my personal problems.
6 I was surprised about all the fuss it caused, but it was just a bit of fun.
7 I often feel isolated from other people.
8 I feel I have changed my personality because of what I do.

b Work in pairs. Discuss these questions.

1 Which of the four people do you think is the most impressive?
2 What are the pros and cons of becoming successful at a young age?

HELP WITH VOCABULARY
Verb + infinitive with *to* or verb+*ing* (2)

5 **a** Look at these pairs of sentences from the articles and complete the explanations with verb + infinitive with *to* or verb+*ing*.

1 a I don't **forget** to have a good time too.
  b I'll never **forget** losing them.
  forget + ________ = looks back to memories of the past
  forget + ________ = refers to now or the future
2 a Neymar **went on** playing for Santos FC throughout his teens.
  b Making beats **went on** to become my life …
  go on + ________ = continue an action
  go on + ________ = begin a new action
3 a … it **means** coordinating really well.
  b Riding was just **meant** to make physiotherapy fun.
  mean + ________ = involve/necessitate
  mean + ________ = intend
4 a He never **regretted** making that decision.
  b I **regret** to say that at school I was trouble.
  regret + ________ = be sorry for what's already happened
  regret + ________ (formal) = be sorry for what you're about to say

TIP • Verbs of the senses (*see*, *notice*, etc.) can be followed by:
a object + verb+*ing* when describing a repeated action or an action in progress: *He noticed me playing.*
b object + infinitive when describing a single action or a completed action: *I saw him get into the car.*

b Check in **VOCABULARY 5.2** p146.

6 **a** Complete these sentences about your own achievements and plans.

1 I (don't) regret …
  I don't regret changing careers. It's the best thing I ever did.
2 I'll never forget …
3 After this course I'm going to go on …
4 Next year I really mean …
5 I must remember …

b Write five questions to ask a partner about their achievements and plans. Use verbs from **5a**.

c Work in pairs. Take turns to interview each other.

YOUNG ACHIEVERS

From musicians to horse riders to campaigners to footballers, they are all people who made an impact at a very early age. Emma Hardy interviews them about their success.

Neymar da Silva Santos Jr.
Often compared to Pelé and Messi, Neymar joined Santos FC in Brazil at 11 years old, made his professional debut at 17 and just turned 20, he scored his 100th goal as a professional football player.

Iris Andrews.
Campaigned for the organisation Peace One Day while still at school. She went on to work for the organisation full-time.

Sophie Christiansen.
European Paralympics horse-riding champion for dressage at the age of 16. Born with cerebral palsy, she did not walk unaided until she was nearly four.

Dizzee Rascal.
The first rapper and youngest person to win the Mercury Music Prize for his debut album in 2003 while still a teenager. He went on to have his own recording label.

Claire

Will

Charlie

Listing

Listening

- In the UK, people leave school at 16 or stay on for another two years to do their A-level (Advanced) exams.

7 **a** CD2 5 Listen to an interview with Claire, Will and Charlie, three 18-year-olds who have finished school or college. Answer these questions.

1. Who has taken a year off to plan his/her future?
2. Who has decided to do research into a range of different jobs?
3. Who changed his/her mind about which subject to do at university?

b Listen again. Tick the true sentences. Correct the false sentences.

1 a Claire has really enjoyed all the different jobs she has been doing.
b She feels there is so much choice these days that it's difficult to make a decision.
2 a Will thinks that his time in the sixth form was quite stressful.
b He has not yet decided what to do after his year off.
3 a Charlie is still not sure she has chosen the right subject.
b She felt that English was not the right choice for her to study at university.

c Do you think life for Claire, Will and Charlie is easier or harder than it was for your parents and grandparents? Is it more enjoyable? Give reasons.

Vocabulary Verb–noun collocations

8 **a** Match the verbs to the noun phrases. Sometimes there is more than one possible answer. Check in VOCABULARY 5.3 p146.

1 come to	a what to do
2 look into	b different options
3 go on	c some time out
4 do	d a decision
5 gain	e an insight
6 work out	f a place at university
7 apply for	g work experience
8 take	h courses

b Work in pairs. Choose four verb–noun collocations from **8a** and write questions to ask another partner.

Have you been able to take some time out from work or studying recently?

c Change pairs. Ask and answer your questions.

Get ready ... Get it right!

9 If you were the Minister of Education in your country, how would you improve schools? Write six suggestions. Use these ideas or your own.

- the range of subjects which are offered
- the curriculum
- how subjects are taught
- whether certain subjects should be compulsory or optional
- the system of exams and assessment
- careers advice
- the standard of teacher training

10 **a** Work in groups. Discuss your ideas. Agree on the best three.

> I think it would be great if music were made compulsory.

b Tell the class your ideas. Which is most popular?

5 Writing

Connecting words time (2)
Spelling *ie* or *ei*
Writing task a formal letter / email applying for a course

1 Work in pairs and discuss these questions.

1 Would you be interested in doing a course in the evening if you had time?
2 What would you most like to learn about?

2 You have seen this notice on a website offering free evening courses. Read the extract from an application. Ignore any mistakes for now. What course does she want to do and what reasons does she give?

Interested in learning something new, completely FREE?

- Apply for the evening course of your choice (see full list for details).
- Funding available for five applicants only!
- Write and tell us which course you are interested in and why you should be the one to get funding.

I would very much like to do this course because I am fascinated by the area I live in, and would be very interested in finding out more about its history. I left school at 16 with reasonable grades and started work straightaway. I was lucky to find a part-time job in a supermarket in our **neighbourhood**, because up until then, I had never worked. However, working behind a till was rather undemanding, so I was **releived** to get a new job a few months later, giving out tickets at a theme park. Although the work itself was not very challenging, I did enjoy the daily contact with people and decided to look into jobs in a **feild** that would allow me to continue this.

Recently, I have been working as a guide in a local museum. I feel I had not done anything very useful previously, but being offered this job was a real **acheivement**. However, I really need to improve my grasp of local history, so on seeing your notice, I instantly **seized** the opportunity to apply. If I **receive** this funding, I'd like to go on to become a tour guide.

3 **a** Complete these words with *ie* or *ei*. WRITING 5.1 ▶ p148.

1 Did you rec _ _ ve a card from Jim on your birthday?
2 Have you met my n _ _ ghbour, Elsa?
3 It takes great pat _ _ nce to do that kind of work.
4 She doesn't have enough exper _ _ nce for that job.
5 The house is surrounded by f _ _ lds.
6 You must be very rel _ _ ved that he is back safely.
7 To ach _ _ ve good grades, you'll have to work hard.
8 She s _ _ zed the money and ran.
9 I like Hal, but he's a bit conc _ _ ted.
10 I will never forgive her for dec _ _ ving me.

b Look at the words in bold in the application. Correct the words which are spelt incorrectly.

4 Rewrite these sentences from the letter with the linking words in brackets. If two answers are possible, write two sentences and add or change any words or verb forms. WRITING 5.2 ▶ p148.

1 I started work straightaway. (immediately)
2 I instantly seized the opportunity. (at once)
3 I had not done anything very useful previously. (before)
4 I was relieved to get a new job a few months later. (after)
5 I'd like to go on to become a tour guide. (eventually)
6 Recently, I have been working as a guide. (lately)
7 Up until then, I had never worked. (prior to this)

5 Decide on a course you would like to apply for and plan your application. Make notes about these topics.

- the course
- your reasons for applying
- your background

6 **a** Write your application. Use language from this unit.

b Work in pairs. Swap and check your partner's writing for:

- correct use of linking words
- correct spelling (*ie* or *ei*)
- use of language from this unit (e.g. reflexive pronouns; verb patterns; verb–noun collocations)

c Discuss any problems. Then try to improve your writing.

7 Read other applications. Who should get funding?

▶ **For more Writing practice: Portfolio 5, Workbook p66.**

Priorities

Vocabulary work expressions
Real World conversational strategies

QUICK REVIEW verb + infinitive with *to* or verb+*ing* Work in pairs. Write a sentence with each of these verbs: *go on*; *forget*. One of you use verb + infinitive with *to*, the other use verb+*ing*. Compare your sentences. What is the difference in meaning between the two verb patterns?

1 **a** Tick the phrases in bold you know. Check in VOCABULARY 5.4 p147.

1 Have you ever been **stuck in a rut** or in a **dead-end** job?
2 Have you ever **taken on too much work** and been **snowed under**?
3 Do you know anyone who always **talks shop**?
4 Are you a good **team player** or would you prefer to be **self-employed**?
5 Which jobs can you think of that either pay a **pittance** or a **fortune**?
6 Would you prefer a **high-powered** or **run-of-the-mill** job?
7 Have you ever been **thrown in at the deep end** when you started a new job?
8 Do you like **deadlines** and working **against the clock**?
9 Are you **up to your eyes** in work at the moment or are you **taking it easy**?
10 How important is it to **climb the career ladder**?

b Work in pairs. Ask and answer the questions in **1a**. Ask follow-up questions.

2 **a** Look at cartoons A–D and their captions. What social issues are they addressing? Do you have similar issues in your country?

b Work in groups of three. Discuss these topics. Talk about each topic for one or two minutes and try to come to some conclusions.

a Is it fair that a company director earns much more than a cleaner?
b How important is work to you? Do you work to live or live to work?
c Is there a legal minimum wage in your country? If yes, do all employers keep to it?
d Should employers be forced to make it easier for mothers to return to work?

3 **CD2 6** Listen to Josh, Tracey and Liz discussing jobs. Match extracts 1–3 to three of the topics in **2b**. Which topic do they not discuss?

A

B

C

D

4 **a** CD2 ▸ 7 Listen again to Extract 1.

1 What do the first two speakers agree on?
2 What counter-argument does Liz mention?

b CD2 ▸ 8 Listen to Extract 2. Which arguments for and against 'living to work' are not mentioned?

a a good income
b illness
c divorce
d enjoying your job
e promotion
f early retirement

c CD2 ▸ 9 Listen again to Extract 3. Then answer these questions.

1 LIZ What I do feel strongly about is that employers make provision for working mothers. (What provisions?)
2 JOSH Well, perhaps they would if it were more accepted. (Who are 'they'? What would they do?)
3 TRACEY The problem is people with no kids. (What problem?)

REAL WORLD Conversational strategies

5 **a** Match strategies a–j with phrases 1–10.

a including someone in the conversation *3*
b adding something to the argument
c stressing an important point
d encouraging someone to continue
e justifying what you say
f getting the conversation back on track
g saying you agree with someone
h conceding someone is right
i disagreeing politely
j asking someone to say more about a topic

1 Not to mention …
2 That's exactly what I was trying to get at.
3 You look dubious, (Liz).
4 I'm with (you) on that.
5 All I'm saying is …
6 Carry on, (Liz). You were saying?
7 Anyway, (assuming you do want promotion) …
8 By (provision) you mean …?
9 You've got me there!
10 Oh, I don't know about (that).

b Match these examples to conversational strategies a–j.

1 You're very quiet, (Josh). *a*
2 That's precisely what I mean.
3 What I'm trying to say is …
4 What were you about/going to say (Tracey)?
5 Well, I can't disagree with that.
6 To get back to what (I) was saying about (promotion) …
7 I'd go along with that.
8 What do you mean when you say (provision)?
9 Actually, I'm not sure you can say (that).
10 And of course there's always …

c Check in REAL WORLD 5.1 ▸ p148.

6 Work in pairs. Change the words in bold in these conversations using one phrase from **5**. You may need to change other parts of the sentence.

1 A Smoking is very expensive.
B **And also** it's a disgusting habit.
Not to mention it's a disgusting habit.
A But I thought you just said you smoked for most of your life.
B That's true. **I admit it**!

2 A Parents should try and leave an inheritance to their kids.
B **I disagree**! What about enjoying your money yourself in your old age!

3 A Becca's invited a few friends round for a sleepover tonight.
B **A few friends?** Two or 20?

4 A I think the prime minister's foreign policy is misguided.
B I agree. And his plans for education are misguided, too.
A Yes, well, but **to go back to** his foreign policy, I think it's dangerous.

5 A It's a waste of time and money buying CDs these days.
B Well, I think it's easier and cheaper just to download them.
A **That's what I meant**.

7 **a** Work in groups of three. Look at Audio Script CD2 ▸ 6 p169. Choose one of the extracts and add at least eight more lines to end the conversation.

b Practise the lines you added. Then act them out to the class. The class decides which extract the lines complete.

c The class votes for the best ending for each extract.

8 Work in groups. Choose a current news issue. Discuss it using the strategies in **5a**.

continue2learn

Vocabulary, Grammar and Real World

- **Extra Practice and Progress Portfolio 5** p118
- **Video (*It's just a job!*)** p128
- **Language Summary 5** p146
- **Workbook 5** p24

Reading and Writing

- **Portfolio 5** An article Workbook p66
Reading an article
Writing personalising language

6A A curious science

Vocabulary words with different but related meanings
Grammar formal and informal ways of comparing

QUICK REVIEW Work expressions
Work in pairs. Use these words/phrases to talk about work: *dead-end*; *deadlines*; *high-powered*; *flexible*; *perk*; *demanding*. A *Have you ever had a high-powered job?* B *Yes, one summer I worked …*

Reading and Vocabulary

1 Work in pairs. Discuss the questions.

1 How do you feel when people break social rules (not waiting their turn, breaking the speed limit, etc.)?
2 Can we influence the way we do things just by thinking differently?
3 Are you good at telling jokes? Can you give an example of a joke you like?

2 **a** Work in pairs. Do you agree with these statements? Why?/Why not?

1 Teenagers are most likely to push in to get ahead of others in a queue.
2 Male drivers are more likely to break the speed limit than female drivers.
3 If you think about old age, it can make you feel and act old.
4 Thinking positively helps you perform better in tasks.
5 Jokes about animals are funnier than other types of jokes.
6 When you smile, it makes you happier (even if you don't feel like smiling).

b Read extracts A–C. What do the extracts say about the statements in **2a**?

c Work in small groups. Discuss these questions.

1 Which of the pieces of research did you find the most interesting? Why?
2 Describe a typical queue where you live. Do you think the way people queue says anything about a culture?
3 Do you agree that most people are 'totally unaware' of why they act the way they do?
4 What kinds of thing do people joke about in your country? Do you think people from other countries would find these jokes funny?

A **JOHN TRINKHAUS**, of the Zicklin School of Business, studies ordinary people going about their everyday lives. One of his specialities is the study of dishonest or anti-social behaviour. In his 25 years of research, one group of people has come to stand out as **decidedly** more likely than others to push boundaries. These are not disaffected teenagers or noisy football supporters. They are women van drivers.

Trinkhaus's finding is perhaps best illustrated by his extensive work, covertly monitoring a supermarket's 'ten items or less'* checkout, over a period of nine years. As many of us may have seen for ourselves, Trinkhaus has found that some shoppers using this lane often had **somewhat** more items than they should in their basket; some cunningly placed their items in groups of ten and paid for each group separately. He found that a very high proportion of these supermarket lane cheats were female van drivers. Furthermore, he has shown that **a good deal** more women than men van drivers break the speed limit, which he suspects is because they may have an unconscious need to out-do behaviour associated with men. Alternatively, this group of drivers may simply reflect a moral decline in society.

* *Ten items or less*: this expression is commonly seen in supermarkets, despite its incorrect grammar. It should, of course, be 'ten items or fewer'!

B

Two recent studies have suggested that most people are totally unaware of their reasons for behaving in the way they do.

In 1998, two Dutch psychologists asked half a group of volunteers to carry out a simple mental exercise that involved imagining the mindset of a typical university professor. The other half imagined a football hooligan. Then, they all had to answer some general knowledge questions. The people in the professor group got 14% more answers correct, despite the fact that there was **barely any** difference in their actual level of intelligence.

Focusing on the body rather than the mind, researchers at New York University asked one group of volunteers to do a mental task involving words relating to old age, such as 'wrinkled' and 'grey'. A second group were shown words unrelated to old age. The researchers then said the experiment was over and secretly recorded the time each participant took to walk down the long hallway to the exit. Those with old age on their mind took **significantly** longer to walk down the corridor.

So, it seems that if people were to have **marginally** more time to prime themselves about what they have to do, it could help them perform either better (or worse!) than normal at both mental and physical tasks.

HELP WITH GRAMMAR

Formal and informal ways of comparing

FORMAL

3 **a** Look at the words/phrases in bold in extracts A–C. Which indicate a big difference, and which indicate a small difference?

INFORMAL

b Look at the informal words/phrases in bold in statements 1–4. Which indicate a big difference? Which indicate a small difference?

1 Eccentric behaviour is **way** more common in older people.
2 You gain **loads** more time by using the '10 items or fewer' checkout.
3 I think the duck joke is **miles** funnier than the others.
4 Women van drivers are probably **a tiny bit** more competitive than men.

TIPS • Some informal phrases with *not as … as* can show big differences:
Cheating in a supermarket ***isn't half/nearly/anywhere near*** *as anti-social as driving too fast. Speeding is much worse.*
• Some informal phrases with *the same as* can show very small differences.
One group's level of intelligence ***was pretty much/more or less/much*** *the same as the other's. There was hardly any difference.*

c Check in GRAMMAR 6.1 p150.

C

Recently, the British Association for the Advancement of Science went in search of the world's funniest joke. The experiment involved people from all over the world posting their jokes on to a website and rating the submissions of others.

Among the jokes entered was the following: 'There were two cows in a field. One said "Moo." The other one said, "I was going to say that."'

The joke was then entered into the archive several times, using different animals and noises. Two tigers said "Grr," two dogs said "Woof" and so on. You would imagine that one animal and noise would be much the same as another. However, the joke rated the funniest was: 'Two ducks were sitting in a pond. One of the ducks said "Quack." The other duck said, "I was going to say that."'

This research supported the widely held theory that some words and sounds are **distinctly** funnier than others. The /k/ sound as heard in 'quack' and 'duck' has always been regarded in the comedy world as especially funny. Why? It may be down to a rather odd facial phenomenon known as 'facial feedback'. When people feel happy they smile but some evidence suggests that the mechanism also works in reverse. The /k/ sound often forces the face to smile, which may explain why the sound is associated with happiness.

4 **a** Complete these sentences with your own ideas.

1 Learning languages is marginally more challenging than …
2 … are a good deal faster than …
3 … is significantly less safe than …
4 … is decidedly more stylish than …
5 … are somewhat less dangerous than …
6 … is distinctly less healthy than …
7 … is barely any more expensive than …

b Work in pairs. Compare sentences. Do you agree with each other?

5 **a** Make comparisons with the adjectives in brackets and the informal phrases in the box.

way	loads	miles	a tiny bit
half	nearly	anywhere near	
pretty much	more or less		
much the same			

1 teenagers / elderly people / (selfish)
Teenagers are way more selfish than elderly people.
2 eating at home / eating in a restaurant (fun)
3 going to work / going to school (tiring)
4 being married / being single (good for your health)
5 having a bath / having a shower (relaxing)

b Work in groups. Say your sentences. Do you agree? Why?/Why not?

Listening and Vocabulary

6 You will listen to some friends telling stories about bizarre behaviour. Before you listen, try to match these words/phrases to story titles A–E.

pockets	patrols	the carriages
line them up	day in, day out	
make holes	the height of fashion	
hopping out of the top of her sweater		
look out	chicken wire	

A Two rabbits
B The perfect seat
C Stuffed toys
D Pebbles
E Odd socks

A

7 **a** CD2 11 Listen to the stories and check your ideas in **6**.

b Listen again. Complete these summaries with one or two words.

1 a Friends often had to look for Martina's rabbits in a ______ .
  b Martina used chicken wire to protect her ______ .
2 a Natalie talked about the man who always gets on at the ______ of the train.
  b He always walks ______ and ______ , looking for the best seat.
3 a The couple on the train used to line up their stuffed toys at ______ .
  b The other passengers always ______ them.
4 a Keith's little girl ______ pebbles and keeps them in her ______ .
  b He thinks she and her friends like to ______ their pebbles.

c Which of this behaviour did you find the most bizarre?

HELP WITH PRONUNCIATION
Showing surprise

- Exclamations often have a rise-falling tone to express surprise or show interest.

8 **a** CD2 12 Listen and notice how the friends use exclamations to show surprise.

Oh, ↗↘**OK**. … How very ↗↘**strange** …

That is very, very biz↗↘**arre** …

↗↘**No** … ↗↘**Gosh** …

b Look at Audio Script CD2 11 on p169 and find more exclamations.

c Work in pairs. Student A, look at picture A and retell the story. Student B, respond with the exclamations in **8a** and **8b**.

d Look at picture B. Swap roles and repeat **8c**.

HELP WITH VOCABULARY
Words with different but related meanings

TIP • Sometimes one word can have completely different meanings:
*I commute on the **train** to work every day. She wants to **train** to be a psychologist.*

• Sometimes one word can have different meanings but the meanings are related:
*The weather's **fine** today. I'm feeling **fine** now.*

9 **a** Look at the words in bold in 1–6. Match them to definitions a–f.

1 **odd** socks	a strange or unexpected
2 It was **odd** that he didn't phone.	b not matching
3 His daughter is really **sweet**.	c sugary
4 Dark chocolate isn't **sweet** enough for me.	d charming, attractive
5 the **top** of her sweater	e the highest part
6 **top** of the class	f the most successful

b Match these general meanings to the pairs of words in **9a**.

- the highest point or part in distance or quality
- unusual or peculiar
- pleasant

c Look at these phrases. All the words in bold are related in meaning. What do you think is the general meaning of each group?

1 a **branch** of a tree; a **branch** of a bank; a **branch** of science
2 feel **flat**; a **flat** piece of land; this lemonade is **flat**
3 have a **break** for coffee; **break** a window; **break** the law
4 **plain** paper; **plain** food; a **plain** face
5 **heavy** traffic; a **heavy** coat; a **heavy** sleeper

d Check in VOCABULARY 6.1 p149.

10 **a** Fill in the gaps with words from **9a** or **9c**.

1 We had ________ snow here at the weekend.
2 I find ________ shoes much more comfortable than heels.
3 I'd prefer a ________ carpet to a patterned one.
4 Where are you going for your summer ________?
5 She has been made ________ manager of a big insurance company.
6 The kitten was so ________ that we had to buy it.

b Work in pairs. Think of five more sentences using words from **9a** and **9c**.

Get ready ... Get it right!

11 Make notes on the unusual habits of four people you know. Use these ideas or your own.

- food
- routines
- superstitions
- clothing
- pets
- travelling

12 **a** Work in groups. Discuss the people you chose in **11**. Ask follow-up questions.

My dad always wears a red tie for good luck.

b Tell the class about the unusual behaviour your group discussed.

6B But is it ethical?

Vocabulary word pairs
Grammar position of adverbials

QUICK REVIEW Words with different but related meanings Work in pairs. Take turns to say a phrase with: *sweet*; *odd*; *plain*; *heavy*; *flat*. Listen and say a phrase with a different meaning: A *sweet coffee* B *a sweet smile*

Reading and Speaking

1 **a** Look at the photos on p61. What do you think was being advertised? How successful do you think the campaigns were?

b Read the article. What is 'stealth' and 'buzz' marketing?

c Work in pairs. Discuss these questions.

1 Why aren't people as easily persuaded by adverts as they used to be?
2 Why may it not be worth spending too much on television commercials?
3 How are current advertising campaigns different from previous ones?
4 In what situations can indirect advertising be tolerated?
5 In what situations can indirect advertising have the opposite effect of what was intended?
6 In what ways has Nike succeeded in gaining good publicity for itself?
7 What is the writer's opinion of Nike's marketing choices?
8 Why does the writer believe that advertising may not be all that important?

2 Find words in paragraphs A–G in the article to match these definitions.

A 1 strong feeling of hatred or disgust
2 believing that people are not sincere
B the long collection of things over a period
C 1 pour
2 new or unusual
D 1 too noticeable, in a way that may be annoying
2 annoys somebody badly
F 1 has no respect for someone or something
2 influence somebody without them noticing
G an attempt to make people feel that something is good by talking about it in the media

3 Work in groups. Discuss these questions.

1 Do you think people are manipulated by the media? Why?/Why not?
2 Are 'stealth' and 'buzz' marketing common in your country? Give examples if possible.

HELP WITH GRAMMAR Position of adverbials

4 **a** Look at the adverbials in blue in the article. Match them to these categories.

1 place (*where*)
2 time (*when*)
3 manner (*how*)
4 indefinite frequency (*how often, approximately*)
5 level of certainty (*how certain*)
6 comment (*the writer's opinion*)
7 definite frequency (*how often, exactly*)

TIPS • Different adverbials have different positions in a clause. We can change the position for emphasis, but these are general guidelines.

Front **comment**: ***Surprisingly***, *it worked.*
Mid **indefinite frequency**: *She's* ***always*** *right.*
level of certainty: *He'll* ***definitely*** *win.*
End **manner**: *They work* ***hard***.
place: *She's* ***at the office***.
time: *The advert came out* ***a year ago***.
definite frequency: *try to exercise* ***every day***.
indefinite frequency (with long adverbials): *I work at home* ***every so often***.

• Where there are several adverbials at the end of the clause, the usual order is manner, place, time:
She sang beautifully in the concert yesterday.

b Focusing adverbials come before the information we want to stress. How does the position of the focusing adverbial in bold in these sentences change the meaning?

1 a Jan and I **only** worked on the Volkswagen advert.
b **Only** Jan and I worked on the Volkswagen advert.
2 a Joe's been everywhere. He's **even** been to Tonga.
b More people are going to Tonga. **Even** Joe's been there.

c Check in GRAMMAR 6.2 p150.

5 **a** Read about an expensive marketing mistake. Why did the stunt fail?

The most expensive mistake in buzz marketing history was General Motors' great Pontiac giveaway. The idea of distributing a free car to every member of the studio audience for the Oprah Winfrey Show achieved its objective. In total, 276 Pontiac G6s – costing $7m – were given away to the audience which consisted of women who had been specially selected as deserving cases. The stunt received vast amounts of positive coverage in news outlets. It emerged, however, that all those deserving women were liable for an unexpected $7,000 income tax bill. General Motors' embarrassment became the talk of America.

b Add these adverbials to the paragraph. Keep the adverbials in the same order. There may be more than one answer.

1 perhaps
2 in September 2004
3 initially
4 only
5 in advance
6 not surprisingly
7 generally
8 quickly
9 now

c Work in pairs. Compare your ideas. Do any differences reflect a change in meaning?

Advertising is Dead – Long Live Advertising!

As advertisers adopt increasingly sneaky ways of selling their products, **Leo Benedictus** charts the rise of 'stealth' and 'buzz' marketing.

A These days, it's quite normal to regard all forms of marketing with loathing. After enjoying a long, golden age of witty, imaginative commercials, the public has now become too cynical – or 'marketing literate' – to be taken in by traditional advertising. The average person is exposed to around 3,000 messages every day so it is difficult for each individual message-maker to get noticed.

B Even more dangerous for the future of traditional advertising has been the accumulation of evidence that it no longer works. There was a study a few years ago which showed that only 18% of television campaigns generated a positive return on investment, suggesting that most TV advertising (however successful and creative) is little more than a fun way for a company to waste its money. It is from this crisis that marketing has emerged into its next revolution. Interestingly, this time it's no longer what brands say that is changing, or how they say it, but where. "Previously, advertising had specific forms," says Tom Himpe, author of *Advertising is Dead – Long Live Advertising!* "If you asked someone, 'What is advertising?' they would say billboards, newspaper ads, cinema and so on. However, these days every possible means of communicating a message is being used and experimented with."

C An extremely innovative and witty example of this experimentation was at a recent whaling conference, where a German animal-welfare group fitted capsules inside the bathrooms, causing the taps to gush 'blood'. A New Zealand television channel found a novel way of promoting its showing of the film *The Invisible Man* by letting a dog roam the streets, wearing a lead with an invisible owner!

D 'Stealth' advertising of this kind overcomes the problem of falling public interest by leaping out at consumers unannounced and grabbing their attention by force. Being intrusive is probably forgivable if the advertising is entertainingly done. However, if overused or done badly, it sometimes antagonises people and increases their resistance to the message.

E One of the most popular ways for a modern brand to win the consumer's heart is by performing good deeds for them, thereby generating positive unofficial information, or 'buzz', about the brand. The company may offer extra value to its customers, or it may perform some act of sponsored public service, such as the renovation of a much-loved swimming pool in the UK, paid for by Evian water. By organising large football and running events, Nike has also generated positive word-of-mouth for itself, as it has with charitable fundraising, such as their 'end AIDS red laces' campaign raising awareness of AIDS.

F Most people, one imagines, would prefer to receive a new swimming pool than an ad campaign out of Evian's marketing budget. Likewise, it is probably a good thing that Nike and many other brands now spend an increasing proportion of their money on charity work rather than commercials. Whether one respects these companies for their efforts or despises them for attempting to manipulate public opinion is a decision that each consumer must make for him- or herself.

G The whole world has a point of view that they hope to convince others to share – whether they are financially motivated to do so or not. We are all free to disagree if we wish. And, sometimes, if we let ourselves, we may prefer to believe the hype. Ultimately, we are the only ones who can decide what we want to believe, and what we want to buy.

Listening

6 Work in pairs. Discuss these questions.

1 Do you think you are influenced by marketing or advertising? If so, how?
2 Would you ever consider a career in marketing or advertising? Why?/Why not?

7 **a** Look at adverts A and B. Do you remember them? What do you think about the designs?

b CD2 13 CD2 14 Listen to two marketing specialists, Graham and Lindsay, talking about the adverts.

1 What aspects of the campaign are they interested in?
2 Why do they think each advert was successful?

8 **a** CD2 13 Listen to Graham again. What does he say about the meaning of the phrase: *it's the real thing*?

b CD2 14 Listen to Lindsay again. List the key words she uses to describe the advert.

c Work in pairs and discuss these questions.

1 Do you agree with Graham and Lindsay's opinions? Why?/Why not?
2 Are these products still widely advertised in your country? If so, how have their ad campaigns changed?
3 Are young people in your country image conscious? What are the 'must-have' products or brands at the moment?

Vocabulary Word pairs

9 **a** Tick the phrases in bold that you know. Guess what the new phrases mean. Then check in VOCABULARY 6.2 p149.

1 A What do you think of TV advertising at the moment?
B It depends what it is. I can **take it or leave it**.
2 A Do you ever buy things you've seen advertised on TV?
B Yes, **on and off**.
3 A Do you think any current ad campaigns are effective?
B A few, yes, but some are a bit **hit and miss**. Also, I do get tired of seeing the same ones **over and over again**.
4 A When you go to the supermarket, do you always choose the same brands?
B No, I tend to go **back and forth** between brands.
5 A What do you think can **make or break** an ad campaign?
B You can't generalise. **Each and every** one is different.
6 A Do you think TV advertising is **part and parcel** of everyday life?
B Sadly, yes. It's so annoying when a good programme is interrupted **time after time**.
7 A Can you think of a product which took off **in leaps and bounds**?
B Yes, the iPod.

b Work in pairs. How would you reply to A's questions in 9a?

Get ready ... Get it right!

10 Choose an advertising campaign that you think is (or was) very effective. Make notes on these topics.

- the product being advertised
- the style and content of the ads
- slogans or catchphrases
- the target market
- why the campaign was successful
- your opinion of the campaign

11 **a** Work in groups of three. Take turns to talk about the advertising campaign you chose. Which campaign does the group think is the best?

b Tell the class about the advertising campaign your group chose.

6 Writing

Connecting words purpose
Punctuation commas
Writing task an article about advertising campaigns

1 Work in pairs and discuss these questions.

1 What makes an advert or advertising campaign memorable? Give examples.
2 Read this extract from the first draft of an article about memorable campaigns. Ignore any mistakes for now. What do you think of the campaign?

[1]Sony is a very well-known and popular brand, which produces a variety of electrical goods, such as camera phones DVD recorders, and so on. They ran a memorable campaign a few years ago **in order launch** a new camera phone. [2]The company hired actors who had to pretend to be tourists, **wander** through US cities. They asked passers-by to take their photo, **so to have** an excuse to show them the camera and the actors then recommended 'their' new camera.

[3]Although a clever effective campaign in itself the problem was that Sony later admitted what they had done and people were outraged. [4]**In order Sony** to make their campaign memorable they used word-of-mouth very successfully. [5]However some people complained about the way the product was promoted.

2 **a** Tick the correct sentences. Then correct the mistakes. WRITING 6.1 p151.

1 The colours need to be bolder **so as to** make the design stand out.
2 **In order** the campaign to be a success, we must increase our budget.
3 We have conducted research **to see** which adverts are the most popular.
4 **So that** we can meet our deadline, we'd appreciate your ideas by tomorrow.
5 I'll send you some possible slogans **in order** you can decide.
6 I'd like to do a copywriting course **so to** go into advertising.

b Read the extract in **1** again and correct the parts in bold with appropriate connecting words. Use words/phrases from **2a**.

3 **a** Add one comma to each sentence.

1 This approach might work in a number of industries, such as fashion book sales and music.
2 If the actors had admitted the truth there would not have been a problem.
3 The advertising campaign which was the first of its kind, was very effective.
4 Tom Hicks, president of the company, said "When people find out they have been fooled, they may feel angry."
5 Buzz marketing requires a confident creative approach.
6 Not surprisingly some people have disagreed with this type of advertising.

b Work in pairs. Decide on the rule about commas in each sentence. WRITING 6.2 p151.

c Add one or two commas to sentences 1–5 in the extract in **1**.

4 Make notes on these questions.

1 What has been a recent memorable advertising campaign?
2 What is it that made this campaign memorable?

5 **a** Write a first draft of an article about the campaign. Focus on the accurate use of these features.

- connecting words of purpose
- commas
- adverbials

b Work in pairs. Read and check each other's articles, using the checklist in **5a**.

c Discuss your articles together and try to improve your work.

6 Read other students' articles. Which campaign sounds the most memorable? Why?

For more Writing practice: Portfolio 6, Workbook p69.

VOCABULARY AND SKILLS 6C Short story radio

Vocabulary dramatic adverbs
Skills Reading: a short story extract; Listening: short stories
Real World telling a story

QUICK REVIEW Word pairs Work in pairs. Take turns to complete these word pairs with *and/or*: *make*; *hit*; *leaps*; *off*; *take it*; *pick*; *each*; *part*; *over*; *back*. A *make or ...* B *make or break*.

1 **a** Work in groups. Do you read or listen to short stories? If so, what genres (crime, sci-fi, etc.) do you like or dislike?

b Read this blog extract. What kind of story do you think would work well?

SHORT STORY RADIO is seeking short stories to be professionally recorded and made available for download. Over 70,000 visitors, including English-language students from around the world, have visited our website.

- Submissions must be in English.
- We don't pay for your stories, but we do arrange for them to be recorded by professional actors.
- Stories must be fictional and work well on radio.

2 **a** CD2 15 John McRae is a professor of literature. Listen to him talking about what makes a good story.

1 What are the three things a story has to have?
2 What examples does he give of what a story can be?
3 What does he say a radio story has to do at the very beginning?

b Listen again to John talking about the components of a short story. Fill in these gaps with one word.

1 The ________ sets the story in its situation and context.
2 The ________ is when another character is introduced.
3 The ________ occurs when something else happens and the story gets more interesting.
4 The ________ happens at the end, when the situation gets sorted out.

3 **a** Read the first part of a story on p65.

1 What genre is it?
2 How is the story organised?
3 What are the premise and development so far?
4 Is the story told in a formal or informal style? Find examples.

b Write a summary of the story in as few words as you can.

c Work in pairs and compare your summaries.

4 Work in groups. What do you think is going to happen next (the complication)? What do you think the resolution is going to be?

5 **a** CD2 16 Listen to the end of the story. What happened? Did you have a similar ending?

b Tick the true sentences. Correct the false ones.

1 Carlos had no idea who Steve was.
2 Steve found Carlos rather frightening.
3 Julie expected Steve to bring his guitar.
4 The customers enjoyed Steve's music.
5 Carlos invited Steve to come back the next day.
6 Steve didn't stay and eat dinner in the restaurant.

6 **a** Complete the extracts with adverbs from the box.

accidentally	meekly	politely	~~unbelievably~~	
uncertainly	clearly	adoringly	expectantly	bitterly

1 I noticed an *unbelievably* beautiful girl smiling at me.
2 I looked up at him and nodded ________ .
3 He sighed ________ and stormed off.
4 They stood next to each other, looking at me ________ .
5 I ________ took the guitar.
6 Julie and Carlos were ________ a couple.
7 I might ________ have exaggerated my musical skills.
8 Julie looked up ________ at Carlos.
9 The couple clapped ________ .

b Check in Audio Script CD2 16 on p170.

7 **a** CD2 17 Listen to John McRae's tips for involving a listener. Fill in the gaps in these notes.

- pauses, [1]________ and stress
- range of lively words (e.g. [2]________ , adjectives, [3]________)
- vary the [4]________ and the [5]________
- build up the [6]________ (perhaps make it more scary or hold something back)
- [7]________ of voice as you tell the story
- give it a flow to make sure the listener enjoys it

b What do you think *a twist in the tail* means?

8 **a** Think of a story, anecdote or joke that you would like to tell. Use these ideas or your own.

- an embarrassing/amusing situation you've been in
- a meeting or relationship that changed your life
- a wonderful or disastrous holiday
- a party or celebration you've attended
- a memory from your childhood

b Plan your story, using John McRae's tips from **7a**. Make notes, but don't write the whole story.

Back in 2005, when James Blunt was still at number one with You're Beautiful, I was away, along with some friends from university. We were 21, we'd just finished our exams, and we were enjoying a well-deserved holiday. It was a beautiful island where the sun always shone, and the water was always warm. We sunbathed all day and danced all night, but there was something missing.

Then one night, my luck changed. I'd just finished exhibiting some of my best dance moves when I noticed an unbelievably beautiful girl smiling at me. Me? Surely she was looking at someone behind me. I turned around, but there was no one else there. I looked back in her direction. She smiled again. "What's happening?" I thought. Yes, she was actually smiling at me. My head spun.

Somewhat to my surprise, I found myself walking over to the girl. Things like this never happened to me. I glanced at my mates who were watching me, as surprised as I was. We found somewhere to chat and she told me her name was Julie. I was so nervous that my conversational skills suffered. I kept wittering on about how beautiful the island was, so much better than home, and wouldn't it be lovely to stay here longer and not have to leave. I told her about myself, and tried to sound interesting ... about what I had been studying, about how good I was on the guitar. To my amazement, she didn't seem to notice that I was talking nonsense. After the best 45 minutes of my holiday had rushed by without me even noticing, Julie said she had to go. I was just figuring out how to ask to see her again, when I heard her saying something about the following evening ... a restaurant called Casa Don Carlos, 7 p.m. "What do you think?" I mumbled a "yes" and tried to sound casual, as if I had a million other things to do. The next moment, she was gone. I went back to my mates.

The next evening, as you might expect, I was outside the restaurant on the dot of seven. It seemed very quiet inside, with no customers. I waited nervously outside for Julie to arrive. Then suddenly, the door swung open and a very large man came out, and eyed me suspiciously.

9 **a** Work in pairs. Take turns to practise telling your stories. Use techniques from the Real World box below.

b Work in groups and tell your stories. Is there one you all prefer?

REAL WORLD Telling a story

- We can use these techniques to add interest to a story.

Short, dramatic sentences	*Me? She smiled again.*
A range of verb forms	*We were 21, we'd just finished our exams, and we were enjoying a well-deserved holiday.*
Descriptive language	*My head spun.*
A mixture of direct and indirect speech	*I heard her saying something about the following evening … a restaurant called Casa Don Carlos, 7 p.m. "What do you think?"*
Idiomatic language	*on the dot of seven*
A comment at the end	*There was still something missing but my dancing was better than ever.*

continue2learn

Vocabulary, Grammar and Real World

- **Extra Practice and Progress Portfolio 6** p119
- **Video (*Ask the public*)** p129
- **Language Summary 6** p149
- **Workbook 6** p29

Reading and Writing

- **Portfolio 6** Letters or emails of complaint Workbook p69
  Reading three letters/emails of complaint
  Writing letters/emails of complaint: content, style, useful phrases

7A Getting away with it

Vocabulary phrases with *get*
Grammar conditionals

QUICK REVIEW Position of adverbials Think of three sentences about yourself using four of these adverbials: *last year*; *to work*; *fast*; *usually*; *every Monday*; *probably*. Work in pairs. Take turns to say your sentences: *I was in a play last year.*

Reading and Vocabulary

1 **a** Look at the photo of a closed prison below and inmates working in an open prison on p67. In what ways do you think 'open' and 'closed' prisons are different?

b Read the article. Why is Bastoey a very different route to rehabilitation?

c Read the article again. What does the article say about these things?

1 where Bastoey prison is situated and what the landscape is like
2 the leisure opportunities there
3 the kind of jobs done by prisoners
4 prisoners' accommodation
5 visits to and from the prison
6 the cost of managing the prison

d Look at the words/phrases in bold in the article. Match pairs of near synonyms.
prison, jail

e Work in pairs. Do you agree with these quotes from the article? Why?/Why not?

1 The biggest mistake that our societies have made is to believe that you must punish hard to change prisoners.
2 The big closed prisons are criminal schools.
3 If you treat people badly, they will behave badly.
4 Individuals will stop their criminal behaviour if they develop a sense of responsibility, as well as empathy.
5 Ecology is a great tool because it shows that what we do has an impact on the future. Criminals often do not think before acting.

Vocabulary Phrases with *get*

2 **a** Choose the correct phrases.

1 It's difficult for prisoners to *get their own back on/get back to* the life they had before they went to jail.
2 It's unlikely that victims will want to *get their own back on/get back to* an offender.
3 It's much more difficult to *get away with/get away from* burglary these days.
4 It's hard for ex-offenders to *get away with/get away from* their criminal record when looking for work.
5 Powerful people are often able to *get round to/get round* the legal system.
6 It takes governments many years to *get round to/get round* changing the legal system.
7 It can be more difficult for close relatives to *get through to/get through* a prison sentence than for the criminals themselves.
8 Education about the consequences of crime is essential, but it can be a difficult message to *get through to/get through* some young people.
9 Women are more likely to *get into/get out of* a prison sentence if they have children.
10 Young men are more likely to *get into/get out of* criminal activity if they don't have a secure family life.

b Match these definitions with *get* phrases in **2a**. Check in VOCABULARY 7.1 p152.

a do wrong and not be punished *get away with*
b leave behind
c become involved in sth
d avoid doing something you should
e do something that you have intended to do for a long time
f find a way of dealing with a problem
g take revenge on
h return to
i finish something
j communicate successfully

c Work in pairs. Do you agree with the statements in **2a**? Give reasons for your answers.

It's a hard life!

It's a summer day on Bastoey island, and Magne Ramstad is making the most of it. Lying on his back in his shorts, the 38-year-old Norwegian is sunbathing. Around him is lush woodland, brightly coloured houses and the sparkling waters of the Oslo fjord. For a prison, it's an idyllic environment. "This place is unbelievable," says Ramstad, who is serving a six-year sentence for drug smuggling. "At the **prison** I was at before this one, we were locked up in our cells 23 hours a day."

On the one-square-mile island, the 115 inmates, who include murderers and fraudsters, enjoy activities not usually associated with **jail**. In summer they can improve their tennis, ride a horse in the forest and go to the beach. In winter they can go cross-country skiing.

But first the **inhabitants** must work. As the island is a farm, there are cattle to tend and organic crops to grow. **Prisoners** have access to tools such as axes, and knives; they cut trees and restore the wooden houses dotted around the island. "It's good training," one prisoner says. "I can do carpentry and I'm hoping to get a certificate in using digging tools."

Afterwards, **residents** retreat to comfortable houses shared between four and six people. As Bastoey is an open prison, **family members** can come at the weekends; the island is accessible via a short ferry ride. Inmates can also leave Bastoey to stay with **relatives** for up to 18 days during the year and 30 if they have children.

All **convicts** must begin their sentences in a traditional, closed prison, from which they can apply to go to Bastoey. The prison selects **individuals** on the basis of whether they want to turn their lives around.

Bastoey is based on the idea that traditional prisons do not work. "The biggest mistake that our societies have made is to believe that you must punish hard to change prisoners," explains Bastoey's governor, Oeyvind Alnaes. "But the big closed prisons are criminal schools. If you treat **people** badly, they will behave badly. Anyone can be a citizen if we treat them well, respect them and give them challenges."

Bastoey's philosophy is that individuals will stop their criminal behaviour if they develop a sense of responsibility, as well as empathy. The way to achieve that is to take care of the nature around them; in the stables, for instance, each person is responsible for a horse or a cow.

"Ecology is a great tool," adds Alnaes, "because it shows that what we do has an impact on the future. **Criminals** often do not think before acting."

The **staff** at Bastoey also run courses designed to challenge prisoners' behaviour and force them to confront what they have done. It is easier to do that in a setting where they have responsibilities than in a closed prison where they lie back on a bunk and wait for their food. Security is deliberately kept low, so there are fewer **employees**, which makes the prison cheaper to run than a closed one.

What sets Bastoey apart from other open prisons is its emphasis on ecology as a tool for rehabilitation, and some **campaigners** would welcome more like it. "This innovative Norwegian model promotes what most criminal justice **reformers** know to work: a requirement that **offenders** take responsibility for their lives and work hard to pay for what they've done, in an environment that is small-scale and from which family contact can be maintained." However good the model is, though, Bastoey cannot easily be duplicated. It's a farm in the middle of a fjord. It wouldn't work in a big city.

Listening and Speaking

3 **a** Check the meaning of these words/phrases.

a forensic scientist   a trace of (saliva)
DNA   sweat   a fibre   a fragment

b Work in pairs. Discuss these questions. Use words/phrases from **3a**.

1 What methods are used to catch criminals?
2 How do criminals often give themselves away?

c CD2 ▸ 18 Listen to the first part of an interview with a journalist.

1 What crimes does she talk about?
2 What usually leads to the criminals being arrested?

d Listen again. Fill each gap with one word.

1 When breaking into a house, try not to break any [1]__________ or scratch any [2]__________ .
2 Wear [3]__________ and [4]__________ to avoid leaving prints, but make sure they're not made of [5]__________ materials.
3 If possible, wear clothes made out of [6]__________ material, such as [7]__________ .
4 It's best to leave the house [8]__________ .
5 Don't be tempted to [9]__________ the stolen goods immediately.

4 **a** Check the meaning of these words. What type of crime do you think Zoë is going to talk about?

an alibi   a maggot   a fly   a weapon
a distinguishing mark   poison
an icicle   a puddle of water

b CD2 ▸ 19 Listen to the second part of the interview. Were you correct?

c Listen to the second part again and answer these questions.

1 What personality traits do many killers have in common?
2 Why can the age of a maggot be useful to forensic scientists?
3 How can flies be useful evidence for forensic scientists?
4 What do you have to do if you keep your weapon?
5 What is the disadvantage of using poison?
6 What would the perfect weapon be, according to Zoë? Why?

d Can you think of any recent murder cases in which forensic evidence played a part in convicting the killer?

HELP WITH GRAMMAR Conditionals

- We can use a variety of verb forms in conditional sentences, not only those used in the four 'basic' conditionals.

5 **a** Match conditional sentences 1–4 to meanings a–d.

a an imaginary past event
b a general truth
c an imaginary present/future event
d a possible future event

1 *If a person doesn't want to leave forensic evidence, they should just slide through a window.* (variation on zero conditional)
2 *If you're going to commit a burglary, you'll have to be careful what you wear.* (variation on first conditional)
3 *If I were committing a burglary, I'd be better off wearing gloves.* (variation on second conditional)
4 *One burglar would have got away with it completely if he hadn't been sweating.* (variation on third conditional)

b Look again at the sentences in **5a**. What verb forms are being used in each of these sentences?

MIXED CONDITIONALS

TIP • In 'mixed conditionals', the main clause and the *if* clause sometimes refer to a different time period. The most common combinations are second and third conditionals.

c Compare these pairs of sentences. Is each sentence referring to a real or imaginary situation?

1 a If the kidnapper hadn't licked that envelope, he wouldn't be in prison now.
  b If the kidnapper hadn't licked that envelope, he wouldn't have gone to prison.
2 a If they weren't such good actors, most of them would probably have been found out much earlier.
  b If they hadn't been such good actors, most of them would probably have been found out much earlier.

d Look at the pairs of sentences in **5c** again and answer these questions.

1 Is each clause referring to past or present time?
2 Which sentences are 'mixed' conditionals? Why are they called 'mixed' conditionals?
3 What is the difference in meaning between the 'basic' and 'mixed' conditional sentences in each pair?

e Check in GRAMMAR 7.1 ▸ p153.

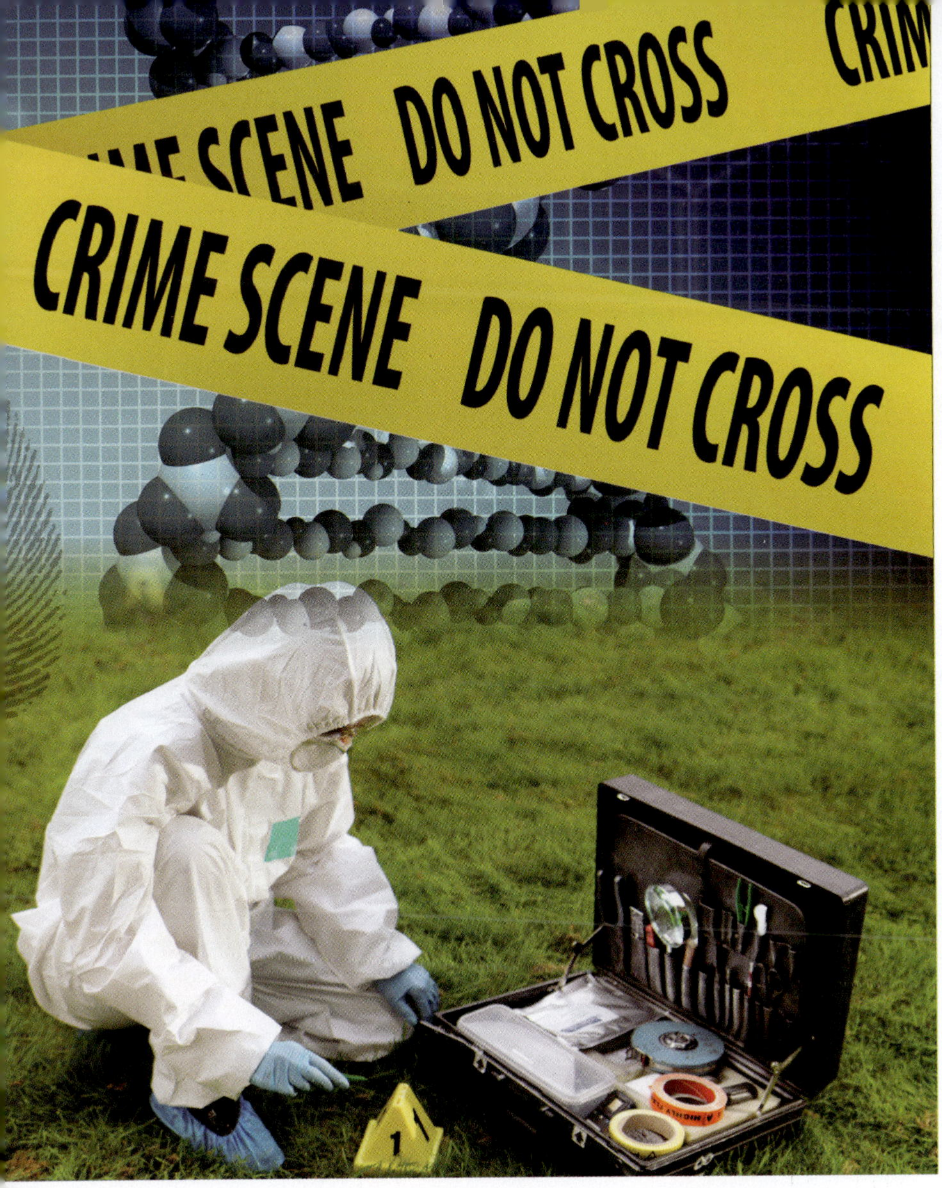

HELP WITH PRONUNCIATION
Leaving out /t/

6 **a** CD2 20 Listen to these sentences. When does the speaker leave out the /t/ sound at the end of words?

a before vowel sounds
b before consonant sounds

1 At one time, if someone committed a crime, you didn'**t** have as much to go on.
2 So, if the kidnapper hadn'**t** licked the envelope, … he wouldn'**t** be in prison now.
3 If a person doesn'**t** want to leave forensic evidence, they should jus**t** slide through a window.
4 One burglar would've got away with it completely, if he hadn'**t** been sweating at the time.
5 So if they weren'**t** such good actors, mos**t** of them would probably have been found out much earlier.

b What happens before a word beginning with /t/?

c Listen again and practise saying the sentences.

TIP • It is not necessary to leave /t/ out to be understood, but an awareness of this feature can help you to understand connected speech and to speak more fluently.

7 **a** Think of possible answers to these questions using different types of conditional sentences.

1 Was it easier to commit a crime in the past?
Yes. If you had committed a crime in the past, it would have been more difficult to find evidence, so it would have been easier to get away with it.
2 Wasn't there a case involving a kidnapper who was caught 20 years later because of an envelope?
3 If you're a burglar, what's the best way to avoid being caught?
4 Is it a good idea to wear gloves and socks?
5 What's the best way to leave a house you've burgled?

b Work in pairs. Role play an interview between a TV presenter and a science journalist. Use the questions from **7a** and add details where possible.

c Change roles and do the interview again. Whose answers were more convincing?

8 Work in pairs. Discuss these questions.

1 Think of an important decision you made recently. Would your life be better or worse now if you hadn't made that decision?
2 If you could choose, what special talent would you like to have been born with?
3 If you hadn't met a very important person in your life (e.g. your husband, business partner or best friend), what do you think your life would be like now?
4 If you had chosen a different career or study option, what do you think you would be doing now instead?

Get ready … Get it right!

9 Work in pairs. What are the advantages and disadvantages of open and closed prisons? Use these ideas or your own.

- Open prisons try to educate people not to re-offend but they can be difficult and expensive to run.
- Closed prisons are often popular with the general public because it's felt that prisoners should be severely punished for their crimes, but they don't help to change prisoners' behaviour.

10 Work in groups. Group A p107. Group B p109.

7B Every step you take

Vocabulary phrasal nouns
Grammar impersonal report structures

QUICK REVIEW Mixed conditionals Complete these conditional sentences about your life: *If I hadn't … , I'd now … ; If I were better at … , I might have …* . Work in pairs and take turns to say your sentences. Ask follow-up questions.

Reading and Speaking

1 **a** Look at the pictures. In which places do organisations often watch or track people's movements? Why?

b Read the article and check your ideas from **1a**.

c Tick the true sentences. Correct the false ones.

1 Identity cards are universally disliked on the grounds that they limit people's freedom.
2 Only the service provider knows which websites people visit.
3 It is likely that RFID tags will soon be on almost all our supermarket shopping.
4 RFID tags can only be used on objects.
5 If you value your privacy, it is better to pay cash when travelling on buses or trains.
6 In certain countries, mobile phones outnumber people.
7 Any organisation is allowed to listen to your mobile phone conversations at any time.
8 It is known that CCTV cameras have been used to check up on employees.

2 **a** Choose the correct collocations from the article.

1 identity *card/records*
2 personal *records/identification number*
3 service *data/provider*
4 CCTV *provider/camera*
5 financial *provider/records*
6 number *tag/plate*
7 smart *travel card/data*
8 medical *provider/history*
9 buying *data/habits*

b Work in pairs. Take turns to explain how the items in **2a** are connected to an individual's privacy.

> ID cards might contain private information about an individual's medical history.

c Work in groups. Discuss these questions.

1 Have you experienced any of the 'tracking' mentioned in the article?
2 Do you feel that a government is justified in tracking people, or is it an 'unacceptable intrusion'? Why?/Why not?
3 How much has the situation changed in your country since this article was written?

WE'LL BE WATCHING YOU

Identity (ID) cards are already widely used in many parts of the world; these often contain information on your race, religion and medical history as well as some form of biometric data such as a fingerprint or an image of your iris. Opinion appears to be divided as to whether this is unacceptable intrusion by the state into the privacy of the individual or simply a useful way to centralise your documentation. Even without ID cards, however, tracking and tagging technology is everywhere you go.

There have been warnings that the newest high-definition CCTV cameras can spot a face half a mile away; and in many city centres you're likely to be spotted at least 300 times a day. Cameras are known to operate in more and more buildings, and there's little control over who sees the footage. Workers at a hotel in Boston in the US took legal action against their employers after finding a tiny camera observing them from one of their lockers, and schools in the UK are known to have installed cameras in pupils' changing rooms.

Simply by going online, you give away information about everything from your political beliefs to your buying habits. 'Cookies' record the websites you visit, so anyone can gain a profile of your Internet activities, not just your service provider.

RFID tags (Radio Frequency Identification tags) – tiny radio-transmitting microchips – are getting smaller and cheaper. It seems that they will soon become the norm on food packaging and clothes; this will allow retailers not only to keep track of what has been stolen, but when stock is running low. However, as well as being used in shops and on everyday objects such as credit cards, tickets and keys, RFID tags are now also being offered as implants. For example, a tag can be implanted in club members' arms, acting as a security pass and allowing cashless bar payments. There also appear to be many hospitals using them as minuscule identity cards for patients.

Buying pre-paid 'smart' travel cards which contain a microchip means that you can be tracked across a city when you use public transport. And in some big cities such as London there is a charge for traffic entering the city centre during busy periods. This tax is often enforced with the aid of a network of cameras, which records the number plates of everyone entering a congestion zone.*

Inputting a personal identification number (PIN) into a cashpoint may be the easiest way of getting your hands on your hard-earned cash, but while you are waiting for your money to appear, your identity (and all the information about you on record) is closely scrutinised. Your withdrawal is also recorded and filed. It is claimed that even your financial records can be accessed if there is a justifiable cause.

There are now estimated to be more mobile phones than people in many countries. As soon as you activate your signal by mobile phone use, any organisation with the appropriate technology – for instance, a car breakdown service – can accurately locate you within seconds. With the co-operation of the phone company, it is possible to listen in on people's conversations. In addition, each mobile has an international identification number, transmitted whenever the phone is on.

*congestion zone = an area with a lot of traffic, in which motorists often have to pay a tax at certain times

HELP WITH GRAMMAR

Impersonal report structures

- We use impersonal report structures when we want to distance ourselves from information which is not necessarily our opinion. They are commonly found in reports and newspaper articles.

REPORTING WITH THE PASSIVE

3 **a** Look at these sentences. Then complete the rules with *that*, or *infinitive with to*.

- ***It is claimed that*** *even your financial records can be accessed.*
- ***Cameras are known to operate*** *in more and more buildings.*
- ***There are now estimated to be*** *more mobile phones than people in many countries.*

To make impersonal report structures we can use …

- *it* + passive + ________ clause
- subject (e.g. *cameras*) + passive + ________
- *there* + passive + ________

TIPS • We can use a variety of infinitive forms with impersonal report structures: *She is known* **to have spent** *five years in India. He is rumoured* **to be resigning** *next month.*

• We often use these verbs to report with the passive: *claim*, *allege*, *estimate*, *believe*, *think*, *fear*, *expect*, *report*, *understand*.

REPORTING WITH *SEEM* AND *APPEAR*

b Look at these sentences. Are the verbs *seem* and *appear* used in the passive?

1 **It seems that** they will soon become the norm.
2 **Opinion appears to be** divided.
3 **There also appear to be** many hospitals using them.

c Check in GRAMMAR 7.2 p154.

4 **a** Use the correct form of the verbs in brackets to make two sentences. Use these passive report structures: *it* + passive + *that* clause; subject + passive + infinitive with *to*.

1 House prices have fallen by 8%. (report)
It is reported that house prices have fallen by 8%.
House prices are reported to have fallen by 8%.
2 The rebels have withdrawn. (know)
3 London is one of the most expensive cities in the world to live in. (say)
4 The senior manager has resigned. (rumour)
5 More than 3,000 people have lost their lives in a devastating earthquake. (fear)
6 The airport strike is affecting thousands of holiday flights. (believe)

b Think of two recent issues which have affected your country. Write about each story using some of the structures in **4a**.

It is feared that eight people have died in an explosion in …

c Work in groups. Share your ideas.

Listening and Vocabulary

5 **a** Look at the newspaper headlines. Check the meaning of any new words. Have any of these topics been an issue in your country?

b CD2 21 Listen to Stefano from Italy, Hiltrud from Germany and Justyna from Poland giving their opinions about how much the state should intervene in people's lives. In which areas do the speakers feel that state intervention is/isn't justified? Why?

c Work in pairs. Answer these questions.

1 STEFANO It's important the government prevents this. (What does he mean by 'this'?)
2 STEFANO That would definitely be too drastic. (What does he mean by 'that'?)
3 HILTRUD It is fairer. (What is fairer and why?)
4 JUSTYNA I think this is a state intervention gone too far. (What does she mean by 'this'?)

d Listen again to check.

6 Work in pairs. Discuss whether the government should get involved in matters such as these.

1 smoking in public places
2 environmental issues
3 relationships and marriage
4 the food people eat

HELP WITH VOCABULARY Phrasal nouns

- Phrasal nouns are compound nouns formed from verbs and a particle (a preposition or adverb).

7 **a** Look at the phrasal nouns in red in headlines A–D. What verbs and particles are they made up of?

TIP • When phrasal nouns begin with a particle, they have no hyphen (*outlook*, *downpour*, *input*). When phrasal nouns begin with a verb, they may or may not have a hyphen (*kick-off*, *breakdown*, *get-together*).
• Not all phrasal verbs can be made into phrasal nouns: *They pulled down two houses.* not *There was a ~~pulldown~~ of two houses.*
• Some phrasal nouns are made up of the same words as phrasal verbs, but have different meanings: *The intake* (= enrolment) *on that course was over 100. He spoke so fast I couldn't take it in* (= understand and remember).

b Look again at the phrasal nouns in headlines A–D.

1 Which phrasal nouns reverse the order of the verb and the particle?
2 Which ones can't be made into a phrasal verb with the same meaning?
3 Which phrasal nouns are countable?

c Check in VOCABULARY 7.2 p152.

8 Match the phrasal nouns in bold to these phrases.

heavy rain
beginning of the football match
contribution
number of people who are accepted
forecast
informal gathering
delay caused by a problem

1 **Kick-off** at Wembley will be at 3 p.m.
2 There has been a **setback** in plans to ban junk food from schools.
3 The **outlook** for the weekend is for yet more rain.
4 Your **input** to that meeting was much appreciated.
5 We sheltered under trees during the **downpours**.
6 My parents are having a **get-together** with friends.
7 The university has restricted its **intake** to those with good grades.

Get ready ... Get it right!

9 Work in groups. Group A p107. Group B p108.

7 Writing

Connecting words condition
Punctuation colons and semi-colons
Writing task an essay giving opinions on an issue

1 **a** Work in groups. Which of these things are you allowed or not allowed to do while driving in your country?

1 drive without wearing a seatbelt
2 use a mobile phone
3 eat or drink

b Read this extract from a student's draft essay. Ignore any mistakes for now. Does the writer agree or disagree with each rule in **1a**?

Due to an excessive concern for health and safety, there are more and more rules and regulations for drivers* these are supposed to make our roads safer for everyone. This essay will discuss the following three factors* seatbelts, mobile phones and eating or drinking while driving. Some current laws make perfect sense, such as wearing a seatbelt. Children, in particular, are not safe [1] ________ they are wearing a seatbelt.

The second issue to be considered is the illegal use of mobile phones* that is, the use of phones to make calls or to send texts. As soon as a driver takes their eyes off the road, they are putting lives in danger, so it seems that texting is unsafe. It is claimed that the same danger applies to talking on the phone* however, [2] ________ the speaker's attention remains focused on the road, they should still be able to drive perfectly safely. Nevertheless, the car must be parked in order to have a mobile phone conversation legally* [3] ________ it is breaking the law.

Finally, it is illegal to eat or drink while driving [4] ________ you put lives in danger. In other words, [5] ________ the car is stationary, a driver is free to eat, drink and make phone calls, but [6] ________ you need to actually drive somewhere? That may be a little more difficult.

2 **a** Choose the correct connecting words. WRITING 7.1 p155.

1 *Unless/In case* ex-prisoners are given help, they are likely to re-offend.
2 We must act now, *unless/otherwise* the prison population will double.
3 Ex-prisoners should be helped financially, *as long as/unless* there is enough money.
4 Prisoners can become responsible citizens, *otherwise/providing* we allow them to.
5 *Imagine/Whether* the governor is right or wrong, there are many who disagree.
6 *Supposing/Otherwise* the prisoners aren't well enough to work, what happens then?

b Fill in gaps 1–6 in the student's extract with connecting words from **2a**. Sometimes more than one answer is possible.

3 **a** Replace one comma in each of these sentences with a colon (:) or a semi-colon (;). WRITING 7.2 p155.

1 There are three sections, the introduction, the main argument and the conclusion.
2 The new traffic laws will be passed early next year, the current laws are no longer sufficient.
3 Learning to drive is not easy, it takes time and a great deal of concentration.
4 The conclusions in this paper are incomplete, further research needs to be done.
5 After the operation, driving is prohibited for 48 hours, however, after that period, you can resume driving as normal.

b Replace the asterisks (*) in the essay with a colon or a semi-colon. Explain why each one is needed.

4 **a** Make notes on your opinions regarding these topics or your own idea.

- prisons
- smoking
- road safety
- alcohol

b Work in pairs. Discuss your ideas.

5 Write an essay, expressing and supporting your opinions on the issue you chose.

1 Decide what aspects of the issue to focus on.
2 Make notes on the laws regarding each aspect and your opinion on each one.
3 Organise your notes into several paragraphs (i.e. one paragraph for each aspect).
4 Think about how to express your ideas using:

- connecting words of condition
- impersonal reporting structures from the unit
- correct punctuation (e.g. commas, colons and semi-colons)

6 **a** Work in groups. Read each other's essays. Is the writer's point of view clear?

b Discuss the issues in each essay. Do you agree or disagree with the opinions raised?

c Make suggestions for any improvements.

7 Improve your essay.

1 Decide on any changes to the content.
2 Check your use of language from the unit.
3 Proofread your essay (e.g. check commas and spelling).
4 Write a final draft.

For more Writing practice: Portfolio 7, Workbook p72.

7C VOCABULARY AND SKILLS Not guilty!

Vocabulary metaphors
Real World functions and intonation of questions

QUICK REVIEW Phrasal nouns
Think of sentences using phrasal nouns made from these phrasal verbs: *pour down*; *break down*; *set back*; *get together*. Work in pairs. Take turns to say your sentences.

1 **a** Look at these pairs of sentences. Which words/phrases in bold have a literal meaning (L)? Which have a non-literal meaning (NL)? What are the non-literal meanings? Check in VOCABULARY 7.2 p152.

1 a I **grilled** the meat for five minutes. *L*
  b The police **grilled** him for hours about what he'd done that night. *NL questioned*
2 a We got a **warm** welcome from my cousin.
  b The pizza wasn't **warm** enough so I put it in the microwave.
3 a The forecast warns a severe **storm** is on its way.
  b The police **stormed** the building and rescued the hostages.
4 a The market is **flooded** with cheap, plastic goods.
  b If it rains any more, the roads will soon be **flooded**.
5 a It was such a **bright** day, I needed my sunglasses.
  b He's a really **bright** lad – I can't believe he'd turn to crime.
6 a I have to get up at **dawn** to drive to work.
  b It suddenly **dawned** on the inspector who the criminal might be.
7 a When I saw the burglar, I **froze** and couldn't move.
  b It was so cold that the lake **froze**.
8 a My parents **flew** to Brazil last week.
  b The crime novel was so exciting, the time **flew**.
9 a Vicky is a good choice for the job because she doesn't **crack** under pressure.
  b I suddenly noticed the large **crack** in the ceiling.

b Write five sentences about yourself. Use metaphors from **1a**.

c Work in pairs. Take turns to say your sentences. Ask follow-up questions.

2 **a** Look at the photo on p75. What do you think is happening?

b CD2 22 Listen to an extract from a TV programme.

1 Why is Mike a suspect?
2 What crime is he alleged to have committed?

3 **a** Listen again. Fill in the gaps with one or two words.

1 Emma is Mike's ______________ .
2 The police think Mike is using Emma as an ______________ .
3 George usually goes out at about ______________ past ______________ on Friday evenings.
4 George had hidden ______________ pounds in the flat.
5 George works as a ______________ .
6 George hid the money under the ______________ .
7 Mike left Emma's house to get a ______________ .
8 He was seen by his ______________ at about 8.20.
9 Mike told the police he watched a ______________ on TV.
10 Mike hasn't got much money because he's ______________ .

b Do you think Mike is guilty? Why?/Why not?

4 What do these phrases from the story mean?

1 it all **strikes me as** very odd
2 we're not **joined at the hip**
3 we **weren't born yesterday**
4 **I lost track of** what was happening
5 must have **hit you hard**, losing your job

REAL WORLD
Functions and intonation of questions

5 **a** CD2 23 Listen to questions 1–5. Which are asking for new information? Which are checking information?

1 What does? ↘
2 Isn't this about the time George usually goes out? ↗
3 How much? ↗
4 So, you went out on your own, did you? ↗
5 How come? ↘

b Listen again and choose the correct answers.

1 We use a *rising/falling* tone to find out new information.
2 We often use a *rising/falling* tone when checking information.
3 We often use a *rising/falling* tone in question tags when we expect the listener to confirm that we are right.

c CD2 24 Listen to questions 1–4 and match them to functions a–d.

1 Could we just go over this one more time?
2 How should I know? / So what?
3 Isn't that a coincidence?
4 He never stays in on a Friday evening, does he?

a giving instructions
b a rhetorical question (expecting agreement)
c aggressive/defensive response to a question
d making a sarcastic comment

d Check in REAL WORLD 7.1 p155.

6 CD2 25 Listen to these questions. Which one is requesting new information?

1 A I haven't got any money on me!
  B Isn't that a surprise!?
2 A So we're meeting at nine, are we?
  B Yes. Sorry, I've forgotten already. Where are we meeting?
3 A Could you put everything in the dishwasher, please?
  B Why should I always do it?
4 A Thank goodness it's arrived at last!
  B What has?
5 A I heard from Terri last night.
  B Oh, so she finally decided to phone, did she?
6 A I believe 200 people are coming to the wedding.
  B Are you sure?
7 A I need some money.
  B Oh you do, do you?

7 **a** Look at Audio Script CD2 25 p172. Listen again and notice the intonation.

b Work in pairs. Listen again and practise saying the exchanges.

8 Work in pairs. Student A, follow these instructions. Student B p113.

1 Student A: You are a police officer. You are going to interview Emma to see if her story contradicts Mike's. Think of questions using a variety of question types, including question tags. Find out the following information.
   - Had Emma been expecting Mike to go round that evening?
   - Did his behaviour seem normal?
   - Why didn't she go out with him to have a pizza?
   - How long did he take to get back with his pizza?
   - What did they do when he got back?
   - When did he leave to go home?
   - Where did he get his phone from?
2 Work with your partner. Ask Emma the questions above and any of your own. Make notes. Does anything Emma says contradict Mike's story?
3 Work in groups of four. Have you changed your mind about whether Mike is guilty or not? Discuss the evidence.

continue2learn

Vocabulary, Grammar and Real World
- **Extra Practice and Progress Portfolio 7** p120
- **Video (*Laying down the law*)** p130
- **Language Summary 7** p152
- **Workbook 7** p34

Reading and Writing
- **Portfolio 7** A review Workbook p72
  Reading A book review
  Writing cohesive devices

Finding time

Vocabulary phrases with *time*
Grammar past verb forms with present or future meaning

QUICK REVIEW Metaphors Work in pairs. Choose four of these words: *bright*; *flood*; *fly*; *freeze*; *storm*; *warm*. Ask and answer questions with each word: first with its literal meaning, then with its metaphorical meaning.

Vocabulary Phrases with *time*

1 **a** What would you like to do if you had more time?

b Tick the sentences that are true for you. Change the others so that they are true for you. Check the phrases in bold in VOCABULARY 8.1 p156.

1 If I **have time to kill** at an airport, I usually read a book.
2 I like to get to class **in plenty of time**.
3 I always **take my time** when I do homework.
4 I usually **have** very little **time to spare** in the morning.
5 **For the time being**, I'm happy doing what I'm doing.
6 **It's only a matter of time** before I change my job/course.
7 I believe in the saying '**there's no time like the present**'.
8 **I've got no time for** people who don't care about climate change.
9 It's difficult to **make time for** important things like environmental issues.
10 I **give people a hard time** when they don't recycle things.

c Work in pairs. Compare your sentences and discuss any differences.

Reading and Speaking

2 Work in pairs and discuss the questions.

1 Read about the people in the photos. What else do you know about them?
2 Do you think it is necessary to be 'great' in order to 'make a difference' to the world?
3 Is it possible for an individual to make a difference?

Gandhi (1869–1948) achieved social and political progress using non-violent means

Rosa Parks (1913–2005) civil rights activist who refused to give up her bus seat to a white man

Marie Curie (1867–1934) scientist famous for pioneering research on radioactivity

Tim Berners Lee (1955–) an inventor of the World Wide Web

3 Read an interview with Eddy Canfor-Dumas, an author, TV scriptwriter and environmental activist. Match the interviewer's questions below to sections 1–3 of the article.

a Do you believe that one person can really make a difference?
b What have you done on a personal level to address the issue of climate change?
c You have recently become seriously involved in green issues. How did this come about?

4 **a** Read the interview again. Use your own words to answer these questions.

1 Why did Eddy want to find out about all the ways the world might end?
2 What did the scientist accuse the US of?
3 What does the scientist suggest global warming is responsible for?
4 Why do you think the head of NCAR was surprised by Eddy's questions?
5 Why was Eddy's conversation with the scientist so significant?
6 What does Eddy suggest about his previous involvement in environmental issues?
7 Why does Eddy think more people will become involved in environmental issues?
8 Why does Eddy mention people like Gandhi and Nelson Mandela?
9 What does Eddy think is the best way to change the world?

b Work in pairs. Compare your answers. Do you agree with Eddy's views about global warming and his proposed solution? Why?/Why not?

5 Work in pairs. Discuss these questions.

1 What do you think this saying means 'If not you, who? If not now, when?'
2 What do you think is involved in conducting an eco-audit on your home?
3 How 'green' do you think your lifestyle is? How could you and your home be 'greener'?
4 What could every person immediately do to fight climate change?

One person can make a difference …

Eddy Canfor-Dumas, television's favourite 'disaster' drama scriptwriter, has recently added politics to his 'to do' list. Irene Core asks why.

1 ____________

Some years ago, I was working on a BBC 'disaster' drama, *Supervolcano*, about the fictional eruption of Yellowstone National Park in the USA. As part of my research I spoke to a scientist who had just written a book about all the ways the world might end. Top of the list was global warming, created by man-made CO_2 emissions. But, he said, one of the worst offenders, the USA, would not start to change until a series of devastating hurricanes hit its Gulf and east coasts.

The next disaster project I was working on was called *Superstorm*. It was about the impact of global warming on hurricanes in the Atlantic, and I visited the National Center for Atmospheric Research in Boulder, Colorado. A number of violent hurricanes were sweeping the Gulf and east coasts of the USA, so I asked the head of NCAR two questions: is global warming a reality, and is it man-made? He looked at me as if I was mad. How could anyone still be asking such basic questions? He gave me a short tutorial on climate science, and after further discussions with other scientists I came home convinced that this was a real and grave issue that needed to be dealt with urgently.

It's high time we all accepted the fact that everyone can make a difference.

2 ____________

Well, I realised I had to be more than just a 'direct-debit environmentalist', paying a small sum of money each month to Friends of the Earth to ease my conscience. So I employed someone to do an eco*-audit on my house to see how my family could become greener, and went along to a meeting of my local Green Party. I left the meeting as the candidate for my area in the upcoming local government elections and the election organiser for a much bigger area!

For the time being I'm OK about doing both jobs but I admit it's hard trying to fit everything in, so obviously I'd sooner someone else was doing one of the jobs. In fact, I would prefer it if a lot more people got directly involved. But I'm confident that this it's only a matter of time before people see that we cannot continue to live as though the planet had unlimited resources and an unlimited capacity to absorb the effects of ever-greater consumption.

3 ____________

There is an ancient Japanese saying: 'One is the mother of ten thousand.' Everything begins with the individual. One person implements change which sets off a change in another person, and so on, even if it takes a great deal of time. If the change in the individual is profound and focused on relieving or preventing suffering, the change he or she sets off in others will be all the greater and far-reaching. Look at the great religious teachers in history or people from more modern times, such as Gandhi and Nelson Mandela.

Of course, we don't need to think in such grand terms. In fact, I'd rather people looked at the small things they could do, bit by bit, right on their doorstep. Otherwise they get put off by thinking they have to change the world. That will happen anyway, if we all do our bit and perhaps just a little more.

*eco = connected to the environment

HELP WITH GRAMMAR

Past verb forms with present or future meaning

- Past verb forms do not always refer to past time.

6 **a** Compare these pairs of sentences. Do any of the sentences refer to past time? Do all the sentences tell us what the speaker would like to happen?

1 a **It**'s time to accept the fact that everyone can make a difference.
  b It's time **we** all accepted the fact that everyone can make a difference.
2 a I'd sooner do one of the jobs.
  b I'd sooner **someone** else was doing one of the jobs.
3 a I'd prefer to get directly involved.
  b I'd prefer it if a lot more **people** got directly involved.
4 a I'd rather look at the small things I could do.
  b I'd rather **people** looked at the small things they could do.

b Look again at the sentences in **6a**. Which verbs (pink or blue) are infinitive verb forms? Which are either Past Simple or Past Continuous?

c Look at the subjects in bold in the sentences in **6a**. Then choose the correct words in the rule.

- When *it's time, would sooner, would rather,* and *would prefer it if* are followed by a subject + verb, we use *an infinitive/a past verb form.*

TIP • We can also say *it's about time …* or *it's high time …* to suggest something is urgent: *It's high time we all accepted the fact that everyone can make a difference.*

d Check in GRAMMAR 8.1 p157.

7 **a** What would you like to change? Complete these sentences.

1 I'd rather people didn't …
2 I'd sooner travel …
3 I'd prefer it if …
4 It's high time people …
5 I'd rather my family …
6 I'd prefer not to …
7 It's about time we …
8 It's time to stop …

b Work in pairs. Discuss your ideas.

Listening and Speaking

8 **a** Check the meaning of these words.

soot   scrub   an incinerator   federal law

b CD3 1 Listen to Eddy talking about Hazel Henderson, an ordinary woman who has made a significant difference to the world. Choose the best answers.

1 All the children who played in the local park in New York were *dirty/ill.*
2 Hazel succeeded in getting *better playgrounds in parks/levels of air pollution made public.*
3 Hazel is now an advisor to *the US president/world governments.*

9 **a** Work in groups of three. You are each going to summarise part of Hazel Henderson's story. Student A, look at list 1 below. Student B, look at list 2. Student C, look at list 3. Which of the items from your list can you already talk about?

1 Bristol, school, qualifications, jobs, New York, an American man, child
2 local playground, soot, pollution, other mothers and children
3 in New York, the quality of the air, ABC news network, weather forecasts

b Listen again. Make notes on your section of the story.

c Summarise your part of the story using the prompts from **9a** and your notes.

d In the same groups of three, compare your summaries. Do you think you have covered all the main points?

HELP WITH PRONUNCIATION Linking sounds

10 **a** CD3 ▶ 2 Listen to these sentences and notice how words within a speech unit are linked together.

1 so // she // er // took a job // in a hotel // as a receptionist
2 the quality of the /j/ air // in New York // was so poor
3 it travelled across the country // to /w/ all sorts of other // erm // cities
4 and // she /j/ enjoyed that // er // for a time

b Find examples of the following features in sentences 1–4.

a a consonant sound at the end of a word is linked with a vowel sound at the beginning of a word.
b a consonant sound at the end of a word is linked with the same consonant sound at the beginning of a word.
c a vowel sound at the end of a word is linked with a vowel sound at the beginning of a word by adding /w/ or /j/.

TIP • It is not necessary to link words in this way to be understood, but an awareness of this feature can help you to understand connected speech and to speak more fluently.

c Listen and practise the sentences.

d Look back at your summary from **9c**. Decide how to break it up into speech units, paying attention to linking sounds.

e Work in pairs. Take turns to read out your summaries.

Get ready ... Get it right!

11 **a** Imagine you can spend an evening with three famous people that have made a difference to the world, positively or negatively. They can be from the present or the past. Which people would you choose to invite and why?

b Write one question you would like to ask each person.

12 **a** Work in pairs. Say who you chose and what questions you would ask. What topics of conversation might your questions inspire?

b Agree on the three most interesting people.

I'd like to invite Rihanna.

Oh, I'd rather we invited Valentina Tereshkova. She had a much greater influence.

c Tell the class who you chose and what topics of conversation are likely to come up.

d Which group would you like to join for the evening? Why?

Rihanna

Valentina Tereshkova

Barack Obama

8B Fear!

Vocabulary word building (2): suffixes
Grammar *wherever, whoever, whatever,* etc.

QUICK REVIEW Past verb forms with present or future meaning Use these prompts to make true and false sentences about yourself: *Most of my friends prefer ... ; I'd sooner ... ; I'd rather I didn't have to ... ; It's about time I ... .* Work in pairs. Take turns to say your sentences. Guess if your partner's sentences are true or false.

Reading and Vocabulary

1 **a** Work in pairs. Discuss these questions.

1 What is the scariest experience you have ever had?
2 What would you do if you heard a burglar trying to break into your home?

b Read the title of the article. What do you think the article is about?

c Read the article and check your ideas. Answer these questions.

1 What happened and what did the writer do about it?
2 Does she see herself as a thrill-seeker or a fear-avoider?

2 **a** Read the article again. Which of these sentences are true, which are false, and which are not mentioned?

1 The writer was terrified when she heard the noise.
2 Her husband was woken by the noise.
3 She would like to be more like the thrill-seekers.
4 She notices people taking risks in day-to-day life.
5 She experienced a lot of fear as a child.
6 She went downstairs with her husband.
7 Her husband saw the burglar.

b Work in pairs and compare your answers.

3 Find words in the article with these meanings.

1 something hard or firm being crushed or broken (para. 1)
2 wood or stone being cut away with a sharp blade (para. 1)
3 set off or cause something bad to start (para. 1)
4 want something badly (para. 1)
5 very ordinary and not interesting (para. 2)
6 making someone seem better in some way (para. 2)
7 unhappy and discouraged (para. 3)

4 **a** Think of someone you know who is a thrill-seeker or a fear-avoider. What examples can you give to justify the description?

b Work in pairs. Talk about the people you know.

Feel the fear

1 What woke me that night were the two loud bangs, one after the other. I stood at the top of the stairs with my heart trying to escape my body. Then the sound of crunching, scraping, chiselling. Whoever was causing this disturbance was obviously trying to enter my house at 4 a.m., uninvited, of course! How long did it take my body to calm down? Well, I have to say, my recovery was slow. Even now, the very thought can trigger the same sensation that raced through me that night and I wouldn't wish it on anyone. But some people, the 'thrill-seekers' actually go looking for this rush of adrenaline. They are the riders of roller-coasters, the fans of horror, the boy car racers. Why do they crave it? Why am I so different?

2 In an article I read about fear, it said there was a clear division between 'thrill-seekers' and 'fear-avoiders'. I immediately put myself down as a fear-avoider. Now, according to the article, it isn't just that I'm not courageous – I could accept that – but supposedly, I hate change, I want the world to stand still. Happiness for me, it seems, lies in being mundane; not very flattering, but at least it shows I have a keen sense of survival.

3 For thrill-seekers, on the other hand, it seems life is too safe, perhaps even too long! They love excitement, growth, change. Nothing pleases them more than a difficult challenge, or better still, an impossible one. And failure to find this bit of danger in the day can leave them despondent. Are these the drivers I see overtaking other cars on the wrong side of the road and jumping red lights? Presumably, just to stop themselves from feeling 'normal'.

4 And what about imagined fear? The article said it's played out all through childhood, and there are clear development markers. A fear of monsters under the bed is common between the ages of four and seven. After that, children leave the world of fantasy and enter the realms of possibility. They develop fears about – and I'm quoting here – "burglars breaking in"!

5 I ended up wondering if thrill-seeking was part of my burglar's motivation. And if so, I wonder if in some small way, I helped him achieve this when I so courageously sent my husband downstairs to investigate.

HELP WITH VOCABULARY
Word building (2): suffixes

NOUNS

5 **a** Look at these nouns from the article. Then answer the questions.

sound	disturbance	recovery	riders
division	change	happiness	survival
excitement	challenge	failure	possibility

1 Which three nouns have a verb in the same form? *sound, a sound*

2 Which seven nouns are made by adding suffixes to verbs? What suffixes are added to the verb?

3 Which two nouns are made from adjectives? What suffixes are added to the adjectives?

VERBS, ADJECTIVES, ADVERBS

b Look at these groups of words. Is each group comprised of adjectives, verbs or adverbs?

1 cowardly, moody, courageous, cultural, sympathetic, talented

2 recently, confidently, finally

3 creative, dependent, remarkable

4 rationalise, widen, clarify

c Complete these sentences with *verbs*, *adjectives* or *adverbs*.

1 To make ____________ from nouns we can use *-ly*, *-y*, *-ous*, *-al*, *-ic*, *-ed*.

2 To make ____________ from adjectives we can use *-ly*.

3 To make ____________ from verbs we can use *-ive*, *-ent*/*-ant*, *-able*/*-ible*.

4 To make ____________ from adjectives we can use *-ise*, *-en*, *-ify*.

d Check in VOCABULARY 8.2 p156.

6 **a** Complete these questions with the correct form of the word in brackets.

1 Would you say all your friends are ______________ dependable? (equal)

2 Do you usually need ______________ to do difficult things? (motivate)

3 Do you consider yourself to be a ______________ person? Why?/Why not? (courage)

4 What would you do if there was a loud ______________ outside your window in the middle of the night? (disturb)

5 Do you agree with the saying that '______________ gets you nowhere'? (flatter)

6 When you were a child, did you or anyone you know have an ______________ friend? (imagine)

b Work in pairs. Ask and answer the questions in **6a**.

Listening and Speaking

7 Work in pairs. Do you agree on which photos, A–F, illustrate each of these emotions: anger; disgust; sadness; fear; joy; surprise?

8 **a** Work in pairs. Discuss these questions.

1 Do you think all cultures experience the same basic emotions?
2 How do you think basic emotions helped our ancestors to stay alive?
3 What other emotions are there besides the basic ones?

b CD3 ▸ 3 Listen to a radio programme about emotions. Check your answers.

c Listen again. Read these quotes and answer the questions.

1 "**Whoever** said that is wrong." (Said what?)
2 "**Wherever** this experiment was carried out, the results were the same." (What experiment?)
3 "**Whoever** saw the photos identified the same emotions." (Which emotions?)
4 "**Whenever** you do this in private … it's unlikely to cause embarrassment." (Do what?)
5 "That's the difference between higher and basic emotions." (What is the difference?)

d Work in groups. Discuss whether this statement is true or not. Consider things such as sports, food, dress, attitude to relationships, attitude to animals, privacy, etc.

> "Things that might make people from one culture proud, embarrassed, guilty, angry, sad, disgusted, happy, etc. might not trigger the same emotion in people from another culture."

HELP WITH GRAMMAR

wherever, whoever, whatever, etc.

9 **a** Read the rule. Then match the words in bold in sentences 1–4 in **8c** to meanings a or b.

When we add *ever* to question words (*wherever, whoever, whenever, whatever, whichever, however*) it usually has one of these meanings.

a It doesn't matter where, who, when, etc. It can be any place, anyone, any time. *Start the experiment whenever you want to.* (it doesn't matter when you start) *Give the results to whoever wants them.* (anyone who wants them)

b An unknown place, person, time, etc. *Whoever wrote this report did a fantastic job.* (I don't know who the person was)

TIPS • *Whenever* can also mean 'every time': ***Whenever** she calls, I'm out.* (= *every time she calls, I'm out.*)

• *Whoever, whichever* and *whatever* can be the subject or the object of the verb:
***Whoever** saw you …* (subject)
***Whoever** you saw …* (object)

• *Whatever* is used in informal English to mean 'It doesn't matter' or 'I don't care'.
A: *Would you like to see that new film?*
B: **Whatever**.

• *However* can be used with an adverb. ***However hard** she tries, she can't please her teacher. **However much** it costs, I'm still going to buy that coat.* (It doesn't matter how hard or how much.)

b Check in GRAMMAR 8.2 ▸ p157.

10 **a** Fill in the gaps with *however, whichever, whenever, whoever, whatever* or *wherever*. There is sometimes more than one possible answer.

1 I can wear ________ I want to work/college/school.
2 ________ much I want to, I don't get much chance to practise my English.
3 ________ early I go to bed, I never feel as if I've had enough sleep.
4 ________ I eat out, I usually order the same thing.
5 ________ people say about this country, I think it's a good place to live.
6 ________ you go in this town, you can always find wonderful architecture.
7 ________ planned the parking in this town did a wonderful job.
8 ________ time of day you travel round this town, there are always traffic jams.

b Work in pairs. Compare answers. Say which of the sentences in **10a** are true for you and where you live. Ask follow-up questions.

Get ready … Get it right!

11 **a** Make a list of things that frightened you as a child and things that frighten you now. Use these ideas or your own.

- imaginary monsters
- the dark
- thunder and lightning
- certain animals or insects
- being a passenger in a car that's being driven fast
- flying
- heights

b Make another list of things you enjoy, which might frighten some people.

riding a motorbike
horror films

12 **a** Work in groups. Discuss the things on your lists. Who is most like you?

> When I was a kid, I needed to leave the light on all night.

b Tell the class how you would describe another person in your group: are they a thrill-seeker or a fear-avoider?

c Do you agree with the description of you? Why?/Why not?

8 Writing

Connecting words/phrases cause and effect (1)
Spelling commonly misspelled words
Writing task an online posting about an issue

1 Work in pairs and discuss these questions.

1 What would you like to improve about your area?
2 What could you do personally to improve the situation?

2 **a** Read this extract from a posting on a website. Ignore any mistakes for now.

1 What is the problem?
2 What are the reasons for the problem?
3 What are the results of the problem?
4 What action is suggested?

b The writer made six spelling mistakes. Find the mistakes and correct them.

CLEAN OUR STREETS!

We should no longer keep silent about this issue. It is high time something was done **to improve** the cleanliness of our streets. During the 15 years I have been living in this neighborhood, the situation has been gradualy deteriorating. This is largely **due to** the lack of services provided by the council. Refuse collection currently ocurs only once every two weeks **owing to** a lack of funds. This **results in** overflowing bins and a build-up of rubbish outside residential areas. It is only a matter of time before this unhigienic state of affairs **leads to** an infestation of some sort; perhaps, in the worst case scenario, of rats.

Clearly, it is necesary for the public to take action **in order to** persuade the goverment to intervene. Please sign our petition and pass it on to your contacts **so that** as many people as possible can support this cause.

27 COMMENTS

3 Choose the correct spelling. WRITING 8.1 p157.

1 receit/receipt
2 accomodation/accommodation
3 colleague/colleage
4 aquaintance/acquaintance
5 business/buisness
6 adress/address
7 medicine/medicin
8 exaggerate/exagerrate
9 admited/admitted
10 beginning/begining

4 **a** Read the posting in **2a** again. Match the expressions in bold to these uses.

To introduce a …

1 purpose *to (improve)* , ________ , ________
2 reason ________ , ________
3 result ________ , ________

b Complete the paragraph below with expressions from **4a**. There is more than one possible answer. WRITING 8.2 p157.

There is far too much traffic on our streets. This ________ traffic jams on major roads every morning and evening, which ________ severe delays and frayed tempers. Most cities suffer from increased pollution ________ the constant traffic on our roads, and many people suffer from allergies ________ the poor quality of the air. It is time we dealt with the traffic situation ________ we can improve the quality of life for those who live in cities.

5 Write a posting for the website about the situation you discussed in **1**. Explain the following points, using connecting words/phrases.

1 what problems there are
2 the reasons for these problems
3 the results of these problems
4 what action should be taken and why

6 **a** Work in pairs. Read your partner's posting. What is the problem, the result and the suggested action?

b Check your partner's posting for accurate use of connecting words/phrases and spelling.

c Discuss possible improvements together.

7 **a** Write a final draft of your posting.

b Work in groups. Read each other's final drafts. Which issue is the most serious? Which suggests the best solution?

For more Writing practice: Portfolio 8, Workbook p75.

8C VOCABULARY AND SKILLS The pros and cons

Vocabulary idiomatic phrases
Skills Reading: a modern poem; Listening: a discussion about gender
Real World Explaining choices

QUICK REVIEW *Wherever, whoever, whatever, etc.* Work in pairs. Take turns to complete these sentences about yourself: *Whenever I go to ... ; Whenever I try to ... ; Whatever I do to ... ; Whoever says ... ; It seems that however ...* . Ask follow-up questions.

1 **a** Work in groups (of the same sex if possible). Make a list of reasons why it's easier or harder to be a member of the opposite sex in your country. Use these ideas or your own.

- jobs
- relationships
- physical strength
- emotions
- appearance
- society's expectations of and attitude towards men and women

b Tell the class your group's conclusions. Do you agree with what the other groups said? Are there any points that the whole class agrees on?

2 **a** CD3 4 Read and listen to Sophie Hannah's poem about a problem she's been experiencing. Then answer the questions.

1 What is her indecision about?
2 Why is the poem called *The Pros and Cons*?
3 How many pros and how many cons does she mention? There may be different interpretations.

b Read the poem again. Match meanings a–g to verses 1–7.

Phoning him means …

a I'll embarrass myself because I'll seem overkeen. 7
b he might think I'm too enthusiastic and I might put him off.
c he'll think I'm a nice person.
d he'll know I'm keen to see him again.
e I won't be wasting time wondering if he's going to phone me or not.
f it's OK because it shouldn't matter who approaches who.
g it'll be less embarrassing for him in front of his colleagues.

The Pros and Cons

1 He'll be pleased if I phone to ask him how he is.
It will make me look considerate and he likes considerate people.

2 He'll be reassured to see that I haven't lost interest,
Which might make him happy and then I'll have done him a favour.

3 If I phone him right now I'll get to speak to him sooner
than I will if I sit around waiting for him to phone me.

4 He might not want to phone me from work in case someone hears
And begins (or continues) to suspect that there's something
between us.

5 If I want to and don't, aren't I being a bit immature?
We're both adults. Does it matter, with adults, who makes the
first move?

6 But there's always the chance he'll back off if I come on too strong
The less keen I appear, the more keen he's likely to be,

7 and I phoned him twice on Thursday and once on Friday.
He must therefore be fully aware that it's his turn, not mine.

8 If I make it too easy for him he'll assume I'm too easy,
while if I make no effort, that leaves him with more of a challenge.

9 I should demonstrate that I have a sense of proportion.
His work must come first for a while and I shouldn't mind waiting

10 For all I know he could have gone off me already
and if I don't phone I can always say, later, that I went off him first.

3 Match meanings h–j to verses 8–10.

Not phoning him means:

h I can pretend I rejected him first if it turns out he doesn't want to see me.
i It's probably better if I leave it to him to do the chasing.
j he'll know I understand that I can't be the most important thing in his life right now.

4 **a** Match these phrases to meanings a–e.

back off   make the first move   go off
make no effort   come on strong

a not try
b stop liking or being interested in someone or something
c stop being involved in a situation
d be the person to take action
e say someone is very attractive, but say it too forcefully

b Work in pairs. Answer these questions.

1 What cultural issue does this poem raise? Did you mention it in your discussion in **1b**? If not, does a similar issue exist in your country?
2 Do you think the writer's predictions about how the man might react are correct? Why/Why not?
3 What would a woman advise her to do? What would a man advise her?
4 Do you think a man would have a similar dilemma? If so, would it be for the same reasons?

5 **a** Do you think men and women would give the same answers to these questions?

1 Do you think that being a man/a woman has ever stopped you from doing something you wanted to do?
2 If you could live your life again as a man or a woman, which would you choose and why?

b CD3 5 Listen to six people answering the questions in **5a**. How many answered 'yes' to question 1?

6 **a** Listen again. Work in groups A and B. Group A make notes on the answers Bana, Mick and Joey give. Group B make notes on Bob, Kay and Leo.

b Work in pairs with a student from the other group. Compare notes.

7 **a** You are going to do a class survey using these questions. Choose two questions to ask other students.

Do you think …

1 men have a much easier life than women?
2 women can do the same jobs as men, just as well?
3 men are not very good at expressing their feelings and communicating?
4 women's emotions interfere with their judgement?

b Interview as many students as you can in five minutes. Make notes on the answers you get.

REAL WORLD Explaining choices

- There's no way that …
- Absolutely! I mean, there may be …
- I'd say that … because I think …
- Even though I think (men/women) have an easier time of it, …
- I reckon it depends on …
- Whatever you think about (women/men), they definitely …
- Whereas/While (men) … , (women) …

c Work in pairs. Compare notes and then answer these questions.

1 Did the men and the women in the class give similar answers?
2 Did any answers surprise you?

d Report the most interesting or surprising results of your survey to the class.

continue2learn

Vocabulary, Grammar and Real World

- **Extra Practice and Progress Portfolio 8** p121
- **Video (*What's stopping you?*)** p131
- **Language Summary 8** p156
- **Workbook 8** p39

Reading and Writing

- **Portfolio 8** An informal email Workbook p75
  Reading an informal email
  Writing informal language

9A The price of happiness

Vocabulary *price* and *cost*
Grammar simple v continuous: verbs with different meanings

QUICK REVIEW Suffixes Change these words into nouns: *recover*; *excite*; *disturb*; *happy*; *fail*. Change these words into adjectives: *coward*; *courage*; *culture*; *sympathy*. Change these words into verbs: *rational*; *wide*; *intense*. Work in pairs and say your words. Are they the same?

Vocabulary
price and *cost*

1 **a** Are you good with money? Why?/Why not?

b Fill in the gaps with the correct form of *price* or *cost*. Check in VOCABULARY 9.1 p158.

In your country ...

1 What's the most ________-effective way of travelling around cities?
2 Do you think basic products are reasonably ________ ?
3 Has the ________ of living risen much over the last year?
4 Do shops often have half-________ sales?
5 Is the ________ of dental treatment very high?

About you ...

6 Do you have anything that you think is ________less?
7 Have you ever bought something that ________ a fortune and regretted it?
8 Do you always check the ________ tag before you buy clothes?
9 Have you bought anything recently that you thought was over________ ?
10 Is there anything you would be willing to buy at any ________ ?

c Work in pairs. Take turns to ask and answer the questions in **1b**. If you're from the same country, do you agree?

Speaking and Reading

2 **a** Work in small groups. Do you think that having more money leads to greater happiness? Why?/Why not?

b Read the first paragraph of the article. Can you answer the questions?

c Read the rest of the article. Does it mention the ideas you discussed?

MORE MONEY, MORE HAPPINESS

If you are a top investment manager taking home $40 million this year, you can afford more than a little luxury. So why strive to take home $50 million next year? This question goes to the heart of one of the most-researched paradoxes in social science: why do people dedicate so much energy to trying to make more money, when having more money does not seem to make them that much happier?

First, a caveat: people who make very little money do become significantly happier when they earn more. But a large survey has shown that the impact of additional income on happiness tends to taper off around an annual salary of $75,000 – well below the top 1%. There is no data suggesting that more money makes people less happy – it's just that it stops making them much happier. Nonetheless, it is abundantly clear that the very rich are forever striving to augment their wealth. Some of the reasons why are surprisingly simple.

People might be happier with their current level of wealth, if it weren't for the curious and apparently irresistible urge humans have to compare ourselves with others in every dimension imaginable: attractiveness; intelligence; height; weight; and crucially, financial success. As H. L. Mencken said, "A wealthy man is one who earns $100 a year more than his wife's sister's husband." The happiness we derive from income is based not only on how much we have, but on how much we have relative to our peers. The pain of seeing someone else make more money is a major motivator when it comes to accumulating wealth. Additionally, people are much more likely to engage in conspicuous consumption when they know that those purchases will get them ahead of their peers in the status hierarchy.

Interestingly, this applies to the other end of the income spectrum as well. A recent study shows that the people who are most opposed to an

increase in the minimum wage are those who make just above the minimum wage. Why? Because if it increases, these people will now tie for 'last place', along with all the people to whom they used to feel superior.

Also, unlike many other things that matter in life, money can be counted. When people reflect on whether they are better off this year than last, questions like 'do I have more meaning in my life?' are too fuzzy. Salary, on the other hand, gives us a measuring stick: 'If I make more this year than last, then yes, I am doing better in life'. This may also explain why people are always buying larger houses and televisions.

Lastly, despite studies contradicting this notion, most people still believe that if they were to have more money, they would definitely be having a better time. In our survey, we asked people to predict how happy they would be if their annual income was anything from $5,000 up to $1 million. We also asked how much money they actually earned, and how happy they were. We found that people generally overestimated the impact of money on happiness; for example, those who earned $25,000 a year predicted that their happiness would double if they made $50,000. More money, more happiness.

When we measured the happiness of people at these two levels of income by having them rate their satisfaction with life on a scale of 1–10, we found that the wealthier group was only 9% happier. This shouldn't be surprising: many of us can think of times when we earned less but were happier. So, if you are thinking of applying for a better-paid job, consider your options carefully.

All of that said, the richest amongst us are better equipped to turn money into happiness, but perhaps not in the way you'd expect. Our research shows that people can gain happiness with money if they simply give it away. It turns out that spending money on other people – donating to charity, or buying coffee for a friend – creates happiness. So the next time you're expecting friends, think about what you can do to treat them. It might bring you more happiness than a pay rise.

3 a Read the article again. Choose the best option a–c for each question.

1 Research has shown that additional income makes people happier if …
   a they have worked hard to achieve it.
   b they earn less than $75,000 a year.
   c they are in the top 1% of earners.
2 The desire to compare ourselves with others …
   a is a particular trait of competitive people.
   b tends to be most common within families.
   c pushes many to improve their financial situation.
3 The writer suggests that people are motivated to …
   a have the same income as their peers.
   b buy possessions which reflect their higher status.
   c rise above 'last place' in terms of their income.
4 Constantly buying bigger houses and televisions is a way to …
   a measure our progress.
   b give our lives meaning.
   c show others that we are better off than we were.
5 The results of the author's research showed that people …
   a were happier when their income doubled.
   b predicted the effect of money on happiness accurately.
   c on a higher income were happier than those on a lower income.
6 Wealthy people are more able to turn money into happiness because …
   a they can buy the things that make them happy.
   b they are able to make good investments for the future.
   c they have the means to spend it on others.

b Work in groups. Discuss these questions.

1 If you earned twice as much money, how much happier do you think you would be?
2 How does it make you feel when you spend money on other people?
3 What do you think is the key to being happy?

HELP WITH GRAMMAR
Simple v continuous: verbs with different meanings

4 **a** Look at the simple and continuous verb forms in bold in these extracts. Match the verbs to these meanings.

a remember c consider e wait for
b possess d believe will happen f experience

1 Most people still believe that if they were to **have** more money, they would definitely **be having** a better time.

2 Many of us can **think** of times when we earned less but were happier. So, if you **are thinking** of applying for a better-paid job, consider your options carefully.

3 The richest amongst us are better equipped to turn money into happiness, but perhaps not in the way you'd **expect**. … So the next time you**'re expecting** friends, think about what you can do to treat them.

b Compare these pairs of sentences. What is the difference in meaning between the verb forms in bold in each sentence?

1 a His clothes **fit** me perfectly.
b They**'re fitting** new brakes on my car.
2 a He **appears** to be fast asleep.
b She**'s appearing** on a TV show.
3 a It **looks** expensive.
b He**'s looking** at a new car today.
4 a She **comes** from London.
b She**'s coming** from London.
5 a He**'s** difficult.
b He**'s being** difficult.
6 a I **imagine** she really likes Canada.
b There's nobody there. You**'re imagining** things!
7 a I now **see** why she found it difficult.
b I**'m seeing** Joe tonight.

c Check in GRAMMAR 9.1 p159.

5 **a** Complete these sentences with the Present Simple or Continuous form of the verbs in brackets. Sometimes both forms may be possible.

1 Most people ____________ (never think) that they have enough money.
2 If you ____________ (have) money problems, it's important to get good advice.
3 It ____________ (appear) that the gap between rich and poor is getting wider in most countries.
4 You can find a job you love doing if you ____________ (look) hard enough.
5 If you ____________ (expect) something bad to happen, then it probably will.

b Work in pairs. Compare your answers. If both are correct, explain why.

c Discuss the sentences in 5a. Do you agree?

Listening and Speaking

6 CD3 6 Listen to Cate, Maureen and Pete discussing whether money can buy you happiness. Which of these sentences best summarises their discussion?

They all agree that …

1 money can't buy you happiness.
2 possessions can't bring you happiness.
3 you only need enough money to cover your basic needs.

7 Tick the true sentences. Then correct the false ones.

1 Two of the speakers believe money can bring you happiness.
2 Maureen believes money can buy you time to do what you want to do.
3 Pete thinks things which bring happiness don't always cost money.
4 Maureen doesn't think money can buy you health.
5 Cate agrees with Maureen that money can buy love.

8 Listen again and fill in these gaps with between one and four words. Then check your answers to **7**.

CATE 'Money can't buy you happiness' is actually a statement I think I would ________________ .
MAUREEN I know a lot of people say that, Cate, but then they're thinking of ________________ .
MAUREEN It can buy you ________________ to do the things ________________ .
PETE What about things that don't necessarily take a lot of money but ________________ ?
PETE It doesn't matter how ________________ you are, you can't buy that ________________ .
CATE Yes, and not having money can really ________________ .
PETE I've been there, worrying about where the next penny's coming from. It's ________________ .
MAUREEN And it's like when they say money can't buy you health – well, ________________ .
CATE I don't ________________ !

HELP WITH PRONUNCIATION
Contrast and contradictions

9 **a** CD3 7 Listen and notice how the speakers emphasise a word which contrasts with a previous point with a step up (↑) in pitch.

'Money can't buy you happiness' is actually a statement I would have to agree with. I mean, I recognise that we need money, we (↑) do need money for our basic needs, but money is (↑) not the route to happiness.

b CD3 8 Listen and circle the words that should be emphasised in this response.

I know a lot of people say that …
But maybe it's the opportunities that, that having money give you that makes me think money can buy you happiness.
So, in that way, I think money really can buy you happiness. I'm not saying it always does.

c Work in pairs. Practise saying the sentences in **9a** and **b**. Use a step up in pitch to say the words that are emphasised.

TIPS • To contrast or contradict a negative statement, we use a positive form of the auxiliary or modal verb (e.g. *can*, *do*) and a step up in pitch. *We* (↑) ***do*** *need money …*
• To contradict or contrast a positive statement, we use *not* or a contraction (e.g. *can't*, *don't*) and a step up in pitch. *Money is* (↑) ***not*** *the route to happiness …*
• We can also emphasise the word that contrasts or contradicts a previous statement (e.g. *always*).

10 **a** Look at this statement. Think about whether you agree or disagree and make notes.

Money can't buy you love or happiness but it is a measure of success.

b Work in pairs. Discuss the statement, paying attention to your pronunciation. Try to reach an agreement.

c Work with another pair and discuss your ideas.

Get ready … Get it right!

11 Make a list of things you have bought and experiences you have had that have given you great pleasure. Which of the experiences didn't involve money?

12 **a** Work in groups. Discuss your lists. Which are the most interesting?

b Tell the class about what your group discussed. As a class, do most of you get more satisfaction from experiences or possessions?

It appears most of us get more pleasure from …

Cash-free

Vocabulary word building (3): productive suffixes
Grammar *a/an* v *one*; *few, a few, quite a few*

QUICK REVIEW ***Price and cost*** Think about the cost of living (food, entertainment, transport, rent, etc.) where you live. Make a list of things you think are reasonably priced and things you think cost too much. Work in pairs and compare lists. **A** *In general, I think the cost of public transport is reasonable.* **B** *Yes, but train fares are overpriced.*

Listening and Vocabulary

1 **a** Can you think of any advantages of travelling without money?

b CD3 9 Listen to the first extract from a programme about Satish Kumar. Answer these questions.

1 What was Satish's plan?
2 What did the teacher say would happen if they had/didn't have money?
3 Did Satish and his companion take any money?

c CD3 10 Listen to the next extract. Make notes on topics a–f.

a 8,000
b two women
c packets of tea
d *No Destination*
e two graves
f the English Channel and the Atlantic

d Work in pairs. Compare answers.

e CD3 11 Listen to the final extract. Fill in the gaps below. What point is Satish Kumar making?

… he learned that if he travels as an Indian with an Indian [1]__________ he'll meet a Pakistani, or a [2]__________ , or a US citizen carrying their [3]__________ . If he goes as a [4]__________ , he'll meet a capitalist. If he goes as a [5]__________ man, he'll meet a [6]__________ man or a [7]__________ man, but if he travels through life as a [8]__________ , he'll meet only [9]__________ .

Satish Kumar, who walked the world for peace

2 **a** CD3 9 CD3 10 CD3 11 Listen again to all three extracts. Are these statements true, false, or the answer is not given?

1 There were anti-war demonstrations in the 1960s.
2 Satish was in his 20s when he began the journey.
3 They often thought of giving up and going home.
4 Satish felt that his journey had been successful in persuading governments to change.

b Work in groups. Discuss these questions.

1 Is Satish Kumar too idealistic?
2 Was his advice right about how to achieve peace?
3 Is the world becoming more peaceful?

HELP WITH VOCABULARY
Word building (3): productive suffixes

3 **a** Look at sentences 1–4 from the radio programme. Choose the correct suffix.

1 There were many community *free/-led* campaigns.
2 The two men, who weren't particularly money-*minded/worthy* anyway, set off.
3 Their 8,000-mile walk certainly wasn't entirely stress *minded/-free*.
4 It's note*worthy/-led* that apart from crossing the English Channel and the Atlantic by boat, they really did walk all the way.

b What do you think the suffixes in **3a** mean?

c What do the suffixes in bold mean?

1 Their journey was totally unpredict**able**.
2 They didn't have water**proof** clothing.
3 They started walking around six**ish**.
4 They were very health-**conscious**.

d Check in VOCABULARY 9.2 p158.

4 **a** What do you think the words in bold mean?

1 an **ovenproof** dish
2 **reddish** hair
3 a **pollution-free** environment
4 a **newsworthy** story
5 an **unforgettable** moment
6 a **government-led** initiative
7 a **politically-minded** person
8 **fashion-conscious** teenagers

b Choose five words or suffixes from **3** and **4a** and write questions to ask a partner.

c Work in pairs. Ask and answer your questions.

Speaking and Reading

5 **a** Work in pairs. Answer these questions.

1. How do you usually pay for things: online, by credit/debit card, in cash, etc.?
2. Do you always have cash on you when you go out? If so, what do you mainly use it for?
3. Do you have smart cards for public transport where you live? Do you use them? Why?/Why not?
4. What do you think 'e-cash' means?

b Read the article. Does the writer think we will become a cash-free society?

6 **a** Find examples of these things in the article.

a three things that mobile phones can pay for
b five advantages of using e-cash for payments
c a disadvantage of mobile-phone payments (from the banks' point of view)

b Work in small groups. Discuss the questions.

1. In your country, have there been changes in how people pay for things recently?
2. What are the pros and cons of a cash-free society?
3. Do you welcome the idea of a world without cash? Why?/Why not?

MOBILE PHONES
the new cash?

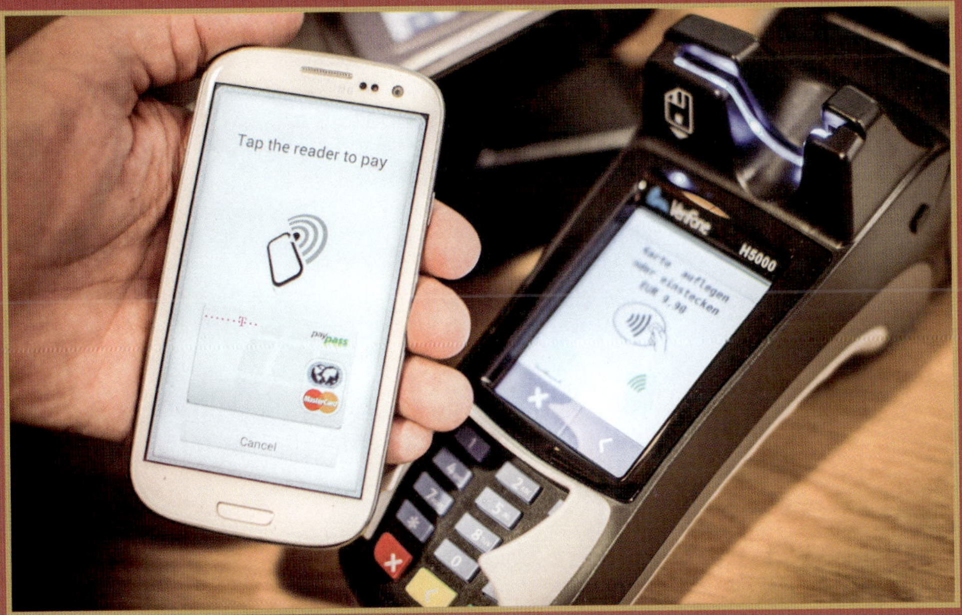

When purchasing goods or paying for services, many of us move from one means of payment to another within the space of one day. We might pay household bills online, use credit cards to pay for food and cash for bus or train fares. However, few financial experts would dispute the fact that some of these methods of payment will soon become a thing of the past. Some experts even believe that one day, we could be living in a totally cash-free society.

Smart cards and mobile phones are becoming an increasingly popular way to make all sorts of payments. In Japan, thousands of purchases, from rail tickets to picking up the groceries, take place every day with customers passing their handsets across a small flat-screen device. Predictions in the world of finance reckon that payments using mobile phones will have risen to more than $50 billion in the very near future.

What's the appeal of e-cash? Compared to cheques or credit cards, it offers the speed of cash, but more so. It takes just one-tenth of a second to complete most transactions and, as no change is required, errors in counting are eliminated. Fraud and theft are also reduced, and for the retailer it reduces the cost of handling money. Sony's vision of having a chip embedded in computers, TVs and games consoles means that films, music and games can be paid for easily without having to input credit card details.

What about the future of the banks? With their grip on the market, banks and credit-card firms want to be able to collect most of the fees from the users of mobile and contactless-payment systems. However, the new system could prove to be a 'disruptive technology' as far as the banks are concerned. If payments for a few coffees, a train ticket and a newspaper are made every day by a commuter with a mobile, this will not appear on their monthly credit card statements, but on their mobile-phone statements. Having spent fortunes on branding, credit-card companies and banks do not want to see other payment systems gaining ground. It's too early to say whether banks will miss out and if so, by how much. However, quite a few American bankers are optimistic. They feel there is reason to be suspicious of those who predict that high-street banks may be a thing of the past. They point out that internet banking did not render high-street branches obsolete as was predicted. On the contrary, more Americans than ever are using local branches. So, whether we're likely to become a totally cash-free society remains open to contention.

HELP WITH GRAMMAR
a/an v *one*; *few*, *a few*, *quite a few*

A/AN, ONE

7 Complete the rules with *a/an* or *one*.

- *a/an* and *one* both refer to one thing and can be used with singular countable nouns. However, we usually use ________ :

a if we want to emphasise the number.
It takes just ________ tenth of a second to complete most transactions. (not two or three tenths)

b when we are thinking of a particular day (in the future or the past), but we don't say exactly which day.
It happened ________ day last month. (but I can't remember which day)
We can see him ________ day next week.

c in phrases with *other/another/the next*.
Many of us move from ________ means of payment to another.

8 **a** Work in pairs. Read the question and choose the best answer in each reply. Give reasons.

> Have you got a five-pound note I could borrow?

> Sorry, I've only got [1]*a/one* ten-pound note.

> Sorry, I've only got [2]*a/one* five-pound note and I need it.

FEW, A FEW, QUITE A FEW

b Match the words/phrases in bold in extracts a–c to definitions 1–3.

a However, **few** financial experts would dispute the fact that some of these methods of payment will soon become a thing of the past.

b If payments for **a few** coffees are made every day by a commuter with a mobile, this will not appear on their monthly credit card statements, but on their mobile-phone statements.

c However, **quite a few** American bankers are optimistic.

1 a considerable number
2 some, but a small number
3 not many, or not enough

TIPS • *Few* is often used in more formal situations.
• *Little/a little* is used with uncountable nouns in the same way *few/a few* is used with countable nouns.
I spend ***very little time*** *with my son.* (not much time at all)
Every evening he spends ***a little time*** *with his son.* (not much time, but some)

c Check in GRAMMAR 9.2 p160.

9 **a** Think about how to answer these questions using words/phrases from the box.

a	an	a lot	one	few	quite a few
a little	a few	very little	quite a bit		

1 How much time do you spend with different members of your family?
2 How many snacks between meals do you have during the day? What about coffees?
3 Do you have a lot of free time during the week?
4 Do you do any activities after work or studying?
5 Do you carry a lot of cash on you?

b Work in pairs. Take turns to ask and answer the questions. Ask follow-up questions.

c Work with a different partner. Explain your previous partner's answers.

> Maria has very little free time during the week.

Get ready ... Get it right!

10 **a** Work in groups. You are planning to raise awareness of an important issue. Decide the following points.

- what you will do (a walk or run, a climb, a bike ride, etc.)
- what issue you will support (a charity, world peace, etc.)

b Now decide the details.

- how you will raise funds (working before the trip, sponsorship, etc.)
- how you will raise awareness of the issue (set up a blog, write articles, seek publicity, etc.)

11 Tell the class about your plan. Which seems the most interesting? Which do you think is most likely to succeed? Why?

9 Writing

Connecting words cause and effect (2)
Spelling *-ible* or *-able*
Writing task making a semi-formal/formal complaint

1 What problems can customers sometimes have with their bank?

2 Read this letter from a customer to a bank. Ignore any mistakes for now. What has happened and what does the customer want to happen next?

Dear Sir,

According to my latest bank statement, I have been charged interest on a loan that I never took out. [1]So, my current account is overdrawn by £50 and [2]because of this, I have been charged £10 for an unauthorised overdraft. [3]As I am not responsable for the mistake and it is [4]because of a bank error, please credit my account with the sum of £60.

There has been a noticable increase in mistakes recently and I believe that customers deserve a more relible service. I find it unacceptable, and quite unbelieveable, that in today's world of computerised banking, such mistakes can still happen. [5]So, I would appreciate some explanation as to why this error has occurred.

3 **a** Look at the letter again. Correct four spelling mistakes with the suffixes *-ible* or *-able*. WRITING 9.1 p161.

b Complete these words with the suffixes *-ible* or *-able*.

Something that …

1. you can eat is ed__________ .
2. you can understand is understand__________ .
3. makes sense is sens__________ .
4. you can see is vis__________ .
5. you can do is do__________ .
6. you notice is notice__________ .
7. you can believe is believ__________ .
8. you can destroy is destruct__________ .
9. is hard to believe is incred__________ .

4 **a** Rewrite these sentences in two different ways using the words in brackets. Make any necessary changes. WRITING 9.2 p161.

1. He's determined. That's why he's successful. (as a result; because)
   He's successful because he's determined.
   He's determined. As a result, he's successful.
2. The weather was bad yesterday. I didn't go climbing. (due; consequently)
3. Three people were ill. The meeting was cancelled. (so; accordingly)
4. My Spanish is really bad. He didn't understand me. (as a result; because)
5. There were terrible floods. They lost all their crops. (therefore; because of)
6. Visibility was poor. There were several road accidents. (because of; consequently)
7. You don't want to help. I'll do it myself. (since; as)

b Read the letter again. Which of these words/phrases could be used to make the underlined connecting words seem more formal? Sometimes there is more than one possible answer.

consequently	therefore	since
as a result	accordingly	due to

5 **a** In your most recent bank statement, you were charged for a purchase you did not make. Because of this, you could not withdraw money from a cash machine. Think of four possible consequences of this situation.

b Work in pairs and compare ideas. What do you think the bank should do?

6 **a** Write a draft letter to the bank, making a complaint and demanding action.

b Work in pairs. Swap letters and check for these features.

- spelling of suffixes
- use of formal connecting words
- appropriate vocabulary

c Discuss how you can improve your letters.

7 **a** Write a second draft of your letter.

b Work in groups. Read other students' letters. Whose situation was the most serious as a result of the bank's mistake?

For more Writing practice: Portfolio 9, Workbook p78.

World issues

Vocabulary world issues and economics
Real World presenting information

QUICK REVIEW Productive suffixes
Write one word for each of these suffixes: *-free*; *-led*; *-conscious*; *-ish*; *-able*; *-minded*; *-worthy*; *-proof*. Work in pairs and swap papers. Say a sentence using words from your partner's list. **A** *sugar-free*. **B** *Sugar-free drinks are much better for you*.

Listening and Vocabulary

1 **a** Work on your own. How much do you know about the economics of your country? Answer these questions. Check new words/phrases in VOCABULARY 9.3 p159.

1 In the last few years has there been **economic growth** or **economic decline**?
2 What steps has your government taken in periods of **economic recession**?
3 Can you name one thing that is **mass-produced** in your country?
4 Does your government send **overseas aid** to **developing countries**?
5 Is your government developing **renewable energy** technology such as wind farms?
6 How strong is the **housing market**?
7 Has your country ever been an **economic superpower**?
8 In what years have there been **record levels** of unemployment?
9 Does your country have **nuclear power**?
10 Are there laws against **gender discrimination** in the workplace?

b Work in pairs. How similar are your answers?

2 **a** CD3 12 Listen to a lecturer talking about studying economics. What are the three sections of his talk about?

b CD3 13 Listen to the next part of the lecture. Tick the true sentence. Correct the false ones.

1 Economics can provide all the answers to world problems.
2 Without it you can't understand world issues properly.
3 You don't need any particular skills to study economics.
4 It is only useful if you want to go into the world of business and finance.

3 **a** Listen again. Answer these questions.

1 What does the teacher say about world food prices and the effect they will have on the world?
2 What does he mean when he talks about "the real cost of a plastic bag"?
3 What type of people does he say are suited to economics?
4 Does he think the study of economics is difficult?
5 Why does he mention careers such as architecture, politics and journalism?
6 At the end of the talk, which four adjectives does he use to describe economics?

b Work in pairs. Compare answers.

4 Work in pairs and discuss these questions.

1 Which of the teacher's arguments do you think would influence a young audience the most and why?
2 Do you know anyone whose job requires a knowledge of economics? If so, why?
3 If you have studied economics, did you enjoy it? If you have never studied economics, do you think you'd enjoy it? Why?/Why not?

REAL WORLD Presenting information

5 **a** Why does the teacher use these sentences in the introduction to his talk?

I'm going to divide the talk into (three sections).
First of all, (how economics is related to real life).
Then I'll go on to (the intellectual challenge).
And finally I'll (discuss future careers).

b Match phrases 1–13 to headings a–e.

a to make the first point *2*
b to refer to a point made earlier
c to signal a new point
d to summarise what's been said so far
e to signal the last point/bring the talk to an end

1 In conclusion …
2 First of all …
3 Now I'll talk about …
4 Let's move on to …
5 So, to sum up …
6 As I said before …
7 Last but not least …
8 Let's start with/by …
9 To go back to …
10 Just to recap …
11 Leaving that aside for a moment …
12 To return to something I mentioned earlier …
13 And finally …

c Look at Audio Scripts CD3 12 and CD3 13 p174. Look at the phrases in bold and notice how the talk is structured.

d Check in REAL WORLD 9.1 p161.

6 **a** Complete these sentences with the correct words.

a First _________ all, let's start _________ looking at the problems that occur when young people can't find work.

b Leaving that aside _________ a moment, let's move _________ _________ the advantages for society in having apprenticeship schemes.

c Now I'll talk _________ how a transfer of skills will benefit individuals both young and old.

d As I said _________ , the benefits will be considerable.

e And to go _________ _________ a point I made earlier, the elderly have skills they can pass on to the young.

f To sum _________ , what we need is to find a way to encourage more apprenticeship schemes.

g _________ conclusion, unless we do something soon, the outcome looks bleak.

b Work in pairs. Answer these questions.

1 What is the talk in **6a** about?

2 Do you think it's a good idea? Why?/Why not?

3 Would it be relevant to your country?

7 **a** Work in pairs. You are each going to give a two-minute talk on the same topic to a different partner. Choose one of these topics (or your own) and follow instructions 1–3.

- Junk mail should be made illegal.
- Public transport should be free.
- Everyone should have a three-day weekend.
- People should retire at 50.

1 Make a list of things you could include in your talk.

2 Put your list in a logical order and make a list about what you could say about each one.

3 Think about how to open and close your talk.

b Work on your own. Make notes on what you are going to say.

c Work with your partner from **7a**. Take turns to practise giving your talk. Give each other advice on how to improve it.

Give clearer signals to show how the talk is structured.
Vary your voice more. Make more eye contact.

8 Work with a new partner who has prepared a different talk. Take turns to give your talk. Was your partner convinced by your arguments?

continue2learn

Vocabulary, Grammar and Real World

- **Extra Practice and Progress Portfolio 9** p122
- **Video (*Cash*)** p132
- **Language Summary 9** p158
- **Workbook** p44

Reading and Writing

- **Portfolio 9** Guidelines and instructions Workbook p78
  Reading information on using a travel card
  Writing connecting words in guidelines/ instructions; questions as headings

10A Be creative!

Grammar subject/verb agreement
Vocabulary noun collocations

QUICK REVIEW Simple v continuous: verbs with different meanings Work in pairs. Make questions with each of these verbs: *have, think, expect, feel.* One of you should use the simple form, the other should use the continuous form. Ask and answer your questions. **A** *Do you have any children?* **B** *Are we having a break soon?*

Reading

1 **a** Work in pairs. Think of different ways in which animals used to help humans in the past.

b Look at the pictures and the title of the article.

1 Which animals do you think will be mentioned?
2 How do you think they improved services?

c Read the article and check your ideas.

2 **a** Fill in gaps 1–7 in the article with sentences a–g. Which words/phrases in the article helped you?

a Further north, mail was being delivered to the icy corners of the world by huskies.
b Cats, meanwhile, were first employed by the Post Office in 1868.
c There was clearly a gap in the market for a swifter service.
d Pigeon post was used first by the Sumerians in 776 BC.
e However, homing birds weren't only used in ancient times.
f Airborne messengers are most useful in time of conflict, however.
g Horses, too, have powered the information superhighway for thousands of years.

b Work in pairs. Use sentences a–g in **2a** to summarise the article.

3 **a** Work in pairs. Look at the words/phrases in blue in the article. What ideas do they refer back to?

b Match the words/phrases in pink in the article with these meanings.

1 surrounded by an enemy
2 made to retire
3 remote
4 taken out secretly
5 employed
6 disappear slowly
7 extremely carefully
8 destroyed

c In what ways do animals help humans today?

Great service

From ancient Greece to the Wild West, animals have had an important part to play in improving vital services. Justine Hawkins reports.

Postal workers these days tend to be human, but it hasn't always been so.

1 ____________ It is known that the ancient civilisations of Egypt, Persia, Mesopotamia, Greece and Rome relied on pigeons to carry messages to far-flung corners of their kingdoms and empires. 2 ____________ In 1850, Paul Julius van Reuter began his news agency by sending information between Aachen and Brussels by pigeon. And until the beginning of the 21st century, the police in the Indian state of Orissa were using a pigeon service to deliver information during floods and cyclones. News comes via email these days, so the birds were pensioned off long ago.

3 ____________ When Paris was besieged during the war in 1870, pigeons provided a vital link to the outside world. The birds were smuggled out in balloons, returning later with much-needed news. During the four-month siege, more than a million letters were delivered to the citizens of Paris by this ingenious method. During the First and Second World Wars, the British army was also dependent on hundreds of thousands of pigeons. With great sadness, these prized flocks were handed over to support the war effort. Many lives were saved by the timely arrival of a pigeon and 32 of these winged heroes each received a medal for bravery in the Second World War.

4 ____________________ No equine postal service is more iconic than the Pony Express. Although it lasted less than two years, the Pony Express came to epitomise the pioneering spirit of the United States. When the gold rush generation arrived in California in 1848, it took 24 days for letters to arrive from loved ones in New York. 5 ____________________ So, in 1860, adverts were placed for 'Young, skinny, wiry fellows, not over 18. Must be expert riders, willing to face death daily. Orphans preferred.' There was no shortage of applicants. Pony Express riders had names like Charlie P Cyclone and Pony Bob, and there were around 400 horses and 100 men. During its short romantic existence, it was the fastest means of delivering messages across the US; 2,000 miles is a long way on horseback, but the riders would travel **this distance** from the railroad station in Missouri to California, across wilderness, in only nine to ten days. The public were fascinated by the Pony Express but **even so**, the team was a financial failure and was put out of business by transcontinental telegraph.

6 ____________________ Commercial dog teams in Alaska and Canada saw their source of income **ebb away** when mail delivery contracts were lost to the aeroplane in the 1920s. The dogs are still going, though, and many of today's dogsled races follow the historic mail routes.

7 ____________________ Initially, only **a couple** were **recruited** when a quantity of money orders was **demolished** by rodents, and an allowance was paid to a Post Office porter for their upkeep. In the decades that followed, dozens of cats were employed at UK sorting offices. Accounts of cats on the payroll were recorded **scrupulously**, but the cats never received a pay rise. Alas, having cats as part of the Post Office workforce is now a thing of the past. Animals have been retired from the communications business and are now found only in the pages of stamp collections.

HELP WITH GRAMMAR
Subject/verb agreement

4 **a** Choose the correct words in sentences 1 and 2.

A verb usually 'agrees' with its subject (i.e. a singular subject has a singular verb and a plural subject a plural verb.)

1 Horses, too, *has/have* powered the information superhighway for thousands of years.
2 Further north, mail *was/were* being delivered to the icy corners of the world by huskies.

b Choose the correct word in these examples.

A 1 if the subject of the verb is a clause
Having cats is/are now a thing of the past.
2 with nouns which end in -*s* but are not plural
News come/comes via email these days.
3 with expressions of quantity, measurement, etc.
2,000 miles is/are a long way to travel.
4 after words such as *everyone*, *anything*, etc.
The information that everyone was/were waiting for.

B 5 for nouns which don't end in an -*s* but are not singular
The police was/were using a pigeon service.
6 after *both of*, *all of*, *plenty of*, *a number of*, *a couple*
Only a couple was/were recruited.

c Choose the correct word in these rules.

- In group A, we use a *singular/plural* verb.
- In group B, we use a *singular/plural* verb.

d Fill in the gaps in rules 1 and 2 with *singular* or *plural*.

Some collective nouns can take a singular or a plural form.

1 When focusing on countries which are a group of states, or an institution or organisation as a whole, the verb is usually ____________ .
The USA **has** *50 states.*
The British army **was** *also dependent on pigeons.*
The team **was** *a financial failure.*

2 When focusing on a collection of individuals, the verb is usually ____________ .
The public **were** *fascinated by the Pony Express.*

e Check in GRAMMAR 10.1 p162.

5 **a** Choose the correct words. Then complete the sentences so that they are true for you.

1 The most interesting news at the moment *is/are* …
2 Personally, I think keeping pets *is/are* …
3 The US *is/are* …
4 In my country, the general public *is/are* fascinated by …
5 Everyone I meet these days *seem/seems* to be interested in …
6 Lots of my friends *like/likes* …

b Work in pairs. Compare sentences.

6 **a** Write a summary of the article in 150 words.

b Work in pairs. Read your summaries and check for subject/verb agreement. Which summary gives a clearer idea of the article?

Listening and Vocabulary

7 **a** Work in pairs. Do the quiz.

b CD3 14 Listen to a radio programme and check your answers.

1 Who invented ice cream?
a the Italians **b** the Chinese

2 Who first started drinking tea?
a the English **b** the Chinese

3 Where did coffee first come from?
a Ethiopia **b** Colombia

4 How high was the first skyscraper?
a 10 storeys **b** 20 storeys

5 Where was the first escalator invented?
a Japan **b** the US

8 **a** Check the meaning of the noun collocations in bold.

1 What does the presenter say about many things we accept as **a matter of course**?
2 How did Marco Polo become **a mine of information** about ice-cream making?
3 Is it generally accepted there is **an element of truth** in the way tea was first created?
4 Are the claims for how people began to eat coffee beans **a matter of opinion**?
5 What was **the centre of attention** in Chicago in 1885?
6 How did it set off **a train of events** which revolutionised city life?
7 What is described as **a stroke of genius**?

b CD3 14 Listen again and answer questions 1–7 in **8a**.

c Work in pairs. Compare your answers.

d Which of the inventions discussed in the programme do you think had the most interesting beginnings? Do you know any others?

HELP WITH PRONUNCIATION
Review: Preparing to give a talk

9 You are going to prepare and give a short talk, focusing on a range of features:

- speech units
- appropriate stress and intonation
- connected speech

Student A p107. Student B p110.

Get ready ... Get it right!

10 **a** Work on your own. Make a list of inventions in your home, both big and small (fridge, toothbrush, coffee machine, etc.).

b Work in pairs. Compare lists. Choose the five most useful inventions and explain why.

11 **a** Work with another pair. Take turns to say which items are on your list and why you chose them. Then agree on the five most useful inventions.

b Work with the whole class. Decide on the top three most useful inventions.

10B Stick with it!

Grammar modal verbs: levels of certainty about the past, the present and future
Vocabulary adjective-noun collocations

QUICK REVIEW Subject/verb agreement Work in pairs. Take turns to complete these sentences with your opinions and information about yourself: *I think having pets … ; Everyone I know … ; I think the police … ; My family … ; My favourite (football) team … ; Only a couple of my friends … .*

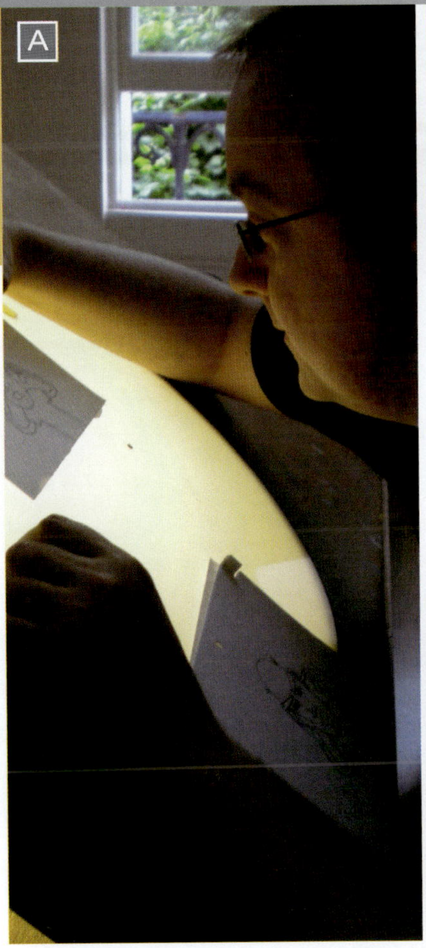

Speaking and Listening

1 **a** Make a list of people you know who have been successful in what they do. Is their success due to luck, talent or the fact that they have been very dedicated?

b Work in pairs. Take turns to tell each other about the people on your list.

2 **a** CD3 15 Listen to Adela and Louie. Who are the people in photos A and B?

b Listen again. Work in Groups A and B. Use these prompts to make notes.

A What does Adela say about: Latin; Martin's talent; Saturday night; his girlfriend; being positive?

B What does Louie say about: luck; Janine Jansen's life; Louie's school; gifted people; being a soloist?

c Work with a student from the same group and compare answers.

d Work with a student from the other group. Use your notes from **2b** to summarise what Adela or Louie said.

e Listen again. Fill in the gaps with one of the verbs in the boxes and a modal verb.

~~work~~	be	be	work	enjoy	find	create

1 Here it is Saturday night and I'm sure he *'ll be working* .
2 He ____________ a new animation character or he ____________ on his next short film.
3 Clearly, he ____________ what he does, why else would he work so hard?
4 But I feel sorry for his girlfriend. It ____________ easy having Martin as your partner.
5 People are just starting to notice his work, so it ____________ long before he gets the recognition he deserves.
6 He's certain he ____________ a buyer for his next animation.

devoted	want	be	have	give up

7 Janine Jansen, for example, you just know it ____________ an easy life for her.
8 She ____________ most of her life to practising.
9 I ____________ some natural talent, who knows?
10 My father says that I ____________ it badly enough or I ____________ .

HELP WITH GRAMMAR
Modal verbs: levels of certainty about the past, present and future

3 **a** Look at sentences 1–10 in **2e**. Complete the rules with *possible*, *definite*, or *probable*.

- We use *will*, *won't*, *can't*, *must*, *would(n't)* when we think something is ____________ .
- We use *should* when we think something is ____________ .
- We use *may*, *might*, *could* when we think something is ____________ .

b Look again at sentences 1–10 in **2e**. Then fill in the gaps with *past*, *present*, or *future*.

1 Sentences 1–4 refer to the ____________ .
2 Sentences 5 and 6 refer to the ____________ .
3 Sentences 7–10 refer to the ____________ .

c What verb form follows the modal verb when it refers to: the present? the future? the past?

d Check in GRAMMAR 10.2 p163.

Reading and Vocabulary

4 Work in groups of three. Student A, follow the instructions below. Student B p110. Student C p112.

1 Look at the picture below of Felix Baumgartner and make notes on these questions, using modal verbs.
   - a What do you think happened before this moment?
   - b What do you think will happen next?
   - c What do you think Felix is thinking and feeling at this moment?

2 Take turns to show your photo and explain your ideas. Do you all agree? Why/Why not?

5 Read this introduction to an article. What kind of person do you think Felix is?

HIS JUMP FROM THE EDGE of space was watched by millions. Now action man Felix Baumgartner wants to talk about the crippling anxiety he had to overcome before falling to earth faster than the speed of sound. In his record-breaking space jump, Felix Baumgartner reached an altitude of 128,000 feet in a small capsule attached to a helium balloon before he plummeted back down again through 24 miles of cold blackness at a top speed of 833.9 miles per hour.

6 **a** Work in pairs. Student A, read the article extract on this page and follow the instructions below. Student B, read the extract and follow the instructions on p113.

1 Answer these questions.
   - a What did Baumgartner find most difficult?
   - b What is his 'message'?

2 Read the extract again. Make notes on the topics below.

1 Baumgartner's early dreams	4 the spacesuit
2 his nickname	5 his replacement
3 his emotional state	6 leadership

b Take turns to summarise your extract. What do you think about Felix and his achievement?

HELP WITH VOCABULARY
Adjective–noun collocations

- Adjectives must collocate with the nouns they are describing. The opposite of a *clear idea* is a *rough idea*. However, the opposite of a *clear sky* is a *cloudy sky*.

7 **a** Look at these collocations expressing opposite meanings. Then choose which words 1–4 do <u>not</u> collocate with *moment*.

*The **toughest moment** was when I lost my team.*
*Baumgartner thinks hard when asked about his jump's **sweetest moment**.*

1 most challenging	3 highest
2 easiest	4 lowest

b Choose words which collocate with nouns 1–4.

thick	big	significant	thin	calm	trivial
slight	huge	important	light	cool	crazy

1 relief	3 gloves
2 message	4 guy

c Which adjectives in the collocations in **7b** are synonyms? Which are antonyms?

d Check in part A in VOCABULARY 10.1 p162.

BORN TO FLY

As a curiously driven man, who had dreamed of flying ever since he was a five-year-old boy in Austria, drawing detailed pictures of himself soaring through the sky, Baumgartner had finally achieved his greatest ambition. Some weeks later, he was sitting in a plush chair in a London hotel and arching a wry eyebrow at his cartoonish nickname. "You and I know 'Fearless Felix' doesn't really exist," he says, quietly, and more thoughtfully than might be expected. "He might seem like a cool guy, but I've had to address a real psychological battle. It's been way harder than stepping out into space."

He may be a certified celebrity, with an American twang to his Austrian accent, but he talks with the zeal of an ordinary man who has just survived an extraordinary experience. Baumgartner also uses the very human confines of psychological frailty, rather than the vast expanse of space, to frame his achievement. A canny publicist, he is smart enough to recognise that there is real strength in admitting moments of weakness. But there is also something surprisingly moving in his revelations that the source of his suffocating anxiety was an old-fashioned spacesuit.

"I feared and hated the suit because of my desire for freedom. I started skydiving because I loved the idea of being free. But you get trapped in a spacesuit, and people

8 **a** Write the correct collocations using the antonyms in brackets. Check in part B in VOCABULARY 10.1 ▸ p162.

1 a a rough surface b a rough sea (smooth; calm)

a smooth surface; a calm sea

2 a a light colour b a light meal (heavy; dark)

3 a a gentle wind b a gentle person (aggressive; strong)

4 a an old person b an old building (young; modern)

5 a a tall building b a tall person (short; low)

6 a a dry wine b a dry day (wet; sweet)

7 a plain food b a plain shirt (patterned; rich)

8 a a strong coffee b a strong possibility (weak; faint)

b Work in pairs. Take turns to say phrases 1–8 in **8a**. Your partner says the antonym.

a rough surface

a smooth surface

Get ready … Get it right!

9 **a** Make a list of things other than language learning that you have done or tried to do. Which have you achieved?

stop smoking – achieved
keep to a regular fitness programme – not achieved

b Look at your list and answer these questions.

1 Why do you think you were successful at some things and not others?
2 Did other people help or encourage you?
3 Would you consider yourself to be someone who generally sticks with things?

10 **a** Work in groups of three. Take turns to tell each other about the things on your list. Ask follow-up questions and take notes on what the other two students say.

b Work in a different group of three. Talk about the other two students in your original group. Decide which person is the most determined.

c Tell the class about the person your group chose and why you chose him/her.

We think Mia is the most determined because it can't have been easy for her to …

are adding weights to it every day. They'd say, 'Right, we need oxygen bottles,' and then a couple of weeks later it would be: 'You need a chest bag.' That chest bag became bigger and bigger and the suit is twice my normal weight. Skydiving is now no fun at all. It's scary. I remember my first dive with this suit. I was standing at the exit at 30,000 feet, and it felt like my very first skydive. It never felt good in that suit because it never became a second skin.

"Normally, when I skydive, even in winter, I wear very thin gloves. I want to be flexible, with fast reactions. But a spacesuit slows you down. You have thick gloves and you cannot move your head very well. … Every skill I had developed over the years became pretty useless as soon as I stepped into the space suit. And after 25 years as a professional, it makes you feel weak and exposed."

Baumgartner's vulnerability was bound up in claustrophobia. The problem became so distressing that he required psychiatric help and walked away from the project for six months. It was only when he saw footage of a replacement doing his job in testing that he was shocked into returning. "I felt jealous," he says, "and I thought, 'You're not supposed to be in my suit.' … It felt like I'd been replaced."

"The toughest moment was when I lost my team after I came back from Austria," he says. "My psychiatrist told me, 'Nobody thinks you can do it any more. You have to get your leadership back.'" As a former soldier and self-proclaimed

team leader and man of action, Baumgartner was shaken by the loss of faith in him. "I thought, whatever it takes to get my leadership back, I'm willing to do it. After five days it was working. Two weeks later, everyone was positive and we knew I was ready."

With regard to his legacy, Felix believes his success in overcoming difficulties is a more important message than flying supersonic. He says, "The suit was my worst enemy, but it became my friend – because the higher you go, the more you need the suit. It gives you the only way to survive. I learned to love the suit up there. That's an even bigger message than flying supersonic."

Go for it!

Vocabulary colloquial language
Skills Reading: a book review; Listening: language-learning strategies
Real World giving advice

QUICK REVIEW Modal verbs Work in pairs. Take turns to make sentences about people you know: *Tomorrow night … will … ; Next month … might … ; Next weekend … won't … ; Last week … wouldn't have had time to … .* Ask follow-up questions.

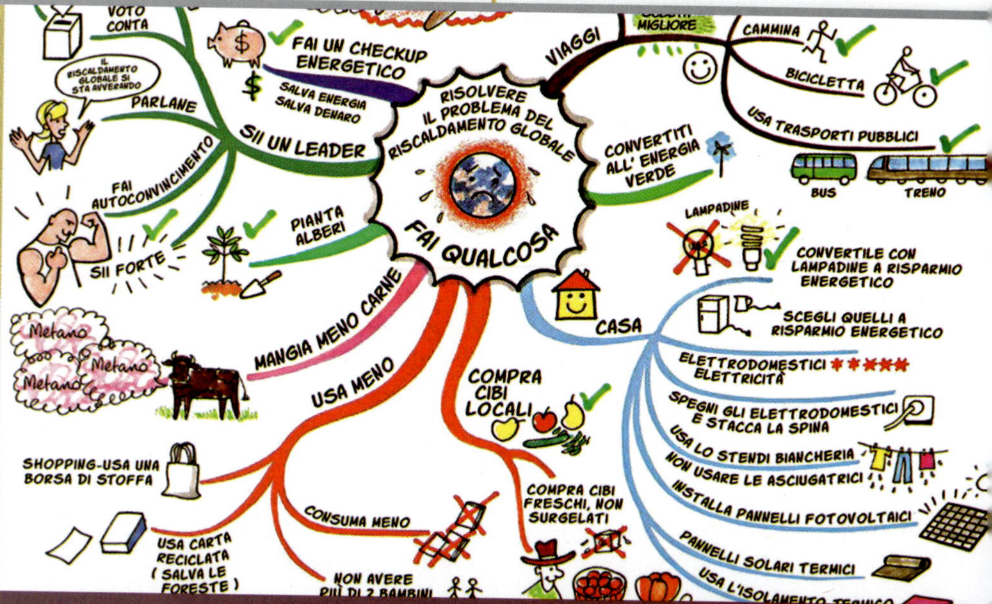

1 **a** What advice would you give to a beginner in English or another language? Make notes on things that helped you to progress. What would you have done differently?

b Work in groups. Agree on a list of 'dos' and 'don'ts'.

2 **a** It is claimed that *Language Revolution*, a language-learning course for beginners, will teach you how to learn a language in just eight weeks. Look at the picture. What technique do you think the series uses?

b Read the review. In what way is this method of learning a 'revolution'?

3 **a** Choose the correct words.

1 Buzan is in favour of *making lists/connecting ideas*.
2 He is inspired by the way *sports people/children* learn.
3 Buzan's claims about mind maps are *convincing/unclear*.
4 Children are believed to learn best by *making links/making maps*.
5 Buzan's approach is based on *linguistic theory/what he believes is self-evident*.

b Work in groups. Discuss these questions.

1 What methods do you use to record vocabulary?
2 Have you ever used mind maps? Do you think they are useful?
3 Would you consider using this method if you were learning a new language? Why?/Why not?

Is this the fastest track to fluency?

Tony Buzan's *Language Revolution* is about learning a language the way a baby would, by absorption and association. Simon Compton investigates.

According to his publicity, Tony Buzan, whose name is invariably associated with the words 'mind guru', has "revolutionised the way people think and remember, in the workplace, classroom and at home." At the heart of all his work are mind maps, a way of graphically organising and developing thoughts.

Mind maps help you to remember by linking words and images in an intuitive way. For example, in his Language Revolution Italian course Buzan encourages learners to draw a mind map of words they can remember associated with a trip to the bar. They are remembered not as a list but as one suggests the other, with colours and pictures as prompts.

Buzan says this reflects the organic and free-flowing way the brain works naturally, meaning we remember better by association. Lists have no associations, so are much harder work. He developed the idea of 'mind maps' as a tool for note taking when he was a student and has since written 95 books and taught his principles to everyone from government departments to the British Olympic rowing team.

Remembering by association, as a child does, permeates Buzan's learning technique. "Babies are the best language learners in the world, but they don't learn grammar," Buzan tells me. "For example, a child will build on the word 'Daddy' with 'Daddy work' and 'Daddy go work' and 'Daddy go car'. And that's a mind map in a baby's head."

Buzan claims that his techniques reflect the workings of the brain, but the science is vague. In the past he has explained it in terms of engaging the parts of the brain that make us creative in memory tasks, as well as the systematic parts of the brain that traditionally dominate. But he prefers to talk to me about natural learning styles. And what he says certainly tunes in with what child development experts know about the importance of learning by association.

Buzan's lack of linguistic expertise is what makes his approach so different. There is nothing miraculous or complex about his techniques; his great knack is to take things that we suspect are true from experience and incorporate them into learning programmes.

4 **a** Work in pairs. What do you think makes learning English at an advanced level different from other levels? What do you need to do in order to be successful?

b CD3 16 Listen to Maria Pia, an advanced Italian learner of English. Does she agree with what you said in **4a**? Answer these questions.

1 What did she do first at elementary level, before learning grammar?
2 What are the advantages of reading newspapers at a more advanced level?
3 What disadvantage does reading the classics have?
4 What helps her learn new language?
5 What has she found useful in order to understand different types of pronunciation?
6 What two tips does she have for remembering vocabulary?
7 What, for her, is the best way to put into practice the language she's learned?

c CD3 17 Listen to Bruce talking about his experience of learning languages. According to him, are these statements true or false?

1 He has learned four languages, all very successfully.
2 He has never liked learning languages in a classroom.
3 When you are advanced in a language, you need to be independent.
4 Learning a language shouldn't take long.
5 You shouldn't worry about making mistakes when speaking.

5 **a** Listen again to Bruce and answer these questions.

1 What does Bruce read in a foreign language?
2 In what ways does he think reading helps?
3 What does he listen to?
4 What does he say about grammar?
5 What technique does he have for learning vocabulary?

b Work in pairs. What do the words/phrases in bold mean?

1 I would just **jot it down** in my little booklet.
2 I'm a very **gregarious** learner … you know, just try and interact with other people …
3 … anything from **trashy** magazines to crime novels.
4 … I'm still a bit **woolly** about some of the grammar.
5 He used to write in English and then he **switched** to French.

6 Work in groups. Discuss these questions.

1 What do both Maria Pia and Bruce agree on?
2 Do you strongly agree/disagree with anything?
3 Do you think that some people have more freedom to express themselves in a foreign language? If so, how?

7 **a** You are going to give a short presentation about your language-learning experiences. Use 1–4 and the Real World box below.

1 How do you still need to improve your English?
2 How are you going to continue to improve your English outside the classroom?
3 What strategies have worked well for you?
4 What advice can you give to other people?

REAL WORLD Giving advice

- Take every opportunity to …
- Make sure you don't …
- Try to avoid …
- If you can, don't …
- It's a good idea to …
- It's absolutely essential to …
- Whatever you do, avoid/don't …

b Work in pairs. Take turns to practise giving your talk. Listen and give feedback.

8 **a** Take turns to give your presentations.

b After each presentation, discuss the strategies and advice. Which will you follow?

continue2learn

Vocabulary, Grammar and Real World

- **Extra Practice and Progress Portfolio 10** p123
- **Video (*Languages*)** p133
- **Language Summary 10** p182
- **Workbook** p49

Reading and Writing

- **Portfolio 10** An extract from a novel Workbook p81
  Reading a description of a scene
  Writing descriptive language in narratives

End of Course Review

Work in groups of four. Read the rules on p105. Then play the game!

START

1 Are both verb forms possible in this sentence?
1 I *saw/'ve seen* Bill this morning.
2 *Having eaten/Eating* a big lunch, I didn't want any dinner.

2 Which prepositions can we use with each of these nouns?
1 average, random, demand
2 times, fault, purpose

3 Talk about things that you have done over the last few months.

4 What does this saying mean?
1 We'll cross that bridge when we come to it.
2 Nothing ventured, nothing gained.

5 MOVE FORWARD TWO SQUARES

6 Are these possible collocations? If not, correct them.
1 firmly enjoy, deeply frustrating
2 vividly unlikely, distinctly remember

7 Complete these sentences for you.
1 I prefer it … I find it hard …
2 I love it … I find it annoying …

8 Put these words in order.
1 a(n) old leather huge suitcase
2 a marble white lovely statue

9 Talk about ways you and your friends try to stay healthy.

10 What is a less formal way of saying this sentence?
1 I received some good advice, for which I am truly grateful.
2 Rarely do I relax.

11 MOVE BACK TWO SQUARES

12 Explain what these words mean. Which has a positive connotation?
1 meticulous, fussy
2 courageous, reckless

13 Correct the mistakes.
1 I wish you went away now. I'm busy!
2 Not only he goes to the gym every day, he runs too.

14 Talk about a person or a place that you think is remarkable.

15 What's the difference?
1 I was going to go out but it started to rain.
2 I was going out when it started to rain.

16 Talk about your top four favourite inventions.

17 Explain the euphemism.
1 He's getting on a bit.
2 This chair's seen better days.

18 Talk about the most frightening experience you've ever had.

19 Correct the mistakes.
1 Did you enjoy at the party?
2 You really must concentrate yourself.

20 Talk about plans that you've made at some point in the past, but which you didn't carry out.

21 Explain the meanings of the verbs in bold.
1 She **appears** to like me. She's **appearing** on TV.
2 This coat **fits**. He's **fitting** new doors.

22 Change the nouns into adjectives and the adjectives into verbs.
1 mood, wide, excitement
2 culture, sympathy, clear

23 Talk about a person you think has achieved something difficult.

24 Make these sentences more formal.
1 It's way better now. It's pretty good.
2 This is loads better. This is a tiny bit cheaper.

25 MOVE BACK TWO SQUARES

26 Make a word with each suffix.
1 -proof, -led, -ish
2 -minded, -worthy, -able

27 Complete the word pairs and use them in a sentence.
1 take it or … , hit and …
2 on and … , over and …

28 MOVE BACK TWO SQUARES

29 Talk about things you are bound to do and are about to do in the near future.

30 What's the difference?
1 Only Pete eats fish. Pete only eats fish.
2 Jo's met everybody, even the Queen. Loads of us have met the Queen, even Jo.

31 What is the meaning of the prefix in these words?
1 semi-circle, semi-professional
2 overhead, overpaid

32 Talk about a recent news story.

33 Use these phrases in a sentence.
1 get round to sth, get away with sth
2 a break-up, a setback

34 Say four words/phrases connected to:
1 work
2 newspapers

35 Talk about how your life would be different now if certain things had or hadn't happened.

36 Are both verb forms possible?
1 I'd prefer it if you *met/'re meeting* me in the café.
2 It *alleged/is alleged* that the minister lied.

37 Talk about the successes that people in your family have experienced.

38 What's the difference in meaning?
1 He went on to do law. He went on doing law.
2 It meant doing it fast. I meant to do it fast.

FINISH

Rules

You need: One counter for each student, one dice for each group.

How to play: Put your counters on **START**. Take turns to throw the dice, move your counter and read the instructions on the square. The first student to get to **FINISH** is the winner.

Grammar and Vocabulary squares: The first student to land on a Grammar or Vocabulary square answers question 1. The second student to land on the same square answers question 2. If the other students think your answer is correct, you can stay on the square. If the answer is wrong, move back to the last square you were on. You can check your answers with your teacher. If a third or fourth student lands on the same square, he/she can stay on the square without answering a question.

Keep Talking squares: if you land on a Keep Talking square, talk about the topic for 45 seconds. Another student can check the time. If you can't talk for 45 seconds, move back to the last square you were on. If a second or third student lands on the same square, he/she also talks about the same topic for 45 seconds.

Pair and Group Work: Student/Group A

1C 7 p15

a Read definitions 1–3. Make sure you understand them and can say them fluently.

1 **rave** /reɪv/ **about something** to talk very enthusiastically about something: *Jan raved about Tarantino's new film. Apparently it's great.*

2 **hit the roof** to get very angry about something: *When June saw how much Pete had spent on his new car she hit the roof.*

3 **call it a day** to decide to stop working or doing an activity usually because you are tired or you have done enough: *I'm really tired. Let's call it a day. We can finish the cleaning tomorrow.*

b You are going to give three definitions of each idiom to Group B: the correct definition and two false definitions. Work together to invent two false definitions and three example sentences for each idiom.

c Decide who is going to give the true definition and the false definitions for each idiom. Then rehearse exactly what you are going to say. Remember you are all trying to convince Group B that your definition is correct.

d Work with students from Group B and follow these instructions. Your group starts.

1 Give your definitions for idiom 1. Group B discusses which definition is correct. Repeat your definitions if necessary.
2 Group B says which definition they think is correct, which are false and why. The student in your group with the correct definition then reads it out.
3 Group B then gives their definitions for idiom a. Continue with the game until both groups have guessed three definitions.

e Which group guessed the most correct definitions?

3B 3 p30

a Read extracts 1–3. Then answer these questions.

a What is the advice? Did it match any of your predictions?
b According to the research, how can the advice contribute to a person's well-being?
c What facts or figures, if any, support the research?

1 Eat more curry. Only recently have experts come to appreciate the health benefits of eating curries. Not only do curries protect against Alzheimer's, stress and depression, but they can also help you lose weight. Apparently, meals containing chillies burn up more calories* than other meals.

2 Get a hobby. Having a hobby can ease depression, lower levels of stress, improve mood and immune systems* and may reduce the risk of high blood pressure. According to research at Maastricht University, men who have hobbies are less likely to be sick and absent from work than men who don't.

3 Drink more coffee. Not until recently has the world's most widely used stimulant been considered good for you. It can lower the risk of diabetes*, relax muscles and improve speed of thought. According to research done at Harvard University, women who drink coffee may reduce the risk of having a heart attack by up to 30%. The research was carried out on 32,000 women over six years. Drinking six or more cups a day also reduces the risk of diabetes by 54% for men and 30% for women.

**calorie* = a unit for measuring the amount of energy that food will produce
**immune system* = system by which your body protects itself against diseases
**diabetes* /daɪə'biːtiːz/ = a serious disease in which there is too much sugar in your blood

b Work with the other people in your group. Take turns to tell each other your answers to the questions.

4B 12 p42

1

2

a Work with another student from Group A. Look at inventions 1 and 2. Then discuss these questions.

1 What were these inventions supposed to do?
2 Why did the inventors think they would be popular?
3 What do you think were the good and bad aspects of the inventions?
4 Do you think they would be popular in your country? Why?/Why not?

b Work with a student from Group B and a student from Group C. Take turns to describe your inventions, explaining what they were supposed to do. The other students should try and draw what you have described.

> The person who invented this obviously thought it was going to help people in rainy climates. It was supposed to …

c Compare your drawings with the original pictures on p109 and p111. Decide which you think is the best and the weirdest invention.

4C 6 p45

a Work with another student from Group A. You are news editors from a tabloid newspaper. Look at these notes for two possible lead stories. Think of photos and a dramatic headline for each story. What extra details could the stories include to have maximum impact?

1 200 drivers trapped in cars and coaches on A66 in north of England last night because of heavy snow and gales. Snow came in very fast, no warning. Some occupants waited for several hours before being rescued by police. Many rescued from A66 were taken to nearby villages. 45 pensioners taken to hotel to wait for a bus. Many motorists arrived on foot, cold and wet. Villagers helped with refreshments, etc. but village hall had no sleeping facilities. Roads now closed.

2 A two-year-old boy has been hailed as a hero after he found his mother collapsed on the floor and calmly dialled 999. He was too frightened to give his name but Joshua Brookes explained to the operator that his mummy wouldn't wake up. Police traced their address and paramedics went to the house but couldn't get in, so Joshua stood on a box and let them in. His mother, Isobel, who suffers from a rare heart condition, was taken to hospital, where she made a full recovery.

b Work in a group of three with students from groups B and C. Listen to the two reporters' presentations of their stories. Decide which should be the main story that day, and give reasons.

5A 11 p49

a You are a personal assistant to a famous person. You are paid well, but these are some things you would like to change about your job. Think of any other ideas.

- You are expected to be 'on duty' from 6 a.m. until midnight six days a week.
- Your employer phones you on your day off.
- You have only one week's holiday every year.
- You have not done any of the overseas travelling you were promised.
- The job advert asked for an educated person to organise your employer's diary. However, your job includes clearing up after the dog, washing clothes and babysitting the children.

b Work with your partner. Complain about your hours and the kind of work you have to do and discuss how your situation could be improved.

5B 2 p50

Neymar da Silva Santos Jr.

Ranked 7th-richest footballer in the world by *France Football* in 2012, you might expect Neymar Jr. to be full of ambition and hungry for success. But it seems that what has always driven him is his love of football. As a child, he was always trying to join older boys playing football in the street. "I just like playing with the ball," he says. "I always have. I play on the street even now. When we're on vacation (it doesn't matter where) I will go and look for a game."

The fact that he appears to be keeping his feet on the ground, despite his success, may be to do with family. His father, Neymar Sr., juggled three jobs to support his family. Of his father's role, Neymar says, "My father has been by my side since I was little. He takes care of things, my finances and my family."

Recruited by Santos FC in Brazil at the age of 11, Neymar Jr.'s talent was spotted at an early age. Although he received offers from top European clubs, Neymar decided to stay in Brazil. He went on playing for Santos FC throughout his teens. But staying at home has not meant keeping a low profile; he is often in the media, not only for his footballing achievements, but for his personal life. In 2010 he hit the headlines when he arrived on the pitch with a Mohican haircut, and a year later he became a father. "Everything in my life has happened very early, personally and professionally," he said. "I'm always learning. I have to."

7A 10 p69

a Work with another student from Group A. You are in favour of closed prisons. You are concerned about the increase in crime and feel that the courts should give tougher sentences to deter criminals. Make a list of reasons why closed prisons are the best way forward.

b You are at a meeting to discuss how best to deal with crime. Work in groups of four with a pair from Group B. Take turns to give your points of view.

c Decide which is the best way to deal with crime: open or closed prisons.

d Tell the class what your group decided.

7B 9 p72

a Work with another student from Group A. Read these newspaper headlines. Choose two and add extra information, e.g. why you think the measures have been introduced and what will happen as a result.

1 **WARNINGS TO BE PUT ON COMPUTER GAMES**

2 ***Football boots outlawed as being 'too dangerous'***

3 **Cameras on beaches to monitor safe sunbathing levels**

b Work with a student from Group B and tell your stories. What do you think about these issues?

c Work in the same pairs. Think of any other similar stories that have happened or could happen in the future.

10A 9 p98

a Work with another student from Group A. Read the talk below silently. Then prepare to give the talk by thinking about these features.

- dividing it into speech units
- marking the stress in each unit
- marking word stress where necessary
- thinking about connected speech within units

Potatoes are the world's fourth largest food crop, following rice, wheat and maize. The Inca Indians in Peru were the first to cultivate potatoes. In 1583, the Spanish Conquistadors, who had conquered Peru, introduced potatoes to Europe. Over the next four decades, potatoes began to be widely cultivated along with other staple crops. The Incas had many uses for this vegetable besides food, for instance, raw slices of potato were placed on broken bones to promote healing. In 1995, the potato became the first vegetable to be grown in space. NASA and the University of Wisconsin (USA) created the technology with the goal of feeding astronauts on long space voyages, and eventually of feeding future space colonies.

b Take turns to practise giving the talk and check your ideas.

c Work with a student from Group B. Listen to your partner's talk. How clear was it? Give feedback, and identify any pronunciation features which you think could be improved.

Pair and Group Work: Student/Group B

1C 7 p15

a Read definitions a–c. Make sure you understand them and can say them fluently.

a **be up for something** to want to do or try something: *We're going clubbing this weekend. Are you up for it?*

b **talk shop** when colleagues talk about work when they could be relaxing and having fun: *Even though it was a New Year's party, Chris and Ben spent all night talking shop.*

c **lose your bottle** when you no longer have the courage to do something: *I went to the bungee-jumping place but I lost my bottle at the last minute.*

b You are going to give three definitions of each idiom to Group A: the correct definition and two false definitions. Work together to invent two false definitions and three example sentences for each idiom.

c Decide who is going to give the true definition and the false definitions for each idiom. Then rehearse exactly what you are going to say. Remember you are all trying to convince Group A that your definition is correct.

d Work with students from Group A and follow these instructions. Group A starts.

1. Listen to Group A's definitions for idiom 1. Discuss which definition you think is correct. Ask Group A to repeat their definitions if necessary.
2. Tell Group A which definition you think is correct. Say why you think the other two definitions are false. Group A then reads out the correct definition. Were you correct?
3. Give your definitions for idiom a. Continue with the game until both groups have guessed three definitions.

e Which group guessed the most correct definitions?

4C 6 p45

a Work with another student from Group B. You are reporters on a tabloid newspaper. Read this outline of a possible lead story.

200 drivers trapped in cars and coaches on A66 in north of England last night because of heavy snow and gales. Snow came in very fast, no warning. Some occupants waited for several hours before being rescued by police. Many rescued from A66 were taken to nearby villages. 45 pensioners taken to hotel to wait for a bus. Many motorists arrived on foot, cold and wet. Villagers helped with refreshments, etc. but village hall had no sleeping facilities. Roads now closed.

b Write a short first paragraph and think of a dramatic photo. Make a note of what else you intend to include. Think of reasons why your story should make the 'splash' tomorrow.

c Work in a group of three with students from groups A and C. Take turns to present your story to the news editor and say why your story is the best.

d Listen to the news editor's reasons for choosing one of the stories.

7B 9 p72

a Work with another student from Group B. Read these newspaper headlines. Choose two and add extra information, e.g. why you think the measures have been introduced and what will happen as a result.

1 **RFID tags soon to check how much food we have in our fridge**

2 ***Cameras in streets to monitor responsible pet ownership***

3 **LOCAL FIREWORK DISPLAY CANCELLED 'IN CASE OF POTENTIAL INJURY'**

b Work in pairs with a student from Group A and tell each other your stories. What do you think about these issues?

c Work in the same pairs. Think of any other similar stories that have happened or could happen in the future.

3B 3 p30

a Read extracts 4–6. Then answer these questions.

a What is the advice? Did it match any of your predictions?
b According to the research, how can the advice contribute to a person's well-being?
c What facts or figures, if any, support the research?

4 **Eat dark chocolate.** Although dark chocolate was once thought to be unhealthy, with its high levels of cocoa beans it is now believed to be good for you in moderation, with research showing it can reduce blood pressure* and bad cholesterol. According to research at Harvard University, flavonoids in dark chocolate reduce the risk of dying from heart disease by 20%.

5 **Brush your teeth.** Not only does good dental hygiene save painful and expensive visits to the dentist, it may also prevent strokes* or heart attacks. Columbia University research based on around 700 people found that those with gum disease were more likely to suffer from narrowing of blood vessels that can lead to heart attacks.

6 **Laugh a lot.** Laughing reduces pain and diabetes* symptoms and also improves the immune system*. Researchers have calculated that laughter burns up calories* at the rate of 2.31 a minute. An average day's laughter gets rid of all the calories in a pepperoni pizza.

**blood pressure* = the force with which blood travels round the body
**a stroke* = when a blood vessel in the brain becomes blocked or bursts
**diabetes* /daɪəˈbiːtiːz/ = a serious disease when there is too much sugar in the blood
**immune system* = system by which your body fights diseases
**calorie* = a unit for measuring the amount of energy food produces

b Work with the other people in your group. Take turns to tell each other your answers to the questions.

7A 10 p69

a Work with another student from Group B. You are in favour of open prisons. Because of recent advances in forensic science, more arrests are being made and there is a danger of overcrowding in prisons. Make a list of reasons why there should be more open prisons for all categories of offenders.

b You are at a meeting to discuss how best to deal with crime. Work in groups of four with a pair from Group A. Take turns to give your point of view. Decide on the best way to deal with crime.

c Decide which is the best way to deal with crime.

d Tell the class what your group decided.

4B 12 p42

3

4

a Work with another student from Group B. Look at inventions 3 and 4. Then discuss these questions.

1 What were these inventions supposed to do?
2 Why did the inventors think they would be popular?
3 What do you think were the good and bad aspects of the inventions?
4 Do you think they would be popular in your country? Why?/Why not?

b Work with a student from Group A and a student from Group C. Take turns to describe your inventions, explaining what they were supposed to do. The other students should try and draw what you have described.

The person who invented this obviously thought it would help office workers. It was supposed to …

c Compare your drawings with the original pictures on p106 and p111. Decide which you think is the best and the weirdest invention.

5B 2 p50

Dizzee Rascal

I started writing lyrics when I was 14. The biggest thing has been learning just to go on doing it – to keep pressing on. I feel alone a lot. All you've got is yourself, so if you're not trying hard enough or working your best, it's you who has to live with that.

I've always had an interest in music. As a person, you hope to get wherever you can, but for me all of this is almost an accident. I regret to say that at school I was trouble – four times I was kicked out of places. At my last school I was walking a tightrope, but the music teacher let me stay there and encouraged me to experiment. Making beats went on to become my life, without me knowing it. If I hadn't had music, I would have been on the streets. I was up to no good, anyway.

Often, I'll be working myself until I'm ill. I'm always trying to find the next song, the next move, the next whatever, and worrying about it. A lot of the time I feel separated from my peers. I didn't try to be a role model. When I do the right thing, I hope I can help. I always try to reach out.

10B 4 p100

a Look at this picture of Felix Baumgartner and make notes on these questions, using modal verbs.

1 What do you think happened before this moment?
2 What do you think will happen next?
3 What do you think Felix is thinking and feeling at this moment?

b Take turns to show your photo to your group and explain your ideas. Do you agree? Why?/Why not?

5A 11 p49

a You are a famous person. You know that your employee is not entirely happy with his/her working conditions. You don't want to lose him/her because otherwise you would have to pay for a housekeeper, babysitter and dog walker as well. Look at the list of some things you know he/she would like to change. Think of ways in which you are prepared to compromise.

- He/She is annoyed about having to work long hours in a six-day week.
- He/She has little holiday time.
- He/She was expecting more administrative work and travel, and less domestic work.

b Work with your partner. Tell him/her about the ways in which you are prepared to compromise.

10A 9 p98

a Work with another a student from Group B. Read the talk below silently. Then prepare to give the talk by thinking about these features.

- dividing it into speech units
- marking the stress in each unit
- marking word stress where necessary
- thinking about connected speech within units

Salt is so common nowadays that it is easy to forget that throughout history, it has been a highly prized commodity. In the not-too-distant past, wars were fought over its possession and civilisations rose and fell in pursuit of what came to be called 'white gold'. The early Romans controlled the price of salt and Roman soldiers were paid in salt. The word 'salt' comes from the Latin word *sal* and the word 'salary' comes from the Latin word *salarium*, which means payment in salt. Besides being used as a seasoning, the discovery of salt as a way to preserve food increased its value. This freed people from their dependency on the seasonal availability of food.

b Take turns to practise giving the talk and check your ideas.

c Work in pairs with a student from Group A. Listen to your partner's talk. How clear was it? Give feedback, and identify any pronunciation features which you think could be improved.

Pair and Group Work: Other activities

4B 12 p42

5

6

a Work with another student from Group C. Look at inventions 5 and 6. Then discuss these questions.

1 What were these inventions supposed to do?
2 Why did the inventors think they would be popular?
3 What do you think were the good and bad aspects of the inventions?
4 Do you think they would be popular in your country? Why?/Why not?

b Work with a student from Group A and a student from Group B. Take turns to describe your inventions, explaining what they were supposed to do. The other students should try and draw what you have described.

> The person who invented this obviously thought it was going to help commuters. It was supposed to …

c Compare your drawings with the original pictures on p106 and p109. Decide which you think is the best and the weirdest invention.

3B 3 p30

a Read extracts 7–9. Then answer these questions.

a What is the advice? Did it match any of your predictions?
b According to the research, how can the advice contribute to a person's well-being?
c What facts or figures, if any, support the research?

7 **Drink tea.** Tea, both black and green, has been associated with a wide range of health benefits, from helping to prevent heart disease and flu, to hair growth and weight loss. A King's College study says that three or more cups a day reduce the risk of heart attack, and there is some evidence that it can improve mental performance.

8 **Get a pet.** Laughter is linked to good health and research shows that dog owners have the most giggles during the day. Pet dogs can lower heart rate and reduce stress, but having a cat reduces the risk of a child developing eczema* and hay fever. Researchers at Rakuno Gakuen University in Japan calculate that 30-minute walks with a dog are 87% more effective for heart health than going for walks on your own.

9 **Chew gum.** Not only is chewing gum good for oral health, especially sugar-free gum, but research at Glasgow Caledonian University shows that people who chew gum eat fewer snacks and 10% fewer calories*. It's also good for face muscles and high blood pressure* and diabetes*. And according to a report published by the University of Michigan, chewing gum may prevent tooth decay.

**eczema* = a skin condition when the skin becomes red and sore
**calorie* = a unit for measuring the amount of energy that food will produce
**blood pressure* = the force with which blood travels round the body
**diabetes* /daɪəˈbiːtiːz/ = a serious disease in which there is too much sugar in your blood

b Work with the other people in your group. Take turns to tell each other your answers to the questions.

5B 2 p50

Iris Andrews

What I do is nothing to do with talent. It's a passion. I have been passionate and aware and asked questions about the world for as long as I can remember but I only began to focus my energy on this stuff when I was 15. I managed to get support from some of my peers by campaigning and holding assemblies and discussions.

Far from being voiceless and insignificant, young people have enormous power. If my generation could screw up just a tiny bit less than previous generations and be slightly more conscious of the impact we have on our planet and our people, I'd be very happy.

Doing this helps me to get a broader perspective on my own life. For me, the biggest struggle has been losing both parents when I was still at school. Although I will never forget losing them and how that's affected me, having opened my eyes to the bigger picture I can see now that this is nowhere near the end of the world. I often feel like I'm a complete fraud – that I'm going to get found out soon – and that what I do isn't that special or impressive. I try to make my little difference. A lot of people think I can.

4C 6 p45

a Work in pairs with a student from Group C. You are reporters on a tabloid newspaper. Read this outline of a possible lead story.

A two-year-old boy has been hailed as a hero after he found his mother collapsed on the floor and calmly dialled 999. He was too frightened to give his name but Joshua Brookes explained to the operator that his mummy wouldn't wake up. Police traced their address and paramedics went to the house but couldn't get in, so Joshua stood on a box and let them in. His mother, Isobel, who suffers from a rare heart condition, was taken to hospital, where she made a full recovery.

b Write a short first paragraph and think of a dramatic photo. Make a note of what else you intend to include in the story. Think of reasons why your story should make the 'splash' that day.

c Work in a group of three with students from groups A and B. Take turns to present your story to the news editor and say why your story is the best.

d Listen to the news editor's reasons for choosing one of the stories.

10B 4 p100

a Look at this picture of Felix Baumgartner and make notes on these questions, using modal verbs.

1 What do you think happened before this moment?
2 What do you think will happen next?
3 What do you think Felix is thinking and feeling at this moment?

b Take turns to show your photo to your group and explain your ideas. Do you agree? Why?/Why not?

3B 3 p30

a Read extracts 10–12. Then answer these questions.

a What is the advice? Did it match any of your predictions?
b How can the advice contribute to well-being?
c What facts or figures, if any, support the research?

10 Eat fish. Very rarely do you hear anything negative about eating fish. That's because according to more than 10,000 pieces of research, fish and its oils can protect you from or treat just about everything, from bad backs to asthma*. It can also contribute to healthy brain cells and good eyesight. One study shows that women who eat fish during pregnancy may have cleverer children.

11 Take up singing. Choral singing increases immunity, reduces depression, improves cognitive function* and mood, and increases feelings of well-being. Research shows that singing helps people cope better with chronic pain, lowers stress levels and boosts the immune system*.

12 Get married. Seldom do people associate being married with being healthy. However, having a good marriage can extend your life, reduce the risk of heart disease, and can lower blood pressure. One study shows that married men are 70% more likely to live longer.

**asthma* = illness that causes breathing difficulties
**cognitive function* = ability to think
**immune system* = system by which your body fights diseases

b Work with the other people in your group. Take turns to tell each other your answers to the questions.

5B 2 p50

Sophie Christiansen

When I first took up riding at the age of six, it was just meant to make physiotherapy fun. I would have to do ten different exercises just to loosen up my muscles, because they get really tight. Riding really helps.

Cerebral palsy has affected all my limbs, so I find coordination difficult. Dressage is about many things – beauty, grace, movement – but above all it means coordinating all of your body in order to control the horse, right down to the most specific movements. It's just an amazing feeling.

It has been hard on my family. When I compete, I get really intense and argue with Mum. She's done very well to put up with that, especially as she's allergic to horses! But competing has turned my life around. I used to be quite shy and self-conscious.

I've always been quite determined and not let anything get in my way. Unless you have the mindset it's no use having the ability to do a sport. I don't let anything stop me. But I don't forget to have a good time too. I still go out clubbing with my mates. I'm a normal teen. My anthem is *Don't Stop Me Now* by Queen.

7C 8 p75

a Work on your own. You are Emma. You are going to be interviewed by a police officer. Read this information and add your own ideas.

- You were surprised when Mike turned up, and he seemed strange. (In what way?)
- You hadn't seen him for a long time before that day. (How long?)
- Mike seemed to be doing well at work – he was wearing new clothes and had a new phone. (What did you think?)
- You offered to make you both some pasta but he seemed very eager to go out and get pizza. (What did you say to him?)
- He was a long time getting back – he said there'd been a queue for pizzas.
- He insisted on staying at your house until late. You couldn't understand why, especially as he obviously didn't want to watch TV. (Why? What do you think he wanted?)

b Work with your partner. Answer the police officer's questions.

c Work in groups of four. Have you changed your mind about whether Mike is guilty or not? Discuss the evidence.

10B 6 p100

1 Read the extract and answer these questions.

a What did Baumgartner find most difficult?

b What is his 'message'?

Despite his daredevil image, Baumgartner was plagued by doubts throughout his adventure. "The worry is I won't fly supersonic or, in the worst-case scenario, I'm not as fast as Joe Kittinger was in 1960. You have to explain to the world that, 52 years later, you're slower than Joe. It's another pressure. I don't think people get what it means to do something when the whole world is watching you."

As Baumgartner floated towards the 24 mile-high mark – it took almost three hours for the balloon to lift his capsule into space – his visor began to cloud as he exhaled. The prospect of doing the jump 'half-blind' threatened the mission, and he had to endure various tests before it was established that his equipment was working. Once he had left his capsule, he began to whirl through space at a speed which sent him into an inevitable spin.

"I had one minute to find a solution. While spinning, I'm thinking, 'Should I push the button to release my drogue chute, to stop that spin? But that would mean it's over and I'm not going to fly supersonic – so should I tough it out and find a solution?' I had to maintain my cool and that's what I've been doing for the last 25 years – being focused and not freaking out." Surprisingly, Baumgartner's main concern was not about personal safety, but about failing to reach a supersonic flying speed. "In the end it was OK, but it was difficult, and that's why Joe held the record for 52 years. Lots of people underestimated it."

Baumgartner thinks hard when asked about his jump's sweetest moment. "I had a couple of good moments," he eventually says. "One was standing with my feet outside the capsule just before I stepped off. We'd been working towards that for five years. As soon as I was standing there – completely released from all the cables – I knew it was going to happen. That was a big relief and a really unique, outstanding moment. And then when you open your parachute, you know it's over – I'm still alive! Mike Todd [his life support engineer] was the last person I saw before going up. He said, 'OK, see you on the ground, buddy.' But you could tell he wasn't 100% sure. I wasn't either. We prepare for the worst, but hope for the best. And then, three hours later, Mike is the guy I see first after it's all over. Mike worried about me like I'm his son. But when he's happy, he looks 16 again. I was looking forward to seeing that smile."

So, how will a man consumed by outrageous challenges rekindle the intensity of his space jump?

"I don't have to," he replies, confirming his plan to become a rescue-helicopter pilot. "I reached a peak and I don't have to top it again." Baumgartner is aware that many see him purely as a daredevil who conquered space, but he hopes to draw attention to an ordinary man who conquered his own demons in order to achieve his greatest ambition. As he says, "that's an even bigger message than flying supersonic".

2 Read the extract again and make notes on these topics.

1 Joe Kittinger
2 Baumgartner's visor
3 spinning in space
4 two good moments
5 Mike Todd
6 future plans

Extra Practice 1

Language Summary 1 p134

1A p6

1 Replace the words in bold with these words/phrases. Use the correct form of the verb.

~~have a row~~	bicker	overhear
come into contact with		
gossip	grumble	butt in

1 Do you often hear people **arguing** in public? *having a row*
2 Do you think it's rude to **interrupt** when someone's talking?
3 Do you ever **complain** about work to your friends?
4 Do you know any couples who continually **argue about unimportant things**?
5 Do you **meet and communicate with** many English-speaking people on a day-to-day basis?
6 Have you ever **accidentally heard** people talking about you or a person you know?
7 Do you like to **talk about people's private lives**?

2 Choose the best ending, a or b, for each sentence.

1 Did you go to rock festivals *b*
2 Have you been to any rock festivals *a*
 a in the last few months?
 b in your teens?
3 So far this morning
4 This morning
 a three people phoned about the job.
 b three people have phoned about the job.
5 I read three of his books
6 I've read four of his books
 a last summer.
 b during the last few weeks.
7 When I've sold my car
8 When I sold my car
 a I'll just use public transport.
 b I just used public transport.

3 Choose the correct verb forms.

1 She *worked*/*'s worked* at home yesterday.
2 During last night's performance, several people *walked/have walked* out.
3 She *came/'s been* here a lot this month.
4 Once I *met/'ve met* her, I really liked her.
5 I've been skiing twice since I *saw/'ve seen* you last.

4 Fill in the gaps with the correct form of the verbs in brackets. Use the Past Simple or the Present Perfect. There is sometimes more than one possible answer.

The flat above mine [1] *has been* (be) empty ever since I [2] ______ (move) in six months ago. But a few people [3] ______ (see) it recently. And three more people [4] ______ (already come) to see it this morning. I [5] ______ (bump into) one of them as I was going out. She [6] ______ (work) in Dubai over the last few years. Apparently, up until now she [7] ______ (always prefer) working abroad, but she [8] ______ (recently offer) a great job here. Anyway, this is the first time she [9] ______ (try) to buy a flat. I hope she gets it. Then after she [10] ______ (move) in, I'll invite her round for dinner.

1B p10

5 Choose the correct prepositions.

1 Are you busy? I'm *on/at* a loose end tonight.
2 I'm *on/at* very good terms with all my neighbours.
3 She bought a lot of clothes *on/at* random.
4 He left his job *on/at* short notice.
5 According to police, burglaries are *on/at* the increase.

6 Rewrite these sentences to emphasise the words in bold.

1 I am very close to **my older sister**. (The person)
 The person who I'm closest to is my older sister.
2 They **sold the house**. (What they did)
3 **We** were responsible. (It)
4 She's tired **because she didn't go to bed until 2 a.m.** (The reason)
5 I didn't start exercising **until I reached 40.** (It)
6 I can't stand **fried food**. (It)

1C p14

7 Complete these sayings.

1 Rome wasn't built in a *day* .
2 Once bitten, twice ______ .
3 Actions ______ louder than words.
4 One man's ______ is another man's poison.
5 Nothing ventured, nothing ______ .
6 Better ______ than never.

Progress Portfolio 1

Tick the things you can do in English.

- [ ] I can describe different ways of communicating.
- [ ] I can talk about the present and the past using a variety of time expressions.
- [ ] I can understand an article in which the writer expresses a specific point of view.
- [ ] I can use various structures to emphasise important or new information.
- [ ] I can use circumlocution and paraphrasing to clarify what I mean.

Extra Practice 2

Language Summary 2 p137

2A p16

1 Fill in the gaps with these intensifying adverbs.

~~deeply~~	bitterly
vividly	entirely

1 I get *deeply* frustrated when I'm stuck in a traffic jam.
2 I ______ remember my first day at school.
3 I always feel ______ disappointed when my country loses an important football match.
4 I ______ agree that men and women should have equal opportunities.

deeply	highly
firmly	completely

5 It's ______ unlikely that I'll ever learn another language.
6 I ______ believe that life improves as you get older.
7 I ______ regret some of the things I've done in my life.
8 I ______ agree with my country's policy on green issues.

2 Fill in the gaps with these phrases.

~~by which~~	both of whom
none of which	on whose
all of which	with whom
for which	after whom

1 The date *by which* all bills must be paid is the 30th of the month.
2 The person ______ I discussed the issue denied all knowledge.
3 I've got two sisters, ______ are younger than me.
4 There are seven Harry Potter books, ______ I've read yet.
5 You have all been very kind, ______ I'm deeply grateful.
6 My favourite singer is Elvis, ______ my son was named.
7 I am grateful to Jack Terry, ______ research I largely depended for this book.
8 I bought myself six games, ______ were reduced by 10%.

2B p20

3 **a** Complete these sentences with a present participle, a past participle or a perfect participle.

eat

1 *Eaten* in moderation, chocolate is good for you.
2 ______ in restaurants all week, Lucy prefers to cook for herself at the weekends.
3 ______ such a big lunch earlier that day, I didn't feel like any dinner.

see

4 ______ the film three times already, she decided to give it a miss.
5 ______ her ex-boyfriend approaching, she ran and hid.
6 ______ from a distance, she looks like a 20-year-old!

read

7 ______ the instructions twice, I began to assemble the desk.
8 ______ out loud, the poem sounded much better.
9 ______ the report so quickly, I missed a lot of mistakes.

give

10 ______ the chance, I'd love to learn how to ski.
11 ______ the job to Fred, she immediately regretted her decision.
12 ______ myself an extra day, I should be able to finish the job.

b Rewrite sentences 1–12 in **3a** using *if*, *because*, *after*, etc. Make any other necessary changes.

If it is eaten in moderation, chocolate is good for you.

4 Read the story. Tick the groups of adjectives 1–6 that are in the correct order. Correct the groups which are not.

When I was 14, my parents went on holiday for a week and I was sent to stay in a(n) 1**beautiful, big old** ✓ house in the country with some distant relatives. My cousin Linda's best friend was a(n) 2**16-year-old attractive** girl called Anna, who had 3**wide, extraordinary emerald-green** eyes and 4**dark, shiny long** hair. I remember evenings around the 5**wooden, round** kitchen table. The following summer, I went back, but Anna had fallen in love with a(n) 6**Italian, tall dark-haired** pilot, so I had no chance!

2C p24

5 Complete these words to describe places.

1 spect_c_l_r
2 st_n_ing
3 h_stl_ and _u_ _l_
4 w_n_i_g
5 _i_h-r_ _e
6 he_it_g_

Progress Portfolio 2

Tick the things you can do in English.

☐ I can define and give extra information in a formal and informal way.
☐ I can emphasise verbs and adjectives using a range of appropriate adverbs.
☐ I can identify points of detail in a complex newspaper article.
☐ I can write concise descriptions using complex clauses.
☐ I can describe places in detail using accurate adjective order.

Extra Practice 3

Language Summary 3 p141

3A p26

1 Match the adjectives and phrases.

~~courageous~~ modest
thrifty meticulous outgoing
innocent deferential

1 doesn't let fear stop them from doing dangerous or difficult things *courageous*
2 friendly and enjoys meeting people
3 doesn't talk about their achievements
4 pays attention to detail
5 respectful and polite
6 not knowing about the unpleasant things in life
7 careful with money

2 Put the words in order.

1 loves / My wife / I / when / it / laugh .
My wife loves it when I laugh.
2 it / Holly / soon / a job / impossible / to get / realised / was .
3 would / wonderful / have / to / It / be / more / free time .
4 if / more / came round / love / it / I'd / you / to / visit / often .
5 the heating / could / appreciate / you / if / I'd / turn down / it .
6 concentrate / there's / I / find / to / difficult / it / when / music on .

3B p30

3 Complete the phrasal verbs.

~~down~~ up (x3) on (x2)
out around

1 Rachel's gone *down* with flu, but the doctor hasn't put her ______ antibiotics.
2 Jake seems to pick ______ every bug that's going ______ .
3 I can't eat strawberries. My face swells ______ and I come ______ in a rash.
4 **A** You sound blocked ______ .
B Yes, I think I have a cold coming ______ .

4 Rewrite sentences 1–5 using these phrases. The meaning should stay the same.

~~only once~~ not until not only
not for a minute
under no circumstances

1 I've only seen him this happy once.
Only once have I seen him this happy.
2 I wasn't just stressed out, I was getting ill.
3 I never once thought I'd enjoy having a dog, but it's great.
4 You should never agree to do overtime for nothing.
5 I didn't realise it was Jin till she spoke.

5 Fill in the gaps with the subject and the correct form of the verb in brackets.

1 Only once before *have I climbed* such a high mountain. (I climb)
2 Not only ____________ the film, I didn't enjoy the meal after either. (I hate)
3 Under no circumstances ____________ a car without insurance. (anyone should drive)
4 Not until she explained it again ____________ what had happened. (I understand)
5 Only by chance ____________ to get tickets for the concert. (we manage)
6 Rarely ____________ a plumber as good as Henry. (you find)
7 Only when Mark walked through the door ____________ I'd met him before. (I realise)
8 Only recently ____________ to play sport on a regular basis. (we begin)
9 Very rarely ____________ such a beautiful sunset. (I see)
10 Seldom ____________ to sleep before midnight. (she go)

3C p34

6 Replace the words/phrases in bold with these euphemisms.

~~challenging~~
a bit on the chilly side
be economical with the truth
bit of a handful
senior citizens
getting on a bit
behind the times
hard of hearing

1 The work I'm doing at the moment is **very difficult**. *challenging*
2 Al's a **naughty and difficult child to look after**.
3 Simon tends to **lie**.
4 My cat's **old**.
5 I think **old people** should be shown more respect.
6 It's **quite cold** in here, isn't it?
7 He's **deaf**!
8 She's **so old-fashioned** – she doesn't know how to send an email.

Progress Portfolio 3

Tick the things you can do in English.

- ☐ I can describe people's character using a wide range of adjectives.
- ☐ I can read, understand and summarise information about health.
- ☐ I can recognise structures used for emphasis in more formal/literary language.
- ☐ I can understand some euphemistic expressions.
- ☐ I can express my ideas tactfully when necessary.

Extra Practice 4

Language Summary 4 p144

4A p36

1 Choose the correct words.

1 *read/receive* a lot of coverage
2 *hold/make* a press conference
3 *seek/issue* publicity
4 *run/hit* a story
5 *follow/issue* the news
6 *receive/hit* the headlines
7 *seek/sue* for libel

2 Choose the correct verb form. Sometimes both are possible.

1 Mandy's *on the verge of/going to* retire in five years' time.
2 The film *will/is about to* start!
3 Clare is *on the brink of having/is due to have* her baby in June.
4 Their new company is *sure to/bound to* make a profit this year.
5 They are *unlikely to/probably not going to* offer a pay rise.
6 Prices *are falling/are set to fall* in the next month or so.
7 He's *on the point of applying/about to apply* for university.

3 Fill in the gaps with these prompts. Use the correct form of the verb.

~~set / rise~~	about / sign
verge / turn back	
to / settle for	due / retire

1 Interest rates *are set to rise* by 1%.
2 Liverpool's chief of police ______ after 40 years of service.
3 Everest's youngest climbers ______ because of poor weather conditions.
4 The singer, Migs, ______ a new recording deal for £10 million.
5 The Workers' Union ______ a 10% pay rise.

4B p40

4 Cross out the wrong word.

1 That's a *big/huge/~~large~~* mistake.
2 I love *watching/gazing at* TV.
3 I *enjoy/like* to learn languages.
4 I was very *cross/furious/angry*.
5 He's so *courageous/reckless*. It's such a good quality.

5 **a** Match words 1–7 with near synonyms a–g.

1	make	a	let
2	infuriate	b	force
3	like	c	city
4	allow	d	enjoy
5	urban	e	exasperate
6	friend	f	large
7	huge	g	mate

b Complete these sentences with the correct form of words from **5a**. Sometimes there is more than one possible answer.

1 I really love *urban/city* life.
2 Dave's got a ______ problem with his boss.
3 Someone left a message for you, Madam. She said she was a ______ of yours.
4 His behaviour ______ me at times. He's so selfish.
5 I ______ to listen to music.
6 They ______ me tell them everything I knew about what Jason had done.
7 I was ______ to leave work early.

6 Tick the correct sentences. Then correct the mistakes.

1 Kelly ~~is~~ *was* going to come, but her car broke down.
2 I had no idea that it will be this exhausting!
3 You've finished! Wasn't Dave supposed to give you a hand?
4 I'm about to leave the house when I remembered you were coming.
5 I'm supposed to call my sister before she left, but I forgot.
6 We are to stay in a hotel near the beach, but it closed down.
7 That day, he made a decision that he would regret forever.

7 Read the story. Then fill in the gaps with the correct form of the phrases in brackets.

Last Saturday Brigit and I [1] *were to meet up* (meet up) in town and join the anti-war demonstration. She [2] ______ (supposed to call) from the station but she didn't. I waited an hour then I decided I [3] ______ (will not stay) any longer. However, just as I [4] ______ (about to leave) another friend shouted my name. I didn't know he [5] ______ (going to be) there. Anyway, we decided we [6] ______ (will join) the march. Then two minutes later I saw my brother and his girlfriend. I had no idea they [7] ______ (going to demonstrate) either. Ten minutes after that, I saw Brigit. Apparently, she [8] ______ (just going to call) me when I spotted her. There were two million people on that march. It's hard to believe that the five of us [9] ______ (will bump) into each other, but we did!

Progress Portfolio 4

Tick the things you can do in English.

- [ ] I can recognise and use phrases which refer to the future.
- [ ] I can keep up with an animated discussion.
- [ ] I can identify near synonyms in a complex text.
- [ ] I can talk about the future when seen from a point in the past.
- [ ] I can recognise and discuss different styles of newspaper.

Extra Practice 5

Language Summary 5 p146

5A p46

1 Cross out the word that doesn't match the prefix.

1 **super** *woman/-rich/~~locked~~*
2 **semi** *action/-circle/-famous*
3 **counter** *balance/foot/-attack*
4 **inter** *action/locked/worked*
5 **over** *worked/-famous/head*
6 **under** *foot/balance/paid*

2 Tick the correct sentences. Correct the mistakes.

1 It's really important to concentrate ~~yourself~~ when driving.
2 He can't come himself, but he'll send a representative.
3 Shall we meet ourselves outside the cinema?
4 The event is open to people such as yourself.
5 Are you feeling yourself ill today?
6 Please feel free to help yourselves to food.
7 I think I'd better take a jumper with myself.
8 He didn't shave himself this morning. He went to the barber's.

5B p50

3 Fill in the gaps with the correct verb form.

1 *to go/going*
   a I'll never forget *going* abroad for the first time.
   b I'm always forgetting *to go* to the bank.

2 *to tell/telling*
   a I regret ______ you that I'm leaving the company.
   b I regret ______ my boss what I thought of him.

3 *to do/doing*
   a Taking up the guitar means ______ lots of practice.
   b I've been meaning ______ a computer course for ages

4 *to study/studying*
   a In the future I'll probably go on ______ a new subject such as business.
   b At school I found it hard to go on ______ maths, because I was hopeless at it.

4 Choose the correct words/phrases.

1 *(come)/go* to a decision
2 *gain/do* an insight
3 apply *at/for* university
4 look *into/in* different options
5 *take/make* some time out
6 go *to/on* courses
7 *make/do* work experience
8 work *at/out* what to do

5C p54

5 Match sentence beginnings 1–7 to sentence endings a–g.

1 My job could be described as **run-of-the-mill**, because *d*
2 There are lots of **perks** with my job, even if I don't **earn a fortune** –
3 I'm **snowed under** at the moment –
4 I'm prepared to **work against the clock**,
5 I don't want to **earn a pittance** even if it means I can **take it easy** –
6 I've worked here for 20 years and feel **stuck in a rut** –
7 I'm not a **team-player**, really,

a I've taken on too much work.
b I get a company car, free lunches and gym membership.
c I need to retrain and do a different kind of job.
d I sit behind a desk doing undemanding work.
e I don't mind **deadlines** as long as the job is **flexible**.
f I'd prefer a **high-powered, well-paid** job.
g I'd prefer to be **self-employed**.

6 Complete the conversation.

~~mention~~ precisely always sure dubious mean got disagree back trying

A Eating ready meals makes life easier, but they're expensive, not to [1] *mention* unhealthy.
B What do you [2] ______ when you say 'unhealthy'?
A What I'm [3] ______ to say is it's healthier to cook your own food.
B Really?
A You look [4] ______ .
B I'm not [5] ______ you can say it's healthier to cook your own food. My cooking is bad!
A You've [6] ______ me there! Anyway, to get [7] ______ to what I was saying, young people should learn to cook.
B Well, I can't [8] ______ with that. I never learned. Of course, there's [9] ______ the argument that I should teach myself, but I never have the time. That's why I buy ready meals. It's easier.
A That's [10] ______ what I mean.

Progress Portfolio 5

Tick the things you can do in English.

- [ ] I can recognise and use prefixes which have multiple meanings.
- [ ] I can take part in a discussion on education and express my ideas clearly.
- [ ] I can summarise a complex written text concisely.
- [ ] I can follow an extended informal monologue even when it's not clearly structured.
- [ ] I can use a range of conversational strategies appropriately.

Extra Practice 6

6A p56

1 Fill in the gaps with a word which can be used in both sentences. You may need to change the form of the word.

1 a I really like Louise, she is so *sweet* and friendly.
b I can't drink tea with sugar – it's much too *sweet* .

2 a Let me get you another coke – that one must be ______ by now.
b Life seems a bit ______ now all the excitement is over.

3 a I won't be long, I'm just on my coffee ______ .
b Have you ever ______ the law?

4 a Have you got any ______ paper for the photocopier?
b Do you want ______ crisps or cheese and onion?

5 a Which ______ of linguistics interests you most?
b The company I work for has ______ all over the world.

2 Look at these pairs of sentences. Do they have the same meaning? If not, what is the difference?

1 a Eating at home costs much the same as eating out.
b Eating at home costs pretty much the same as eating out.
Both sentences have the same meaning.

2 a Organic food is significantly more expensive than non-organic food.
b Organic food is barely more expensive than non-organic food.

3 a Having a cat is marginally easier than having a dog.
b Having a cat is distinctly easier than having a dog.

4 a Theme parks are way more fun than museums.
b Theme parks are loads more fun than museums.

5 a Travelling by plane isn't half as stressful as driving.
b Travelling by plane is miles more stressful than driving.

6B p60

3 Fill in the gaps with these words.

~~forth~~ break leave off bounds parcel every

1 I keep going back and *forth* between the two options.
2 You can't treat children all the same. Each and ______ one is different.
3 I usually have coffee for breakfast but to be honest I can take it or ______ it.
4 I think stress is part and ______ of modern life.
5 In my opinion, the choice of music can make or ______ a party.
6 I think my English vocabulary has improved in leaps and ______ .
7 I go to the gym on and ______ .

4 Read the conversation and look at the adverbials in bold. Tick the adverbials that are in the correct position. Correct the mistakes.

A Hi, Clare, I've been trying to get hold of you all morning.
B Sorry, I've been **at the Town Hall** to see Monica's show. ✓
A Was it good?
B I thought she **brilliantly** performed, especially given the lack of rehearsal time. The only problem is we had a power cut.
A **Unfortunately, often** that happens. I don't know why.
B Are you going to see the show?
A Yes, I'll go **probably** and see it **next Thursday**, if I can get tickets.
B Yes, I think it's **every day** on until the end of March.

5 Put the adverbials in brackets in the correct place in these sentences.

1 *Obviously* , I dislike ______ having to do housework ______ . (at weekends; always; ~~obviously~~)
2 I will ______ do the run ______ to raise money for charity. (probably; on Saturday)
3 ______ one of my essays will ______ be finished ______ . (definitely; by then; only)
4 ______ , my car ______ breaks down ______ . (without any warning; annoyingly; often)
5 That actress is ______ more popular than her brother ______ . (even; these days)
6 ______ , it's ______ going to snow tomorrow – even though it's March. (definitely; surprisingly)
7 I ______ book my flights ______ because it saves a lot of money. (generally; in advance)
8 She works ______ in the office ______ , ______ on Fridays. (even; late; every day)

Progress Portfolio 6

Tick the things you can do in English.

- [ ] I can compare things in both an informal and formal way.
- [ ] I can understand words with different but related meanings.
- [ ] I can give my views and respond to opinions on advertising and marketing.
- [ ] I can work out the meanings of words and phrases from context.
- [ ] I can follow established conventions to tell a personal anecdote.

Extra Practice 7

Language Summary 7 p152

7A p66

1 Fill in the gaps with these words/ phrases.

~~round~~	into	round	at
away	through	my own back	

I've never got [1] *round* to learning how to cook, even though I've lived on my own for years. I get [2]______ the problem by buying lots of ready-made meals, but I know I won't be able to get [3]______ with it forever. My friends are always getting [4]______ me about how lazy I am. I get [5]______ by pointing out how much time they waste in the kitchen. However, all the publicity about eating healthily is finally getting [6]______ to me, although I really don't think I'll ever get [7]______ cooking.

2 Choose the correct answer. Sometimes both are possible.

1 If Lorraine *is going/might go* into town later, she'll post this letter for you.
2 That wasn't bad driving, but if you had *taken/been taking* your test, you'd have to be more careful than that.
3 I'd feel much happier if you *phoned/would phone* me later.
4 If you wash wool, you *use/should use* cold water.
5 If you'd *been telling/told* me about your problem, I'd have helped you.
6 If I *want to catch/'m going to catch* that train, I should leave.
7 They wouldn't have caught the burglar if he hadn't *dropped/been dropping* his wallet.
8 If the police *were hoping/hoped* to make an arrest, they would need to do it now.

3 Fill in the gaps with the correct form of the verb in brackets to make mixed conditionals.

1 If I'd invested that money, we *would be sitting* (sit) on a tropical beach now.
2 If I hadn't lost my keys, I ______ (give) you a lift. But I'm afraid I can't find them.
3 I'd still be living in Wales if I ______ (not change) my job.
4 If I hadn't taken out a huge bank loan, I ______ (not have) this car.
5 If Jess wasn't so lazy, she ______ (finish) her coursework.
6 If you had taken my advice, we ______ (not be) so late now!

7B p70

4 Fill in the gaps with these particles to make phrasal nouns.

~~down~~	in	off	on	back

1 Take your coat. There's going to be a *down*pour later.
2 Because the roads were busy we missed kick-______ .
3 The ______ set of her illness began when Julie was very young.
4 Due to an unavoidable set______ , our departure has been delayed.
5 Try and reduce your ______ take of saturated fat.

5 Fill in the gaps with the correct form of the verbs in brackets. There is sometimes more than one possible answer. The verbs in bold should be in the present.

1 Recently burglaries *are reported to have increased* in this area. (**report** / increase)
2 It ______ that the cost of the Olympic stadium will be over budget. (fear)
3 Mike and Jane ______ a divorce. (**rumour** / seek)
4 People ______ divided over the issue. (**appear** / be)

7C p74

6 Complete the sentences with words from the box.

~~bright~~	crack	fly	storm
freeze	flood	dawn	warm

1 My room is small but *bright* .
2 We got a very ______ welcome when we went to Scotland.
3 He said he will ______ out of the meeting if he doesn't get what he wants.
4 If I have any more work, I will ______ .
5 The pyramids have been there since the ______ of civilisation.
6 There will be a pay ______ next year – our salary won't be increased.
7 We had a great holiday. The time really ______ by.
8 After I finished my degree, I was ______ with job offers.

Progress Portfolio 7

Tick the things you can do in English.

- [ ] I can understand a radio interview in detail and make notes on it.
- [ ] I can understand and use a range of more complex conditional forms.
- [ ] I can report information in an impersonal way using a range of structures.
- [ ] I can identify and use a variety of questions and intonation patterns.
- [ ] I can recognise and use a range of idiomatic and metaphorical language.

Extra Practice 8

Language Summary 8 p156

8A p76

1 Match sentence beginnings 1–8 with sentence endings a–h.

1 The flight is at ten, so if we leave at seven, *c*
2 Take your time –
3 My parents used to give me such a hard time
4 We're very different. I usually put things off,
5 I'm so busy these days,
6 We can't move into the new flat yet,
7 I've got no time for Suzy –
8 It's only a matter of time

a before there's another oil crisis.
b but for Joe, there's no time like the present.
c we'll get there in plenty of time.
d but I really must make time to see my parents.
e there's no need to hurry.
f for not studying enough.
g so for the time being we're staying with my brother.
h as far as I'm concerned she's lazy and selfish.

2 Tick the correct sentences. Then correct the mistakes. Sometimes there is more than one possible answer.

1 I'd rather people ~~don't~~ *didn't* drop litter in the streets.
2 I'd sooner travel by car than by bus.
3 I'd prefer more people were environmentally conscious.
4 It's high time people stop using cars in cities.
5 I'd rather my family spend more time together.
6 I'd prefer it if people don't use their mobiles on public transport.
7 It's time I had a holiday.
8 I'd prefer I live nearer to the sea.

3 Fill in the gaps with the correct form of the verbs in brackets.

1 A Is it OK if I call by this evening, or would you prefer me *to come round* earlier? (come round)
B I'd rather you ______ this afternoon. (come)
2 A What would you prefer ______ this evening, go out for a meal or stay in? (do)
B I'd sooner ______ a film, actually. (see)
3 A Look, isn't it about time you ______ to your sister? (apologise)
B What for? I know she'd rather I ______ the first move, but she started the argument. (make)
4 A You look exhausted. It's high time you ______ a break from work. (have)
B I'd prefer ______ this, then I can forget about it. (finish)
5 A It's time the kids and I ______ home. Thanks for looking after them. (go)
B A pleasure. Shall I get you a taxi, or would you prefer it if I ______ you a lift to the station? (give)
6 A Vince says it's time for him ______ on. So, he's leaving this Friday. (move)
B Yes, I know. I'd prefer it if he ______, though. (stay)

8B p80

4 Rewrite these sentences. Begin with the words in brackets.

1 I don't know who made this cake, but they must have a great recipe. (Whoever)
Whoever made this cake must have a great recipe.
2 You can rely on me for anything that needs doing. (Whatever)
3 No matter how many times I wash my hair, it always looks greasy. (However)
4 It doesn't matter what you do, don't tell my mum I've lost her camera. (Whatever)
5 It doesn't matter which road you take to get to the station, it'll take the same amount of time. (Whichever)
6 I don't know who wrote this, but they certainly can't spell. (Whoever)
7 It doesn't matter when I ring Mick, he's always out. (Whenever)

5 Complete these sentences with the correct form of the words in brackets.

1 I'm quite a *moody* person, especially in the mornings. (mood)
2 He ______ left at 11 p.m. (final)
3 There are plans to ______ the motorway in order to cut traffic jams. (wide)
4 There's a strong ______ she will be promoted. (possible)
5 She's an extremely ______ person. (create)
6 There are a lot of ______ events here in the spring. (culture)
7 I need to ______ the situation – can you tell me exactly what happened? (clear)

Progress Portfolio 8

Tick the things you can do in English.

- [ ] I can recognise and use past verb forms which refer to present or future time.
- [ ] I can use suffixes to change a word from one form to another.
- [ ] I can describe people's feelings and emotions.
- [ ] I can understand a modern poem.
- [ ] I can summarise the results of a survey.

Extra Practice 9

Language Summary 9 p158

9A p86

1 Fill in the gaps with these words.

~~fortune~~ tag reasonably half effective over

1 How could he afford to buy that car? It cost a *fortune*!
2 I expected this to cost a lot more, but it's ______ priced.
3 It was originally €60, but I got it ______ price – €30.
4 Excuse me, this hasn't got a price ______ . How much is it?
5 Underfloor heating is a very cost-______ way of heating your home.
6 That's ______ priced. I've seen cheaper elsewhere.

2 Choose the correct verb form. Sometimes both are possible.

1 Have you heard that Maria *looks/is looking* for a new job?
2 Do you think Ahmed *comes/is coming* out tonight?
3 They *have/'re having* their own furniture business.
4 I *expect/'m expecting* you'll be very tired after such a long journey.
5 There's someone at the door. *Are you expecting/Do you expect* anyone?
6 She *feels/'s feeling* very relaxed.
7 This chair *feels/'s feeling* very comfortable.
8 A I *think/'m thinking* he's very controlling.
B Yes, I *see/'m seeing* what you mean.
9 That *doesn't fit/isn't fitting* in the kitchen. It's too big.
10 She *appears/'s appearing* in a new production of *Hamlet*.
11 It *appears/is appearing* you were right. He's going to resign.

9B p90

3 Complete definitions 1–7.

~~worthy~~ proof ish free able related conscious

1 Someone you can trust completely is trust *worthy*.
2 Someone with sort of green eyes has green ______ eyes.
3 Something you can afford is afford ______ .
4 Someone who considers safety is important is safety-______ .
5 When an illness is due to stress it is a stress-______ illness.
6 A room that doesn't let sound in or out is a sound ______ room.
7 A place where you can't smoke is a smoke-______ environment.

4 Fill in the gaps with *a/an*, *the*, *one* or no article (–). Sometimes there is more than one answer.

[1] *A* little boy from [2]___ poor village used to walk [3]___ long distances from [4]___ village to another, selling baskets. Then [5]___ day [6]___ little boy was given [7]___ bicycle. [8]___ villagers went to [9]___ Zen master and said, "This is [10]___ wonderful thing to happen to [11]___ boy – [12]___ few children from this village will ever get [13]___ chance to own [14]___ bicycle." [15]___ Zen master said, "Let's wait and see." [16]___ month later [17]___ little boy fell off [18]___ bike and broke [19]___ leg. [20]___ injury was serious. [21]___ villagers went to [22]___ Zen master and said, "Isn't it [23]___ terrible thing the boy has broken [24]___ leg?" [25]___ Zen master said, "Let's wait and see." Then, [26]___ few months later, [27]___ country went to war with [28]___ neighbouring country and [29]___ young men of [30]___ village were called to join [31]___ army. However, [32]___ boy, now [33]___ young man, wasn't allowed to join because of his injury. [34]___ villagers went to [35]___ Zen master and said, "Isn't it [36]___ wonderful thing he doesn't have to go to war?" "Let's wait and see," said the Zen master.

5 Choose the correct words in these sentences. Sometimes both are possible.

1 He's so fortunate. He has *a few/few* problems compared to me.
2 I've got *a/one* friend who really doesn't care about money.
3 I first met Max *one/a* day last summer.
4 I'm so busy I only have *one/a* free day a week.
5 She's working late, so sadly there's *little/a little* chance she'll be home before eight.
6 Quite *few/a few* people I know upload their photos to the Internet.

9C p94

6 Choose the correct words.

1 mass-*superpower/produced*
2 *renewable/developing* energy
3 *overseas/economic* aid
4 developing *resources/countries*
5 record *superpower/levels*

Progress Portfolio 9

Tick the things you can do in English.

- [ ] I can follow complex interaction between a group of people.
- [ ] I can talk about complex issues concerning money and finance.
- [ ] I can recognise when the simple or continuous form of a verb can change its meaning.
- [ ] I can recognise and use suffixes which have meaning.
- [ ] I can follow a short presentation on a subject I may or may not be familiar with.
- [ ] I can plan and give a talk on a subject I am familiar with.

Extra Practice 10

Language Summary 10 p162

10A p96

1 Tick the correct sentences. Then correct the mistakes.

1 Eating fish ~~are~~ *is* good for you.
2 Have the mail arrived yet?
3 The police are on their way.
4 Only a few people has arrived.
5 The news today are very bad.
6 The public are voting today.
7 Anything are better than school!
8 The team was winning until half-time.

2 Fill in the gaps with the present form of the verbs in brackets.

1 Both of my parents *prefer* dogs to cats. (prefer)
2 Everyone ______ that economics ______ a really interesting subject. (say; be)
3 Five litres of water ______ too much to drink in one day. (be)
4 Mathematics ______ not a subject I enjoy at all. (be)
5 The army in my country ______ people from the age of 16. (recruit)
6 The staff ______ really friendly. (seem)

10B p99

3 Write the opposite of phrases 1–10 using the words in the box.

~~strong~~	smooth	rich	wet
calm	short	sweet	
patterned	dark	weak	

1 a gentle/ *strong* wind
2 plain/______ food
3 dry/______ wine
4 a rough/______ surface
5 a plain/______ shirt
6 a strong/______ coffee
7 a light/______ colour
8 a tall/______ person
9 a rough/ ______ sea
10 a dry/______ day

4 Choose the correct adjectives to complete the collocations.

1 I live in quite a *young/ modern* building – it was only built 10 years ago.
2 There is a *faint/weak* possibility that I might be promoted next month.
3 I have a *smooth/clear* idea about what's going to happen next.
4 It's best not to have a *heavy/ strong* meal too late in the evening.
5 There are no skyscrapers where I live – the buildings all tend to be very *short/low*.
6 I think the storm has passed – there's just a(n) *easy/gentle* wind blowing now.

5 Work in pairs. Look at the modal verbs in bold and explain their meanings in context.

1 a He **must** hate that job. I wouldn't do it for the world. *I am sure he hates that job.*
b You **must** try to be more punctual. *I want you to be more punctual.*
2 a He **won't have** paid yet.
b He **might not have** paid yet.
3 a We **should have** bought her that violin, but we couldn't afford it.
b She **should** be back soon. Why don't you wait?
4 a John **will** still be sleeping now. He gets up late.
b They**'ll have** eaten by now. It's 3 o'clock.
5 a They **couldn't have** left already.
b I **couldn't** swim until I was six.
6 a Lucy **wouldn't** forget to phone.
b He **wouldn't** often talk about his experiences in the war.
7 a You **may** see me later, if I can make it.
b You **may** start now.

6 Write sentences with the same meaning, using the correct form of the modal verb in brackets.

1 It's possible that she went to see Martin. (might)
She might have gone to see Martin.
2 It's obvious he didn't practise enough. (can't)
3 I'm fairly sure the parcel will arrive tomorrow. (should)
4 It's possible that Jan's having lunch now. (may)
5 Clearly, they're not enjoying the holiday as they're coming home early. (can't)
6 Don't call him now because I'm pretty certain he's sleeping. (will)
7 They got there late, so I don't see how they had time to visit the exhibition. (won't)
8 She probably won't have problems finding the place. (should)

Progress Portfolio 10

Tick the things you can do in English.

- ☐ I can recognise devices for making a complex text cohesive and coherent.
- ☐ I can identify and use a range of antonyms and their collocations.
- ☐ I can use a range of modals to talk about levels of certainty in the present and past.
- ☐ I can follow extended speech on a complex topic.
- ☐ I can give a clear, well-structured talk on improving my English in the future.

VIDEO

Unit 1 Let's talk!

Lead-in

1 Work in small groups. Discuss these questions.

1. Do people who speak your language have different accents? Do you have an accent?
2. What determines people's accents in your country and are there some accents that are more or less popular?
3. Do you know anything about particular English accents? Are there any that you find especially easy or difficult to understand? Can you say why?

Viewing

2 **a** Decide which statements about British English accents you agree with.

a Some individual sounds tell us whether an English person comes from the north or south of the country.

b People may not be aware of their own accents but they know which accents they like and don't like.

c The accents are based on region, but some are likely to die out in the future.

b VIDEO 1.1 Watch the whole video. Does it suggest that the statements above are true, partly true or false? Give reasons.

3 **a** VIDEO 1.2 Complete these sentences with one or two pieces of information. Sometimes there is more than one possible answer.

1. Jonnie Robinson was chosen for the interview because …
2. He says UK northern accents …
3. The pronunciation of English underwent some changes …

b Work in pairs and compare answers.

4 VIDEO 1.3 Match the person with the sentence they might say next.

Carolyn — 5 (example)
Denise
Andrew
Sheniz
Susan
Jane

1. Of course, I don't usually speak like that myself!
2. But only a tiny bit when I'm talking to my mates.
3. In fact, *all* English people have got accents to me.
4. Not all Scottish accents are the same, you know.
5. But then, I think *they've* got really strong accents.
6. It's a bit different from the way they speak in the *city* of Oxford.

5 **a** VIDEO 1.4 Work in groups of three. Watch and make notes.

Student A: What generalisations does Jonnie make about different accents?

Student B: Write all the different types of accents Susan and Sheniz mention and whether they are positive or negative about them.

Student C: Note reasons people give for disliking certain accents.

b Compare your information and summarise this part of the video. Are Jonnie's generalisations true, do you think?

6 VIDEO 1.5 What were Jonnie and Denise referring to (a–c) when they used words/ phrases 1–8?

a received pronunciation

b Australian accents

c the evolution of English accents

1. a Yorkshire speaker and a London speaker
2. adopted by the BBC
3. almost unique RP
4. been around 150–200 years
5. come into face-to-face contact
6. 'ocker'
7. of the 19th century
8. North Shore

b Watch again and check your answers. Note what exactly they were referring to.

c Work in pairs and compare answers.

Discussion

8 **a** Rank these statements 1–5 (1= strongly agree, 5 = strongly disagree). Make notes on reasons why.

- Learners hardly ever pick up their teacher's accent.
- Teachers should teach 'standard' English accents.
- We should practise listening to as many different accents as possible.
- It is just as important to understand non-native varieties of English as different native accents.
- I aim to speak with a native-like English accent.

b Work in groups. Tell each other your opinions and give reasons. Is there a consensus in your group?

VIDEO

Unit 2 Remarkable!

Lead-in

1 Work in groups. Discuss these questions.

1 When you visit a new city or country, do you like sightseeing? If so, what kind of sights do you particularly like or dislike visiting?
2 Which buildings in your city or country have an interesting history?
3 What do you know about these well-known sights in London: the Tower of London; Big Ben; Buckingham Palace.
4 Do you know about any other sights in London?

Viewing

2 **a** VIDEO 2.1 Watch the whole video about the Tower of London and choose the best title (1–3).

1 London's Most Romantic Tower
2 The Tower of London – 900 years of history
3 Tower of London – from palace to prison to crowd-pleaser

b Work in pairs. Take turns to explain what title you chose and why.

3 **a** VIDEO 2.3 Watch again. Make notes on these questions.

1 Why were Sheniz and Bettina impressed by the Tower of London?
2 Why has Daniel been asked to explain the history of the Tower?
3 Why did William the Conqueror build the Tower?
4 Why was the Tower very different to most other buildings in England at that time?

b Work in pairs and compare answers.

4 VIDEO 2.3 Watch again. Are these statements true, false or there is no information given? Correct the false statements.

1 The White Tower was the last part of the tower to be built.
2 It took 10 years to build.
3 It was the most impressive castle in England at one time.
4 King William lived in the Tower.
5 The arches over the windows had a special function.
6 Most people are interested in the Tower because it was a place of punishment.
7 This was the only castle King William built in England.

5 **a** VIDEO 2.4 Watch again. Tick the events of Anne Boleyn's life that are mentioned.

- how old she was when she met Henry VIII
- how she met Henry VIII
- her wedding day
- the night before her coronation
- her children with Henry VIII
- why Henry VIII turned against her
- her trial
- her execution

b Watch again and make notes on the events you ticked.

c Work in pairs. Compare notes.

Discussion

6 **a** A museum wants to create an exhibition on the best of your country's history and culture. Think of six things that best represent different aspects of your country (e.g. a historical object, a building, a work of art, etc.). Be prepared to justify your choices.

b Work in pairs. Tell each other your ideas and agree on the same six exhibits. (If you are from different places, imagine it is a joint project between your countries.)

7 **a** Discuss these questions.

1 How will you attract visitors to your exhibition?
2 How much should visitors pay for admission?
3 How will information be made accessible to people who speak different languages? Which languages will be catered for?
4 How will the exhibition bring its content to life?

b Work in groups with another pair. Tell the other pair about your exhibition and the exhibits you chose. Do you agree with each other's ideas?

c Present your group's best ideas to the rest of the class.

VIDEO Unit 3 Well-being

Lead-in

1 Work in groups. Discuss these questions.

1 How important is it for you to stay fit and healthy?
2 Do you do anything to keep in good condition? If so, what? If not, why not?
3 Do you do anything that you think is bad for you? Or are there things that would be good for you that you don't do?
4 What responsibility should the following take for improving the fitness of a nation: government; schools; doctors; the media; parents; individuals?
5 Think of five suggestions you would give to someone who wanted to become healthier.

Viewing

2 **a** VIDEO 3.1 Watch an interview with Esther Mills (a nutritionist), and interviews with members of the public.

1 Does Esther give the same suggestions you did in exercise 1?
2 Overall, how healthy do you think the interviewees are?
3 Do you agree when Esther says, "I've been really encouraged by what I've seen on the streets today."

b Work in pairs and discuss your ideas.

3 VIDEO 3.2 Watch the interview with Esther again. What do these phrases refer to?

1 three popular health magazines
2 every single day
3 the rest of your life
4 positive things
5 eight hours
6 at least 3 times

4 **a** VIDEO 3.3 Watch part 2 again. Work in pairs. **Student A:** make a note of food mentioned that you consider healthy. **Student B:** make a note of food mentioned that you consider unhealthy.

b Work in pairs. Compare your lists. Do you have any foods in both lists? If so, explain why.

5 **a** Read points 1–4 below. Tick the ideas below you agree with.

1 If it tastes good, it does you good.
2 Live for today!
3 Knowing is one thing, doing is another.
4 You should eat a little of what you fancy each day.

b VIDEO 3.4 Watch again. From what Esther says, do you think she would agree with points 1–4?

c Work in pairs. Discuss your answers and give reasons.

Discussion

6 Look at these radical ideas to improve health. Decide how much you agree with each one.

1 Price food according to its nutritional value.
2 Completely prohibit the sale of cigarettes.
3 Companies should pay for all their employees' healthcare.
4 Ban cars from city centres, but there are free bicycles everywhere.

7 **a** Work in small groups. Discuss these questions.

1 Which ideas would be most/least effective?
2 Which would be possible/impossible?
3 How could the ideas be adapted to make them more feasible or more effective?

b Do you have any other radical ideas for improving health and fitness? Prepare to present your ideas to the class.

Unit 4 Civilised: TV addicts

Lead-in

1 Work in groups. Read all the questions. Choose three or four to discuss.

1 How many televisions have you got?
2 How many hours a week do you watch TV?
3 Who comes up with the ideas for TV programmes?
4 Is there such a thing as a fresh idea in TV these days?
5 Do you think that ideas are often recycled in programme making?
6 What kind of things do you watch?
7 Should parents restrict the time their children watch TV?
8 Do you think TV has a positive influence on us in general?
9 Do you think that TV programme makers have a responsibility to educate viewers?
10 What would you change about TV programming?

Viewing

2 **a** VIDEO 4.1 Watch some interviews about television. Sometimes you hear a question and sometimes you only hear the answer and have to guess the question. Which questions from 1 do you think were asked?

b Work in pairs and compare answers. Were many of the answers you heard similar to your own ideas in 1?

3 VIDEO 4.2 Watch again. Choose the correct answers. Sometimes there may be more than one possible answer.

1 When the interviewer says, 'Love it or hate it', she means …
  a she's got mixed feelings about TV.
  b people have very strong feelings about TV.
  c whatever you think of it.
2 When the interviewer says, 'everyone's a critic', she means …
  a nobody really likes TV nowadays.
  b everybody has something to say about it.
  c there are too many professional TV critics about.
3 When Lissa mentions 'people who commission the programmes', she means the people who …
  a make the programmes.
  b choose somebody else to make them.
  c decide what will be on TV.
4 When Lissa says 'it's throwing a lot of things at them and seeing what sticks', she means …
  a TV companies choose programmes randomly.
  b production companies send in a lot of ideas and are sometimes lucky.
  c if a programme is popular, it will be continued.

4 Work in pairs and discuss these questions.

1 Why do you think people have such strong feelings about TV?
2 How has the internet helped to make everyone a critic?
3 What kind of programmes have 'stuck' (become very successful) in your country?

5 **a** VIDEO 4.3 Watch again. Tick the programmes that people mentioned they like watching. Which was mentioned twice?

comedy cartoons documentaries
Do It Yourself entertainment shows
music news reality TV sport

b Work in pairs. Discuss these questions.

1 Do you have strong feelings about any of these types of programme?
2 Which types are popular in your country?

6 VIDEO 4.4 Watch again. What do the interviewees say about these topics?

1 violent crime
2 schools
3 documentaries
4 reality TV
5 Africa

Discussion

7 **a** Work in pairs. Think of at least two reasons why somebody could agree with the statement below and two reasons to disagree.

- TV's main responsibility is to educate and inform rather than entertain.

b Decide whether you mainly agree or disagree with the statement. Join other people with a similar view. Pool your ideas to support your argument.

8 **a** Work in groups with people with different views. Take turns to speak for one minute.

b As a class, vote on whether you agree or disagree with the statement.

VIDEO

Unit 5 It's just a job!

Lead-in

1 Work in pairs. Discuss these questions.

1 As a child, what job did you want to have when you grew up?
2 How much does school prepare pupils for the world of work?
3 Do you know anyone who loves or hates their job? How does it affect their lives?

Viewing

2 **a** VIDEO 5.1 Watch the whole video about work and answer the questions.

1 Do the children know what they want to do when they grow up?
2 According to Nick, the headmaster, how do schools nowadays aim to prepare children for the real world?
3 Are the other interviewees talking about a past or a future career, or both?

b Work in pairs and discuss these questions.

1 Did anything surprise you about the children's, or Nick's answers?
2 Did the other interviewees remind you of people you know?

3 **a** VIDEO 5.2 Watch and make notes on how these ideas can be compared.

1 The girls' and the boys' answers.
2 Nick's preparation for the world of work and the preparation pupils get now.
3 Being a barrister and being a headhunter.
4 Lucy and Connor's attitudes.

b Work in pairs and discuss your notes.

4 **a** VIDEO 5.3 Watch again. Are these statements true, false or no information is given?

1 Nick only has one regret about his career.
2 Nick was a headmaster for longer than he was a teacher.
3 Mary didn't study what she wanted to.
4 Michael has only one complaint about his job.
5 Michael is looking for a new job.

b Work in pairs. Compare your answers.

5 **a** Work in pairs. How many jobs or employers can you remember that were mentioned in the video? Make a list.

b VIDEO 5.1 Watch again. Tick the jobs and employers you wrote and add any others you hear.

c One of the children gave the wrong name for a job. What is the proper name for the job?

Discussion

6 Look at the list of jobs you wrote in **5a**. Discuss these questions. Be prepared to justify your answers.

1 Which would be the best job and the worst job for someone who …
- is generally pretty laid-back?
- is highly articulate?
- is an arty type?
- loves wide, open spaces?
- is a bit of a loner?
- is kind?
- is highly sociable?

2 Which job …
- would you hate to do?
- would you do if you were desperate?
- doesn't sound very exciting but would be OK for you?
- sounds perfect for you?
- would have sounded great when you were a child?

Unit 6 Ask the public

Lead-in

1 Discuss these questions in pairs.

1 How do shops try to persuade you to buy certain products?
2 Do you ever complain to shops or companies? If so, give an example. If not, why?
3 Have you ever answered any market research questions?

Viewing

2 **a** VIDEO 6.1 Watch the whole video. In what order were these issues discussed?

a why companies use market researchers
b what makes people buy certain products
c the market research process
d more knowledgeable and aware customers
e complaining

b Work in pairs. Were any of the views you heard the same as yours?

3 **a** VIDEO 6.2 Watch again. Are these statements true, false or no information is given?

1 The interviewees usually get what they want after complaining.
2 Martin suggests it's quite easy to write good market research questions.
3 Martin stresses that companies need to use their intuition.

b Work in pairs and compare your answers.

c What phrases are used to express these ideas?

1 isn't as good as I expect (Susan)
2 give your opinion (interviewer)
3 deal with the most important thing (Michael)
4 a guess or feeling without proof (Michael)

4 **a** Look at these reasons for buying products. Which ones do you think affect your buying choices? Consider different types of product (food, clothes, electronics, media).

- practical necessity
- media exposure
- brand loyalty
- word of mouth
- placement in shops
- celebrity endorsement
- quality
- cost
- personal taste
- multi-buy offers
- packaging

b VIDEO 6.3 Tick the reasons from **4a** that you hear.

c VIDEO 6.4 Answer these questions in your own words.

1 Why do manufacturers need to employ specialist market researchers?
2 What's a professional consumer?

d Work in pairs and discuss your answers.

Discussion

5 Work in groups. Choose one of the language-learning 'tools' below. Imagine you are market researchers. Your client, a publisher, wants to produce an improved type of this tool.

- a coursebook
- a website
- a mobile app
- a dictionary
- an online video channel
- a self-access course

1 Decide on three questions that would give your client useful information.
2 Ask your questions to as many people in the class as you can in five minutes. Also answer their questions from the perspective of a language learner.
3 Analyse the responses you gathered. What recommendations could you make to your client? Present them to the class.

VIDEO Unit 7 Laying down the law

Lead-in

1 Work in groups. Discuss these questions.

1 Would you rather live in a country with a lot of laws or one with not many? Why?
2 Do you think people in your country are quite law-abiding or not? Why?
3 How are lawyers regarded in your country?

Viewing

2 VIDEO 7.1 Read the list of topics. Then watch the whole video and put the topics in order.

- different types of lawyers in the UK
- qualifying to become a lawyer
- laws people don't like
- breaking the law
- the number of laws
- reciprocal laws between nations

3 **a** VIDEO 7.2 Watch and choose the correct answers.

1 The majority of interviewees think the number of laws is …
  a about right
  b too low
  c too high
2 Both solicitors and barristers …
  a are qualified lawyers
  b work in court
  c have exactly the same training
3 Jenny mentions child abduction as an example of a law which is …
  a usually different in different countries
  b the same in different countries
  c sometimes agreed to by different countries

b Work in pairs and compare answers.

4 **a** Match the beginning and ends of these phrases.

1 Sunday	a wrong
2 burning	b change
3 morally	c Trading law
4 career	d desire

b VIDEO 7.3 Watch and find out what the phrases refer to.

c Work in pairs. Discuss your answers. How much detail can you remember?

5 **a** Look at the sentences from the dialogue. Decide which phrases sound best.

CONNOR I *shouldn't say / wouldn't say* I've broken the law *to any major extent / to any main extent*.

EMILY No, *beside from / aside from* the occasional parking ticket, I've never *really done much with / really had much to do with* being on the wrong side of the law.

LUCY No, *apart from / except from* speeding!

TOM *No more than every other / Only the same than any other* teenager's broken the law.

b VIDEO 7.4 Watch and check your answers.

Discussion

6 **a** Accept, reject or modify these statements so they reflect your opinion. Be prepared to give reasons for your choices.

1 There are too many laws.
2 The law treats everyone equally.
3 There should be international laws.
4 Speeding should carry heavy penalties.
5 Shops should be able to open whenever they like.
6 Lawyers are underpaid.

b Work in groups. Compare your answers. Give reasons.

Unit 8 What's stopping you?

Lead-in

1 Work in pairs. Discuss these questions.

1 Have you ever made a big change in your life? If so, describe what happened and why? If not, is there a change you would like to make?
2 What is the most satisfying thing you've done?
3 How do you feel about giving to charities?

Viewing

2 **a** VIDEO 8.1 Watch nine people talking about changes they made, or would like to make to their lives. Which of these changes are mentioned?

- attitude to other people
- new job
- ending poverty and injustice in Africa
- starting a business
- buying from ethical suppliers
- the way people buy presents
- raising children to have better values

b Work in pairs and compare your answers.

3 VIDEO 8.2 Watch part 1 again. Are the statements true, false or no information is given?

1 Rachel's present job involves public relations.
2 She didn't feel her previous job helped the people who needed help.
3 Her trip to Africa made her change her career.
4 She had always been a supporter of Oxfam's work.
5 She was excited about the possibility of meaningful change.

4 **a** VIDEO 8.3 Put these events in the order they were mentioned.

- Someone dreams of a change.
- Someone made a change.
- Someone didn't need to change.

b What were the changes?

5 **a** VIDEO 8.4 What is the relevance of these words/phrases?

nosy	catalogue	bubble bath
poor country	goat	fridge magnet
makes a real difference		

b Work in pairs and compare answers.

6 **a** Complete the sentences with the correct form of the verbs in the box.

do (x2)	make (x2)	change	consider	donate

1 they ________ a lot of charity work in Africa
2 the people I recruit ________ a difference to the organisation I work for
3 occasionally ________ to charities and ________ voluntary work
4 I had an accident and it ________ my outlook completely – I'd never ________ anyone else before
5 Whichever job you're in, you can actually ________ a contribution to society

b VIDEO 8.5 Watch and check your answers.

Discussion

7 **a** Work in groups. Discuss what you could do to make a difference to these people/situations.

- a neighbour who doesn't speak the language
- your local community that has nowhere for children to play
- unemployed people in your city
- victims of a natural disaster in another country
- global warming

b Which actions you discussed would you be most prepared to do? Which would make the biggest difference? Give reasons.

VIDEO

Unit 9 Cash

Lead-in

1 Work in pairs. Discuss what these proverbs about money mean and whether you agree.

1. Money doesn't grow on trees.
2. The best things in life are free.
3. Look after the pennies, and the pounds will take care of themselves.
4. You can't take it with you.
5. Money is the root of all evil.

Viewing

2 **a** VIDEO 9.1 Watch the whole video. Answer these questions.

1. Whose attitude to money is most like your own?
2. Did you learn anything new about the history of money? If so, what?
3. Think of one more question that you'd like to ask either Dr Singh or the interviewees about money.

b Work in pairs. Discuss your ideas.

3 **a** VIDEO 9.2 Watch again. How are these ideas linked?

1. cash and money
2. cheques and women
3. exchanging things and money
4. the Chinese and the Greeks

b Work in pairs. Compare your answers.

4 **a** VIDEO 9.3 What do you think the speakers meant when they said these phrases?

1. CONNOR err on the side of caution
2. CONNOR tend to be reasonably … careful
3. SUE I just get on with it.
4. JAZ That's what it's there for.

b Work in pairs and discuss your answers.

5 VIDEO 9.4 According to Dr Singh, the statements below are not correct. What are his arguments against them?

1. The value of money depends on what you are buying with it.
2. Money is the root of all evil.
3. A lack of money is causing global warming.

6 VIDEO 9.5 What did the speakers mean when they used these words/phrases?

1 LUCY lavish
- a extravagant
- b wealthy

2 AZIN disposable income
- a money you waste
- b money to enjoy after the necessities are paid for

3 ALASTAIR I don't think anyone can ever have too much money.
- a Nobody should be extremely rich.
- b There's no such thing as being too rich.

4 MELISSA you're comfortable
- a you don't mind being poor
- b you've got enough to buy what you want

Discussion

7 **a** Choose three of these questions and complete them in any way you like.

- Do you think that money is … ?
- Do you think that being rich means … ?
- When it comes to spending money … ?
- Do you often feel … about money?
- Do you blame money for … ?
- Do you think the rich … ?

b Ask as many people as you can in the class your three questions. Ask them to justify their answers. Answer their questions too.

c Work in groups. Report back on the most interesting observations.

VIDEO

Unit 10 The key to success: languages

Lead-in

1 Work in pairs. Discuss these questions, giving examples from your own language-learning experiences.

1 What reasons do people have for learning other languages?
2 What reasons do people give for not speaking other languages?
3 If you were a native English speaker, would you learn another language?

Viewing

2 **a** VIDEO 10.1 Watch the whole video. Answer these questions.

1 Do the interviewees seem like confident language learners?
2 Does the teacher, Rene, think his students lack motivation for languages?
3 What reason was given several times for English people's lack of foreign languages?
4 According to Rene, are the British worse at learning languages than other countries?

b Work in pairs and compare your answers.

3 **a** Work in pairs. Do you think gender makes a difference in language learning?

b VIDEO 10.2 Answer these questions.

1 Did you notice any general differences between the answers of the male and female interviewees?
2 What does Rene think about the gender difference?

c Discuss your answers with your partner. Do you think that what the video suggests is true? If so, why could that be?

4 Match words 1–6 to words a–f to make collocations.

1 new	a students
2 failed	b spoken
3 widely	c language
4 unmotivated	d challenge
5 native	e franca
6 lingua	f miserably

5 VIDEO 10.3 Watch and check. What does the speaker say about each of the phrases?

new challenge – *He likes the **new challenge** of learning languages.*

6 **a** VIDEO 10.2 Work in pairs. Watch again and discuss these questions.

1 Why do you think Nic found that English wasn't enough? What advice would you give him?
2 Why do you think Sheila speaks those four languages?
3 Why do you think the students are excited?
4 Why do students find vocabulary difficult?

b VIDEO 10.3 Watch again and discuss these questions.

1 Why do you think Seb, Josh and James feel they failed at languages?
2 What advice would you give them?
3 Why do you think English is the *lingua franca* if Chinese is the most widely spoken native language in the world?

Discussion

7 **a** Work in groups. You have been asked to advise on a new TV advertising campaign to encourage people to learn languages. Discuss these questions.

1 What are the benefits of learning a foreign language?
2 What stops people from learning them?
3 What would persuade them to?
4 How could these ideas be used in the advertisement?
5 Do you have any ideas about images or soundtrack?
6 What about a slogan?

b Present your ideas to the class.

Language Summary 1

VOCABULARY

1.1 Communicating 1A 2 p6

make eye contact (with) when two people look into each other's eyes at the same time
come into contact with be in communication with people or ideas
gossip (about sb/sth) talk about other people's private lives
butt in (to) interrupt someone who is talking
overhear accidentally hear what other people are saying without their knowledge
have a row (with sb/about sth) /raʊ/ argue, especially loudly
intervene to get involved in a difficult situation, in order to help
witter (on) /ˈwɪtə/ talk about unimportant things for a long time
grumble (about) /ˈgrʌmbl/ complain about something
eavesdrop (on) intentionally listen to others' conversations
bicker (about) /ˈbɪkə/ argue about unimportant matters
chat (sb) up talk to somebody in a way that shows them that you are sexually attracted to them

TIPS

- In the Language Summaries we only show the **main** stress (•) in words and phrases.
- We can sometimes combine a verb and a noun to describe an action: *They had a gossip over coffee.*
- We do not use *butt in*, *witter* or *bicker* in formal contexts.

1.2 Prepositions and phrases 1B 7 p12

on a broader scale relating to the size or level of something (especially when large): *To get more accurate results, the research needs to be done on a broader scale.*
on the same wavelength /ˈweɪvleŋθ/ with similar views/opinions: *I can't work with him – we're simply not on the same wavelength.*
on average /ˈævrɪʤ/ typically: *On average, I go to the cinema twice a month.*
on purpose intentionally, not by accident: *We can't prove it but we're sure he broke it on purpose.*
on good terms have a good relationship with one another: *Jerry always tries to stay on good terms with ex-girlfriends.* (opposite: **on bad terms**)
on a regular basis /ˈbeɪsɪs/ happening or doing something often: *She sees her ex-husband on a regular basis, so they still get on.*
on demand whenever needed or asked for: *She's up all night; she feeds the baby on demand.*
on the increase increasing: *Poverty is on the increase.*
at fault /fɔːlt/ responsible for a problem: *Nobody was at fault for the accident.*
at arm's length a distance: *We're not close. She keeps me at arm's length.*
at a loose end with nothing to do: *Could I do that for you? I'm at a loose end.*
at a glance immediately: *We knew at a glance that she was upset.*
at times occasionally: *He's a bit bad tempered at times.*
at hand easily available: *They need to know that help is at hand.*
at random by chance: *The winner was picked at random.*
at short notice only a short time before something happens: *They cancelled the meeting at short notice.*

TIP

- Make a note of nouns together with their prepositions and try to learn them as 'chunks' of meaning.

1.3 Sayings 1C 1 p14

Rome wasn't built in a day.

Rome wasn't built in a day. to emphasise that you can't expect to do a lot of things in a short period of time
Don't make a mountain out of a molehill. don't make a slight difficulty seem like a serious problem
Once bitten, twice shy. when you are frightened to do something again because you had an unpleasant experience doing it the first time
Actions speak louder than words. to emphasise that what you do is more important and shows your intentions and feelings more clearly than what you say
One man's meat is another man's poison. to emphasise that people like different things
Engage brain before mouth. think about something before saying anything about it
Nothing ventured, nothing gained. to emphasise that you have to take a risk in order to obtain a benefit
Better late than never. said when you think that it is better for somebody or something to be late than never to arrive or to happen

1.1 Past Simple and Present Perfect

1A 1 p6

PAST SIMPLE

- We can use the **Past Simple** for a single completed action in the past: *How old **were** you when you **had** your first English lesson? When **was** the last time you **spoke** English outside class? **Did** you have to write anything in English last month?*
- For a repeated action or habit in the past: *My son **had** some lessons at that school.*
- For a state in the past: *I **was** always good at languages.*
- We also use the **Past Simple** with expressions such as the *first/last time*: *The last time I **bought** a dictionary was when I was at school.*

PRESENT PERFECT SIMPLE

- We use the **Present Perfect** to talk about things that connect the past and the present.
- We often use the **Present Perfect Simple** for experiences: ***Have** you ever **read** a novel that was written in English?*
- For states or activities that started in the past and continue in the present: *I**'ve had** this dictionary for years.*
- For completed actions that happened recently, but we don't say exactly when: ***Have** you **seen** any films in English recently?*
- With superlatives: *It's the easiest language I**'ve learned.***
- To talk about change: *My English **has improved** since this course started.*
- We often use the **Present Perfect Simple** to say that something is completed: *I**'ve read** that book.* (= the book is finished now)

PRESENT PERFECT CONTINUOUS

- We often use the **Present Perfect Continuous** for longer actions that started in the past and continue in the present: *I**'ve been working** on this for two hours.*
- For longer actions that have recently finished, but have a result in the present: *I'm tired because I**'ve been revising** for an exam.*
- For actions that happened repeatedly in the past and still happen in the present: *How long **have you been coming** to this school?*
- We often use the **Present Perfect Continuous** to emphasise the action we've been doing rather than the result: *I**'ve been reading** this book.* (= we don't know if the book is finished or not)

1.2 Time expressions with the Past Simple and Present Perfect 1A 6 p8

- We can use the **Present Perfect** with time expressions which mean up to and including now: *I**'ve bought** quite a few self-help books over the past few months.*
  *I**'ve read** about 150 pages so far. During the last couple of weeks I**'ve** actually **been trying** out some of Carnegie's suggestions.*
  *Until now, I**'ve** never really **had** any contact with the guy in the ticket office.*
- We use the **Past Simple** with definite time expressions in the past (*yesterday, a few weeks ago, last year*, etc.): *... in 1937 the book's runaway success **meant** the publishers **had** difficulty keeping up with demand.*
- Some time expressions can be used with both the **Present Perfect Simple** and **Past Simple**. Compare these sentences:
  A ***I told** at least ten people about it at work this week.*
  B ***I've told** at least ten people about it at work this week.*
  Speaker A uses the **Past Simple** because he/she considers the period of time (this week) as finished. Speaker B uses the **Present Perfect** because he/she considers the period of time (this week) as still continuing.
  A *I **read** it during the summer holidays.*
  B ***I've read** a lot of books during the last month.*
  Speaker A uses the **Past Simple** because the event (reading the book) was completed at a definite time in the past (during the summer holidays). Speaker B uses the **Present Perfect** because the time period (during the last month) is still continuing.
  A *Since Ann **suggested** this one, I've read a couple of his other books.*
  B *I've read lots of his books since **I've been** unemployed.*
  Speaker A uses the **Past Simple** after *since* because the event (Ann's suggestion) was completed at a definite time in the past. Speaker B uses the **Present Perfect** because the event (being unemployed) is continuing to happen.
  A *As soon as I **finished** reading it, I gave it to my brother.*
  B *As soon as **I've finished** reading it, I'm going to give it to my brother.*
  Speaker A uses the **Past Simple** because the event (reading the book/magazine, etc.) was completed at a definite time in the past. Speaker B uses the **Present Perfect** because the event (reading the book) started in the past but is continuing to happen.

TIPS

- We can replace *as soon as* with *once/when/after: I'll lend it to you **once** I've finished it.*
- We use *during* or *in + the last few days/weeks/months/years*, etc.: ***In the last couple of months** I've read three of her books.*
- We use *up until/until/till/up to + now: I've written four pages **up to now**.*
- We use *It's (not) the first time* with the **Present Perfect** to talk about the first instance of something happening: ***It's the first time** I've read a book like this, really.*
- We can also say *This is / That's the first (second, third, fourth, etc.) time ...* : ***This is the fourth time** I've written a review of a book.*

1.3 Cleft sentences: *what* and *it* clauses

1B **3** p10

- Cleft sentences divide a message into two parts, using *what* or *it* clauses. They can focus attention on new, more important or contradictory information.

  (I can get a bit stressed by work.) ***What*** *I do if I get stressed* ***is*** *talk to my friends.* (new information)

  (I get on well with my parents.) However, ***it's*** *my friends* ***that*** *I talk to if I have a problem.* (contradiction)

WHAT CLAUSES

- Cleft sentences with *what* are very common in spoken English.

Known information (subject)	***be* (main verb)**	**New information (clause/complement)**
What we talk about	*isn't*	*deep and meaningful.*
What I do if I get stressed	*is*	*talk to my friends.*
What happens	*is*	*we bottle things up.*

- The new information comes in the last part. This can be a complement, describing the subject (*deep and meaningful*), or a clause (*talk to my friends*).
- We join the known and new information in this type of cleft sentence with *be*.
- The *what* clause is the subject and contains known information. We know that they talk because of the speaker's previous sentence.
- To focus on an action we can use *what* + sb/sth + *do* + *be* (+ subject) + infinitive clause.
- To focus on a whole sentence, we can use *what happens* + *be* + clause.

TIPS

• When we use *who, why, whose, when, where,* etc. instead of *what*, we usually use an expression such as *a person, the reason,* etc. with or without the *wh-* word: ***A person (who)*** *I tend to confide in* ***is*** *my hairdresser.* ***The reason (why)*** *we meet there* ***is*** *because they put up with all our noise.*

• To give a reason we can follow *be* with *to*+infinitive. *The reason (why) she left so early was* ***to finish*** *her essay.*

• We can reverse the order of the clauses in *wh-* cleft sentences without changing the meaning: *The person (who) I used to sound off to most was my hairdresser = My hairdresser was the person (who) I used to sound off to most.*

• We can use *the thing/something/all/anything/one thing,* etc. in place of *what/whatever* in cleft sentences. These phrases are especially common in informal spoken language: ***The thing*** *I hate is men chatting me up.*

IT CLAUSES

- In cleft sentences with an *it* clause, the speaker emphasises the information in the *it* clause. The verb that follows *it* is *be*. ***It'd*** *probably* ***be*** *my parents* ***who*** *I'd talk to first.*

TIPS

• In cleft sentences with an *it* clause, *who* can be used instead of *that* when referring to a person/people: *It's Keith* ***who*** *left, not Mark.*

• When there is a plural noun in the *it* clause, we still use a singular form of *be*: ***It's*** *his friends that I can't stand.* not ~~*It are his friends ...*~~ .

• We use an object pronoun after *it* + *be:*
He's always gossiping. → *It's* ***him*** *that's always gossiping.*

WRITING

1.1 Connecting words: addition **3** p13

- We sometimes use connecting words to join clauses and sentences that add information.
- We usually use ***as well*** and ***too*** at the end of a clause: *She's been running the company since November. She's got three children to look after* ***as well/too****. Chinese food is very tasty. It's quite cheap* ***as well/too****.*
- We can use ***also*** at the beginning or in the middle of a clause: *The traffic is really heavy at this time of day. The roads are* ***also*** *extremely icy, so be careful/****Also****, the roads are extremely icy so be careful.*
- We usually use ***not only*** with ***but***: *The village is* ***not only*** *remote,* ***but*** *totally inaccessible by road.*
- We use ***what's more*** and ***besides*** at the beginning of a sentence: *I haven't got any change on me.* ***What's more/ Besides****, you already owe me money from last time. The probelm we were set was extremely difficult to solve.* ***What's more/Besides****, we didn't have much time to do it.*

TIP

• We do not usually use *also, too,* or *as well* in negative clauses. Instead we use phrases such as *either: I haven't read the Harry Potter books or seen the films* ***either****.*

1.2 Spelling: homophones **4** p13

- Homophones are words that sound the same, but have different spellings and different meanings.
- Some common homophones are: *whose/who's, there/they're/their, of/'ve, you're/your.*

REAL WORLD

1.1 Explaining and paraphrasing

1C **3** p15

- When we need to clarify, simplify or explain something we have already said, we often use phrases which signal to the listener that we are going to say the same thing again in a different way.

  Which simply/just/basically means ...
  And what it/this/that means is ...
  What I mean by that is ...
  By which I mean ...
  What I'm trying to say is ...
  Which is to say ...
  To put it simply, ...
  That is to say, ...
  Or to put it another way, ...
  In other words, ...

TIP

• We can also say *i.e.* /aɪjiː/ (= *that is*) or *meaning* to paraphrase: *We'll meet there,* ***i.e.*** *at the station. He said he was a bit busy, meaning he wasn't going to come.*

Language Summary 2

VOCABULARY

Preview

GRADABLE AND NON-GRADABLE ADJECTIVES

- We can modify gradable adjectives with adverbs such as *very* or *a bit* to say something has more or less of a quality: *It was* ***very*** *interesting. I was* ***a bit*** *tired.*

  Modifying adverbs: *very, extremely, rather, really, a bit, a little, fairly,* etc.

  Gradable adjectives: *interesting, scared, surprised, difficult, tired,* etc.
- We do not talk about non-gradable adjectives such as *impossible* or *perfect* in the same way. We combine non-gradable adjectives with intensifying adverbs such as *absolutely* or *completely* to emphasise their quality.

  Intensifying adverbs: *absolutely, completely, entirely, totally,* etc.

  Non-gradable adjectives: *impossible, terrible, excellent, huge,* etc.
- We can often use *really* to intensify non-gradable and gradable adjectives: *The lecture was* ***really*** *fascinating/good.*

2.1 Intensifying adverbs 2A 7 p19

- We can use some adverbs with adjectives or verbs to amplify or intensify their meaning.
- Some intensifying adverbs go naturally with particular adjectives or verbs. Look at these examples:

1 ***thoroughly/really*** *enjoy*
2 ***deeply/totally*** *frustrated*
3 ***highly/extremely*** *(un)likely*
4 ***strongly/firmly*** *believe*
5 ***bitterly/deeply*** *regret*
6 ***bitterly/extremely*** *disappointed*
7 ***completely/entirely*** *agree*
8 ***vividly/distinctly*** *remember*

TIPS

- We can use *quite* in front of non-gradable adjectives or adverbs to mean 'truly' or 'completely': *He's quite remarkable. I saw him quite clearly.*
- We usually use the adverb *quite* in front of a gradable adjective or adverb to mean 'fairly' or 'rather': *It's quite expensive.*
- We use different stress and intonation with the different meanings of *quite.*

He's quite remarkable. (= truly remarkable)

It's quite expensive. (= rather expensive)

- We do not use *quite* in front of comparative adjectives or adverbs. Instead we use *a bit/a little/slightly: The city is a bit more peaceful than I had expected it to be.* not ~~*The city is quite more peaceful ….*~~

2.2 Adjective word order 2B 7 p22

- When describing a noun, there is an order that adjectives usually follow. Notice that opinions come before facts, the general before the specific.

opinion	size	age	colour	origin	material	noun
beautiful			white		sandy	beaches
stark		modern			log	cabins
	massive	100-year-old				tortoises
charming				rustic	stone	cottages
breath-taking	high				snow-capped	peaks
delicious				Thai	fish and coconut	curries
extravagant			white		marble	buildings
picture-book		medieval		Italian		villages

- When speaking, we try not to put too many adjectives in front of the noun. We avoid doing this by adding phrases beginning with *and, with* or *in* or adding a relative clause: *a stunning modern bike with an aluminium frame.* (not ~~*a stunning modern aluminium-bodied bike*~~), *an original watercolour painting (which is) signed and dated* (not ~~*an original watercolour signed and dated painting*~~).
- A compound noun (e.g. *dressing-gown, address book*) cannot be separated by other words: *a leather address book* not ~~*an address leather book*~~.

2.3 Describing places 2C 2 p24

high-rise very tall and having a lot of floors: *Chengdu is a modern city, full of traffic and high-rise department stores.*
spectacular /spekˈtækjʊlə/ very exciting to look at: *Beyond the city, you can experience the spectacular Huanglong Valley.*
snow-clad /ˈsnəʊklæd/ covered in a layer of snow: *The valley is bordered by snow-clad peaks and glaciers.*
golden the colour of gold: *A golden dragon seems to surge forth from the forest.*
heritage /ˈherɪtɪdʒ/ important historical features, such as traditions, languages or buildings: *Home to the Terracotta Army, the city has a historical heritage second to none.*
searing /ˈsɪərɪŋ/ extreme: *Despite the searing heat, Xi'an is a joy to visit.*
winding /ˈwaɪndɪŋ/ following a route which turns in different directions: *Many people say that the real culture of Beijing lies in the winding lanes known as hutong.*
hustle and bustle /hʌslənˈbʌsl/ all the noise and activity: *Shut away from the hustle and bustle of the city outside, the hutong dwellers enjoy a peaceful existence.*
icebound /ˈaɪsbaʊnd/ fixed in a state of ice: *While northern China is snowy and icebound, in Hainan it is possible to swim in the sea and enjoy warm sunshine all year round.*
stunning /ˈstʌnɪŋ/ extremely beautiful: *In addition to stunning golden beaches, Hainan boasts such tropical scenery as the Dongjiao Coconut Plantation.*

GRAMMAR

Preview

RELATIVE CLAUSES

Defining relative clauses tell you which person, thing, etc. the writer or speaker is talking about: *The singer who you admire so much is giving a concert next month.*

- In defining relative clauses we use:
  - a *who/that* for people: *The **singer who** you admire so much is giving a concert next month.*
  - b *which/that* for things: *I'd love to go and see that **show which/that** everyone's talking about.*
  - c *where* for places: *That's the **café where** we met last time.*
  - d *whose* for possessives: *Have you met the **woman whose** daughter babysits for us?*
- We don't use commas with defining relative clauses.
- We can leave out *who*, *that* or *which* when these words aren't the subject of the defining relative clause: *That was the car (which) I was telling you about.*

TIP

- We can't use *what* in defining relative clauses: *The woman that has just left must have forgotten her coat.* not ~~*The woman what has just left must have forgotten her coat.*~~

Non-defining relative clauses add extra non-essential information: *I'm meeting Michael Jones, who is joining our firm very soon.*

- We don't use *that* in non-defining relative clauses: *I didn't buy his latest book, which was unusual for me.* not ~~*I didn't buy his latest book, that was unusual for me.*~~
- We can't leave out *who, which, whose*, etc. in non-defining relative clauses: *His first book, which I haven't read, is meant to be his best work.* not ~~*His first book, I haven't read, …*~~
- We must use commas with non-defining relative clauses.

2.1 Relative clauses with prepositions

2A 2 p18

- In more formal, usually written English, we tend to put the preposition before the relative pronoun: *Daniel has described how he does it in a book, **in which** he writes about his life.*
- In less formal, usually spoken English, prepositions at the end of relative clauses are common: *Daniel has described how he does it in a book **that** he writes about his life **in**.*
- Here are some rules for transforming informal sentences of this type to more formal, usually written English.
  - a We change the relative pronoun *that* (if it refers to a person) or *who* to *whom*.

    *He's the man **that/who** I spoke to.*
    → *He's the man **to whom** I spoke.*
  - b We change the relative pronoun *that* (if it refers to a thing) to *which*.

    *It's Kim's life **that** an Oscar-winning film, Rain Man, was based **on**.*
    → *It's Kim's life **on which** an Oscar-winning film, Rain Man, was based.*
  - c We move the preposition from the end of the clause/sentence to before the relative pronoun.

    *One skill **that** all savants are known **for** is an extraordinary memory.*
    → *One skill **for which** savants are known is an extraordinary memory.*

NONE/BOTH/ALL/ONE/NEITHER/MOST … OF WHICH/WHOM

- Determiners (*both, all, one, neither, most, none*, etc.) combine with *of which* or *of whom* in non-defining relative clauses. They refer to words/phrases in the previous clause: *It was difficult being at school surrounded by children, **none of whom** understood his condition.*
- In formal written English we can use:
  - a *both of whom* in relative clauses instead of *who both*: *He also has a brother and a sister, **both of whom** are exceptionally clever …*
  - b a relative clause with *all of which* instead of a normal clause with *all*: *Daniel's condition allows him to achieve extraordinary mathematical feats. He finds all of them simple.* → *Daniel's condition allows him to achieve extraordinary mathematical feats, **all of which** he finds simple.*

TIPS

- When we are speaking informally, we can use *both of them, all of them*, etc. Notice the change in word order: *He would find it impossible to fit a 9–5 job around his daily tasks. **He does all of them** in the same order every day.* → *He would find it impossible to fit a 9–5 job around his daily tasks, **all of which** he does in the same order every day.*
- In non-defining relative clauses, prepositional phrases, e.g. *at which point, in which case*, can be used to comment on the whole situation in the previous clause: *When he was a child, doctors advised putting him in an institution, **at which point** his parents took him home instead and introduced him to books.*
- We can combine other determiners such as *each, part, some, very little/few*, a number, and superlatives (*the biggest, the best*, etc.) with *of which/whom*: *There were many great films in 2013 and I think **the best of them** were European.* → *There were many great films in 2013, **the best of which** I think were European.*
- We can combine certain nouns with a preposition + *which*, e.g. *the level/degree/stage (at/to which), the effect/anniversary (of which): … we must celebrate the discovery of DNA, **the anniversary of which** …*
- In formal written English, we can use *whose* after a preposition in relative clauses: *I was inspired by the philosopher Dante, **whose** work this quotation has been taken **from.*** → *I was inspired by the poet Dante, **from whose** work this quotation has been taken.*
- We can use *where* instead of *in/at which* in relative clauses to talk about location. We do not use prepositions with *where*: *This is the house **where/in which** she was born.*

Preview

VERB+*ING* AND PAST PARTICIPLES

We use verb+*ing*:

- as an adjective: *We found giving a talk rather* ***frightening****.*
- in reduced relative clauses: *People who are leaving should do so quietly.* → *People* ***leaving*** *should do so quietly.*
- after certain verbs: *However much I ask her not to, she can't* ***resist spoiling*** *her grandchildren.*
- after prepositions: *According to the manual, that switch is* ***for opening*** *the boot.*

We use past participles:

- in reduced relative clauses where the original clause contains a passive verb: *The castle, which was built in the tenth century, is just round the corner from where we're staying.* → *The castle,* ***built*** *in the tenth century, … .*
- as an adjective: *Karen was soon* ***bored*** *out of her mind by the guided tour.*

2.2 Participle clauses 2B 3 p20

- Participle clauses give more information about a verb or idea in a sentence. They are often used to make a piece of writing more varied and sophisticated.

  Because *we arrived late, we couldn't find a room.* → ***Arriving*** *late, we couldn't find a room.*

- There are three types of participle clause.
  - a Present participle clause: … ***acting as a vital means of communication*** *between remote villages and crowded towns.*
  - b Past participle clause: ***Poured very slowly across your forehead****, the oil feels like a cow is licking you.*
  - c Perfect participle clause: … ***having had an indulgent lunch****, I'd lie in a hammock …*

- Past participles are used in passive clauses, and present participles are used in active clauses.

  (Having been) Caught locally every day*, it's always wonderfully fresh.*

  (As you are) Gliding silently along in a canoe*, you get to see a rural Kerala … .*

- Participle clauses can replace connecting words such as *so, while, because, if, after,* etc. When we use participles instead of connecting words, we usually leave out the subject and sometimes the auxiliary. We also change the verb to the present, past or perfect forms of the participle. Compare the following sentences:
  While you *glide silently along in a canoe, you get to see a rural Kerala.*
  Gliding silently along in a canoe, *you get to see a rural Kerala.*

- Participle clauses often give information about the causes, results, conditions or time of the events described.
  (result) … ***acting as a vital means of communication*** *between remote villages and crowded towns.*
  (time) ***Gliding silently along in a canoe****, you get to see a rural Kerala.*
  (time) ***Having had an indulgent lunch****, I'd lie in a hammock.*
  (cause) ***Caught locally every day****, it's always wonderfully fresh.*
  (condition) ***Poured very slowly across your forehead,*** *the oil feels like a cow licking you.*

TIPS

- The subject of a participle clause is usually the same as the subject of the main clause: *Looking out of the window, Verity noticed the sun had almost set.* (the subject of both clauses is Verity) not ~~*Looking out of the window, the sun had almost set.*~~ (This suggests that the sun is looking out of the window.)
- When we use *not* in a participle clause, it usually comes before the participle: *Not knowing much about Kerala, we bought a guidebook.* not ~~*Knowing not*~~ *much about Kerala, …* ('not' refers to 'knowing much about Kerala' which means that he didn't know much about Kerala). However, *not* can also follow the participle: *Pretending not to notice him, she walked straight past.* ('not' refers to noticing him, which means that she pretended that she hadn't noticed him).
- We use a perfect participle (*having* + past participle) instead of a present participle if the action in the main clause is the result of the events in the participle clause: ***Having*** *lost our credit cards, we had to get some money sent to us.* (We had to get some money sent to us because we had lost our credit cards.) not ~~*Losing our credit cards*~~.
- We can use prepositions such as *after, by, in, while, with, since,* etc. with a present or perfect participle clause to make the meaning clearer: *After visiting / having visited several temples, we returned to the hotel for a rest. By not eating between meals, she managed to reach her target weight.*

Pretending not to notice him, she walked straight past.

WRITING

2.1 Punctuation: apostrophes 2 p23

WE USE AN APOSTROPHE ('):

- in contracted forms of *be*, *have* and modal verbs and between 'n' and 't' in contracted forms with *not*: *I'm, I've, I'd* (= *I had* or *I would*), *don't, didn't, shouldn't, there's.*
- in front of an 's' added to a noun, or after a plural noun ending in 's' to show a relationship of possession: *Sally's friend, the friends' relationship.*
- in front of an 's' added to an irregular plural to show a relationship of possession: *the children's father.*

WE DO NOT USE AN APOSTROPHE:

- in possessive pronouns such as *his, hers, ours or theirs.*
- in the possessive adjective *its*: *The house has its own swimming pool.* not ~~*The house has it's own swimming pool.*~~

2.2 Connecting words: time (1) 3 p23

WE CAN USE:

- ***the moment/as soon as*** at the beginning of a clause to say something will happen immediately after something else has happened. When we refer to a point in the future we usually use the **Present Simple** after *the moment/as soon as* rather than a future form: ***The moment*** *I* ***get*** *home, I'm going straight to bed.* not ~~*The moment I will get home*~~ … .
  We use the **Past Simple** after *the moment/as soon as* when talking about the past: ***The moment*** *I* ***arrived*** *there, I wanted to make it my home. Tourism improved* ***as soon as*** *they* ***renovated*** *the centre.*
- ***ever since*** at the beginning of a clause to mean 'continually since that time': ***Ever since*** *the canals were built, the city has suffered from flooding.*
- ***first/originally*** at the beginning of a clause, in front of the main verb or after the verb *be* to talk about something as it was in the past: *The town was* ***originally*** *inhabited by farm workers, but they've all left now.*
- ***while*** at the beginning of a clause to say that something happens during the same period of time that something else happens: *I visited some old friends* ***while*** *I was staying there.*
- ***afterwards/then*** at the beginning of sentences to talk about an event that happens after the time mentioned or later: *I decided to stay in a cheap hotel.* ***Afterwards****, I regretted it. He began asking the boss about his plans.* ***Then*** *he realised the mistake he'd made and changed the subject quickly.*
- ***meanwhile*** at the beginning of a sentence to talk about an event that happens while something else is happening: *I sat anxiously waiting for the call.* ***Meanwhile****, I tried to get on with some work but kept looking at the clock.*

TIP

• We can use ***from then on*** at the beginning of a sentence to mean 'continually since that time'. However, *from then on* refers to information in a previous sentence or clause. Note that we can also use *ever since then* instead of *from then on*: *I bought a new computer last month. From then on/Ever since (then) I've had nothing but trouble with it.*

The moment I get home, I'm going straight to bed.

I sat anxiously waiting for the call. Meanwhile, I tried to get on with some work but kept looking at the clock.

Language Summary 3

VOCABULARY

3.1 Positive character adjectives

3A 1 p26

Courageous /kəˈreɪdʒəs/ people have the ability to control their fear in a dangerous or difficult situation: *It was very courageous of her to resign without finding another job first.*
Decisive /dɪˈsaɪsɪv/ people are able to make decisions quickly and confidently: *It's lucky that my wife's so decisive, because I find it difficult to make important decisions.*
Deferential /defəˈrenʃəl/ people are respectful and polite: *He is always deferential towards older people.*
Innocent /ˈɪnəsənt/ people have no knowledge or experience of the unpleasant or evil things in life: *It is difficult for children to remain innocent with the influence of TV and the internet.*
Meticulous /meˈtɪkjʊləs/ people are very careful and pay great attention to every detail: *I can't believe this was written by Paul – it's so inaccurate! He's normally meticulous in everything he does.*
Modest /ˈmɒdɪst/ people talk little about their skills or achievements: *She's so modest that I never realised how successful she is.*
Outgoing /aʊtˈgəʊɪŋ/ people are friendly and like meeting people: *She has a very outgoing personality; she has loads of friends and is always out having a good time.*
Spontaneous /spɒnˈteɪniəs/ people do things in a natural, often sudden way, without any planning or without being forced: *She's always been a spontaneous sort – flying off all over the place at a moment's notice.*
Thrifty /ˈθrɪfti/ people are careful with the use of money, particularly by avoiding waste: *He earns a lot of money these days but he's still quite thrifty.*

3.2 Connotation: positive and negative character adjectives

3A 13 p29

- *Connotation* means a feeling or idea that is suggested by a particular word. Sometimes two character adjectives can describe similar traits, but one may have a positive connotation and one may have a negative connotation.
- Both *arrogant* and *confident* refer to someone who is very sure of themselves, but *arrogant* means the person also thinks they are better than other people. *Confident* has a positive connotation. *Arrogant* has a negative connotation.

negative connotation	positive connotation
arrogant	confident
reckless	courageous
tight-fisted	thrifty
fussy	meticulous
forceful	decisive
submissive	deferential
reserved	modest
impetuous	spontaneous
loud	outgoing
naive	innocent

Reckless people do dangerous things and do not care about the risks and the possible results.
Tight-fisted people are unwilling to spend money.
Fussy /ˈfʌsɪ/ people are difficult to please.
Forceful people express opinions strongly and demand attention and action.
Submissive /səbˈmɪsɪv/ people are easily controlled by other people.
Reserved /rəˈzɜːvd/ people tend not to show their feelings or thoughts.
Impetuous /ɪmˈpetjʊəs/ people act on a sudden idea without considering the results of their actions.
Loud people tend to seek attention and dominate situations.
Naïve /nɑiˈjiːv/ people have unrealistic expectations about life.

3.3 Phrasal verbs: health

3B 1 p30

come on start to feel ill, often with a cold or flu
swell up when a part of your body becomes larger and rounder than usual, often because of an illness, injury or insect bite
pick up catch an illness from somebody or something
be blocked /blɒkt/ **up** when a part of your body, e.g. your nose, is filled with something that prevents anything getting past
go down with sth become ill, usually with a disease that is not very serious
go around when a lot of people get an illness in the same time period because the illness passes from person to person
put sb on sth give somebody a particular type of medical treatment or food
come out in sth when spots or a rash appear on your skin
come off sth stop taking a type of medicine
flare up when a condition worsens after a period of improvement

3.4 Euphemisms

3C 1 p34

- A euphemism is a word or phrase used to avoid saying something unpleasant or offensive.

economical /iːkəˈnɒmɪkl/ **with the truth** not tell the truth; lie
a senior citizen an old person
behind the times be old-fashioned
see better days be old and in bad condition
get on a bit get old
hard of hearing not able to hear well
be/feel under the weather be or feel ill
a bit of a handful difficult to look after, especially children and animals
challenging very difficult
a bit on the chilly side cold

GRAMMAR

3.1 Patterns with *it* 3A 7 p28

IT AS SUBJECT

- If the subject of the verb is a long and grammatically complex structure, we often put it at the end of the clause/sentence and use *it* as the subject of the verb at the beginning of the clause/sentence. Compare these sentences. The subject of the verb is underlined.

  That no one was hurt is incredible.
  It's incredible that no one was hurt.

- We can use several structures with ***it*** as subject.

  it **+ verb**:

  a + adjective + (*that*): ***It's clear that …***
  b + (*not*) + noun + (*that*): ***It's not an aspect …***
  c + adjective + infinitive with *to*: ***it's difficult to know …***
  d + *that* clause: ***it follows that not winning*** *is stressful.* Other verbs we use with this structure include *appear, transpire.* The *that* clause cannot go in initial position in these sentences, e.g. not ~~*That not winning is stressful it follows*~~.
  e + object + infinitive with *to* + *that*: ***it surprised him to discover*** *that …* . Other verbs we can use with this structure are connected with feelings, e.g. *amaze, annoy, concern, frighten, hurt, scare, shock, upset, worry.*

IT AS OBJECT

- We often use *it* as the object of a verb where *it* refers to a clause later in the sentence.
- We can use these structures with ***it*** as object.

  verb + ***it***:

  a + *when*: *… we all* ***hate it when*** *we lose.* Other verbs we use this structure with include: *can't bear, can't stand, dislike, enjoy, like, love, prefer, resent, understand.*
  b + adjective + infinitive with *to*: *…* ***find it difficult to cope*** *with losing.*

TIP

• Common expressions with *it*: ***It's no good*** *getting all upset about it.* ***It's no use*** *asking her, she's busy.* ***It's no wonder*** *that he got ill.* ***It's no coincidence*** *that they arrived together.*

Preview

SUBJECT AND VERB INVERSION

- In statements, the verb usually follows the subject: *I don't know him.*
- Sometimes, we invert the subject and verb so that the verb comes before the subject.
- We use inversion:

  a after *so, neither/nor*: *I need an eye test. So* ***do I****. I didn't know there was sugar in this. No, neither* ***did I****.*
  b in the phrases *Here comes/come* + noun and *There goes/go* + noun: ***Here comes*** *the doctor.*
  c in question tags: *She's a doctor,* ***isn't she****?*

- We do not put the verb before the subject:

  a when we include a question in another question. Instead, we use a normal word order of subject + verb: *Where* ***are my glasses****? → Have you any idea where* ***my glasses are****?* not ~~*Have you any idea where are my glasses?*~~
  b when we include a question in another sentence: *What's his* ***diet*** *like? → I wonder what his* ***diet's*** *like.*
  c when we are using a question word to introduce a relative clause in phrases such as *I don't know* ***what his problem is****.* not ~~*I don't know what is his problem*~~.
  d in indirect speech. We use *if* when we report a *yes/no* question. We usually (but not always) change the verb form in reported speech: ***Are you*** *taking any vitamins? → He asked me if* ***I was*** *taking any vitamins.*

3.2 Inversion 3B 5 p31

- Inversion is a way of adding emphasis or dramatic effect.
- An adverbial is any word or phrase which functions as an adverb. When we begin a sentence with a limiting adverbial (e.g. *seldom*) or a negative adverbial (e.g. *under no circumstances*), the subject and the auxiliary or modal verb are inverted: ***I am rarely*** *able to get out before seven.* ***Rarely am I*** *able to get out before seven.*
- Look at the underlined examples of inversion structures in these sentences:

  a *People seldom associate being married with being healthy.* → ***Seldom*** *do people associate being married with being healthy.*
  b *You should not, under any circumstances, exercise immediately after eating a heavy meal.* → ***Under no circumstances*** *should you exercise immediately after eating a heavy meal.*
  c *Dental hygiene saves painful visits to the dentist, as well as saving money …* → ***Not only*** *does dental hygiene save painful …*
  d *He didn't agree to stop smoking until last week.* → ***Not until*** *last week did he agree to stop smoking.*
  e *You very rarely hear anything negative about eating fish.* → ***Very rarely*** *do you hear anything negative about eating fish.*
  f *Experts have only recently come to appreciate the health benefits of eating curry.* → ***Only recently*** *have experts come to appreciate …*

- When using inversion with Present Simple and Past Simple, the subject must agree with the auxiliary not the main verb: *Not only does he enjoy …* . not ~~*Not only do/does he enjoys …*~~.
- Inversion can occur after another complete clause beginning with *not until, only when, only if, only after*: ***Not until*** *she learns to relax* ***will things get*** *any better.* ***Only when*** *we got the dog* ***did we start*** *going for long walks.*
- We use inversion after *neither* or *nor* when it introduces a negative clause that is related to one mentioned previously: *Unfortunately, Colin didn't listen to me, and* ***neither did he take*** *the doctor's advice.*

TIPS

- Although inversion is usually found in literary and formal texts, we also use it in less formal spoken and written English when we want to add emphasis or dramatic effect: ***No way** should people drive to work if they can possibly walk.*
- We don't use inversion when we use *not … either; I don't like fish and I don't like curry either.* not … ~~*either do I not like curry.*~~
- We can find inversion in literature after adverbials of place: *Into the room walked Johan.*

WRITING

3.1 Spelling: one word, two words or hyphenated 4 p33

- ***Everyday*** is an adjective which we use to describe something which is normal and not exciting in any way: *This is an **everyday** occurrence.*
- ***Every day*** is an adverbial. If something happens every day, it happens regularly each day: *I eat pasta **every day.***
- We use ***everyone*** to refer to all the people in a particular group: ***Everyone** is coming.*
- We use ***every one*** to emphasise that something is true about each of the things or people you are talking about: *I take **every one** of my jobs seriously.*
- When we make an adjective from a number and unit of measurement, we hyphenate the number and its unit of measurement and we use the singular form of the unit: *The fence was two metres high.* → *It was a **two-metre high** fence.* With ages and times we hyphenate the complete phrase: I work ***twelve hours a day.*** → It's a ***twelve-hour-a-day*** job.
- We use ***anyone*** to talk about people in general, or about each person of a particular kind: *Is there **anyone** you know who can help?*
- We use ***any one*** to emphasise that you are referring to only one of something: ***Any one** of you can do this. There isn't **any one** person here who opposes the proposal.*
- We use ***anyway*** when you are adding a remark you have just thought of to something you have just said. Usually the remark makes the previous statement seem less important than it did: *I can't ask him out. **Anyway**, I think he's seeing that girl.*
- We use ***any way***, usually in the phrase *in any way*, to mean 'in any respect' or 'by any method': *Is there **any way** I can make it up to you?*
- We use ***maybe*** as an adverbial to indicate that something is possible: ***Maybe** we should offer to pick them up.*
- We use ***may*** + ***be*** as a modal verb + infinitive to indicate that something is possible: ***He may be tired***.

3.2 Connecting words: contrast (1) 5 p33

WE USE:

- ***although/even though*** to contrast two clauses in the same sentence: *I've decided to give up my job, **although/even though** I love my work.* (*I've given up my job* contrasts with *I love my work.*) ***Even though*** is similar in meaning to *although* but it is more emphatic: *I never bother to lock my car, **even though** I know I should.* We can also put *although* and *even though* at the beginning of sentences: ***Although/Even though** I was planning to say no at first, I've changed my mind.*
- ***whereas*** to introduce a subordinate clause which you are comparing with what you are saying in the main clause: *Travelling gives you time to think, **whereas** working full-time doesn't.* We can also put *whereas* at the beginning of sentences: ***Whereas** I was awake for hours, they slept.*
- ***but*** to contrast two clauses in a sentence: *I very much enjoy writing the column, **but** I've always wanted to travel.*
- ***however*** to contrast two sentences. We usually put *however* at the beginning of a sentence and we put a comma (,) after the word *however*: *I know this is not ideal. **However**, I hope we will work together again.*

REAL WORLD

3.1 Being tactful 3C 4 p34

- We sometimes soften a message by using particular words/ phrases.

USING PAST FORMS
We **were planning** to go the cinema tomorrow.
USING MODALS
They **could** do with being (a bit looser). It **could have** been a bit hotter. I'**d** go for black instead if I were you.
USING VAGUE LANGUAGE
We must all get together **some time.** (They could do with being) **a bit looser.** It was **sort of** interesting in parts. The steak was **on the tough side.**
NOT SOUNDING NEGATIVE
I think darker colours **suit you better.** **I've seen better** performances.
USING ADVERBS OF ATTITUDE
Quite honestly, I've seen better performances. **Unfortunately,** the steak was …

Language Summary 4

VOCABULARY

4.1 News collocations 4A 1 p36

follow* the news
seek publicity*
hold a press conference*
go to press*
make the front page
hit the headlines
run a story
sue for libel*
receive a lot of coverage*
issue a press release*

***follow** to be interested in an event or an activity
***seek publicity** the activity of making certain that somebody or something attracts a lot of attention in the media
***a press conference** a meeting at which a person or organisation makes a public statement and reporters can ask questions
***press** a machine used to print books or newspapers
***libel** writing which contains bad information about someone which is not true
***make the front page** a news story thought to be important enough to go on the front of a newspaper
***coverage** the reporting of a particular important event or subject
***a press release** a statement given to the press to publish if they wish

4.2 Near synonyms 4B 5 p41

- We often avoid repeating the same words (particularly nouns, adjectives, verbs and adverbs) so that what we say or write sounds less repetitive and more interesting: *The Industrial Revolution brought* ***important*** *change to the* ***entire*** *country. The* ***whole*** *of Britain was forced to address* ***fundamental*** *questions.*
- Examples of synonyms from page 41 are as follows.

homo sapiens	man	human beings
village	settlement	
country folk	rural inhabitants	villagers
improvements	developments	
rise	increase	growth

TIPS

- Synonyms are not always interchangeable.

a **formality**: *kid* and *child* are similar but *kid* is more informal. *How are the kids?* (informal)

b **collocations**: *huge* and *large* are similar but do not always collocate with the same words.
A huge / large house; I've got a huge ~~large~~ problem.

c **grammatical agreement**: We can say either *I like / enjoy travelling.* However, we cannot use *enjoy* + infinitive: *I like/~~enjoy~~ to travel.*

d **connotation**: *determined* and *obstinate* are similar but *determined* has a more positive connotation. *I admire her because she's so ~~obstinate~~ / determined.*

GRAMMAR

Preview

FUTURE VERB FORMS

- We use the **Present Simple** for a fixed event on a timetable or a calendar: *The new airport tax* ***comes*** *into effect on Monday.*
- We use the **Present Continuous** for future arrangements: ***Who's meeting*** *you at the station?*
- We use ***be going to*** for a personal plan or intention: ***I'm going to*** *stop reading this paper, it's so right-wing.*
- We use ***be going to*** for a prediction that is based on present evidence: *Look at the time. We****'re going to*** *be late.*
- We use ***will*** for a prediction based on opinion rather than evidence: *I think they****'ll*** *have an early election.*
- We use the **Future Continuous** for something that will be in progress at a certain time in the future: *This time next week we****'ll be having*** *talks with the Prime Minister.*
- We use the **Future Continuous** for something that will happen in the normal course of events – not because you planned it: ***I'll be passing*** *the post office, so I can post that for you.*
- We use the **Future Perfect** for something that will be completed before a certain time in the future: *By the end of the year we****'ll have built*** *10,000 new homes.*

TIP

- We also use the **Present Simple** in clauses beginning with *as soon as, by the time, before, after, until* and *when*: *As soon as he* ***arrives****, I'll tell you.*

4.1 Phrases referring to the future 4A 5 p38

- Newspaper journalists often use phrases in headlines such as *due to/set to/about to/on the verge of* to refer to the future: *Shocking environmental data* ***set to*** *be released.*
- To make a headline into a sentence we might need to add other words such as articles or missing auxiliary verbs, e.g. *be*.

Driving age about to rise → ***The*** *driving age* ***is*** *about to rise.*
Crowded space on the verge of catastrophe → Crowded space ***is*** *on the verge of catastrophe.*
Restrictions set to improve safety on the road → Restrictions ***are*** *set to improve safety on the road.*
Size of fish to shrink as sea temperatures rise → ***The*** *size of fish* ***is*** *to shrink as sea temperatures rise.*
Patients to be entertained by electric drill. → Patients ***are*** *to be entertained by* ***an*** *electric drill.*
Shorter week due to be introduced → ***A*** *shorter week* ***is*** *due to be introduced.*

- We use (*be*) *due to / set to / about to / on the verge of* or *am/is/are to* to talk about something that is ready to happen, probably in the near future.
- We use (*be*) *likely to, unlikely to, sure to, certain to, bound to* to say how certain we are that something will happen.
- We use a noun or verb+*ing* after *on the verge of*: *She's* ***on the verge of leaving*** *her job.*
- We use an infinitive after (*be*) *due to / set to / about to / likely to / sure to / unlikely to / certain to / bound to / is to.*

TIPS

- *due to* is often used when we state a particular time. *Building work is due to start in March.*
- We sometimes use *not about to* when we mean 'not willing to': *I'm not about to drop everything just to pick her up from the station.*
- We can say *on the point/brink of* + verb+*ing* (or noun) to refer to things in the near future. *On the brink of* usually refers to something that is bad, exciting or very important and is usually used in formal English. *A large bank is on the brink of collapse.*
- We can't refer to specific time after *on the verge of/on the brink of*: ~~*He's on the verge of/on the brink of resigning next week*~~.

4.2 Future in the past 4B 10 p42

Compare these two sentences:
We didn't know our ideas were going to be successful.
We believe our ideas are going to be successful.

In the first sentence we know the result (our ideas were successful). In the second sentence we are predicting the result (our ideas are going to be successful).

Look at the diagram. In the first sentence we are talking about the future seen from a point in the past. In the second sentence we are talking about the future seen from now.

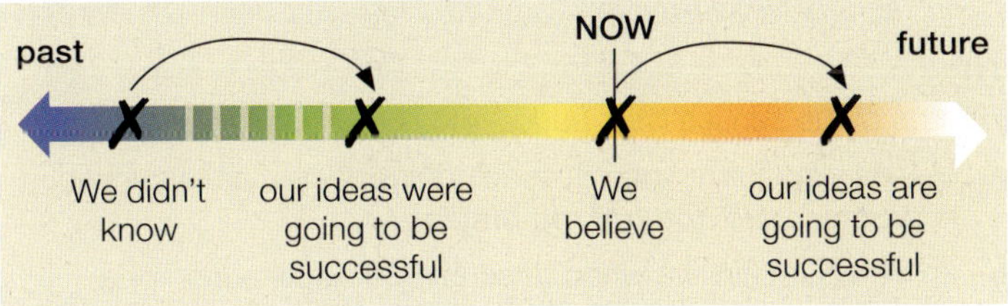

To talk about the future seen from the past, we use the past tenses of the verb forms we would usually use to talk about the future. Compare these sentences:

The future seen from now	The future seen from the past
am/is/are going to + infinitive *… our ideas* ***are going to be*** *successful*	*was/were going to* + infinitive *… our ideas* ***were going to*** *be successful …*
will + infinitive *… these young fans* ***will*** *go on to spend …*	*would* + infinitive *… these young fans* ***would*** *go on to spend …*
is/are supposed to + infinitive *… Star Trek* ***is*** *just* ***supposed to*** *offer …*	*was/were supposed to* + infinitive *… Star Trek* ***was just supposed to*** *offer …*
am/is/are about to + infinitive *… these bits of cardboard and plastic being used on set* ***are about to*** *be …*	*was/were about to* + infinitive *… these bits of cardboard and plastic being used on set* ***were about to*** *be …*
is/are to + infinitive *… they* ***are to find*** *out …*	*was/were to* + infinitive *… they* ***were to find*** *out …*

TIP

- We often need to change time expressions when we talk about the future seen from the past: *There is to be a meeting about it* ***tomorrow***. → *There was to be a meeting about it* ***the following day***.

WRITING

4.1 Punctuation: capital letters and full stops 3 p43

We use capital letters for:

- new sentences: *For instance, Nevertheless*, etc.
- names: *Sam Baker*
- streets and roads: *25 Lime St*
- towns and cities: *Bradford*
- postcodes: *BD5 8LM*
- countries/nationalities/language: *UK*
- titles: *Mr, Mrs, Ms, Dr, Sir, Madam*, etc.
- days of the week: *Sunday, Monday*, etc.
- months of the year: *January, February*, etc.
- places: *Waterloo Station, River Thames*, etc.
- the pronoun 'I': *I'm sorry I'm late.*

TIP

- We sometimes use full stops after abbreviated words such as *Dr., etc., U.S.A.* This is a personal style and is not necessary in most contexts.

4.2 Connecting words: contrast (2) 4 p43

We use:

- ***but*** to introduce something which contrasts with what you have just said: *Viewing figures are down,* ***but*** *the programme has not been cancelled.*
- ***although/though*** to introduce a subordinate clause which mentions something that contrasts with what you are saying in the main clause: ***Although*** *she has been contacted, we have had no reply.*
- ***nevertheless/nonetheless/however*** to introduce a simple clause which contrasts, in an unexpected way, with what has just been said. *I dislike reality TV.* ***Nevertheless,/ Nonetheless,/However****, Callow's new series is worth watching. Nevertheless/nonetheless/however* usually come at the beginning of a sentence (or after a semi-colon) and are followed by a comma: *Few people have the money to spend on great house designs. Nonetheless, these people seem to have unlimited funds.*
- We can also use ***nevertheless/nonetheless*** after *but* to emphasise the contrast: *He only got 50% in his exam, but* ***nevertheless****, that's better than last year.*
- ***despite/in spite of*** to contrast two clauses in the same sentence when we are talking about circumstances which surprisingly, do not prevent something from happening or being true: ***Despite/In spite of*** *all their hard work, they failed to make the deadline. The film was finally completed* ***despite/in spite of*** *the budget issues.*
- ***despite/in spite of*** introduces a subordinate clause: + noun phrase; + verb +-*ing*; + *the fact that* + clause: *Despite / in spite of* ***being*** *late, their proposal will be considered. Despite / In spite of* ***the fact that*** *he was ill, he went into work.*
- We do not use *in spite of/despite* as a conjunction. We use *although/though*: *Although he was late, he stopped to buy some flowers.* not ~~*In spite of/Despite he was late …*~~ .

Language Summary 5

VOCABULARY

5.1 Word building (1): prefixes with multiple meanings 5A 4 p48

- If we don't know the meaning of a noun, adjective or verb, we can often guess from its prefix.

prefix	meaning	example
inter-	between (two things, people, etc.)	interaction
	joined together	interlocked
counter-	in opposition to	counterbalance
	as a reaction to	counter-attack
super-	more than usual	superwoman
	extremely	super-rich
over-	too much	overworked
	from above/on top/across	overhead
semi-	partly	semi-famous
	half	semicircle
under-	not enough	underpaid
	below	underfoot
pseudo-	not real	pseudo-friendship

Preview

VERB + INFINITIVE WITH *TO* OR VERB+*ING*

- When we use two verbs together, the form of the second verb usually depends on the first verb.
- The verbs in **bold** in the table have more than one verb pattern. Both verb patterns have the same meaning.
  I began to watch soaps while I was ill at home. = I began watching soaps while I was ill at home.
- The verbs in red in the table have a different meaning when they are followed by verb+*ing* or infinitive with *to*.
  I remember telling him about tomorrow's training session.
  (= I told him and now I can remember that I did that.)
  I remembered to tell him about tomorrow's training session.
  (= I remembered and then I told him.)

keep on miss **stop** avoid **begin continue** don't mind end up enjoy finish **hate** keep **like love** **forget** **prefer** **regret** **remember** **start** try	+ verb+*ing*
need expect manage **stop** **try** learn **begin continue** decide **forget** **hate** hope **like love** plan **prefer** pretend refuse **regret** **remember** seem **start**	+ infinitive with *to*
help let make	+ object + infinitive
persuade allow encourage **help** ask convince expect force pay teach	+ object + infinitive with *to*
would can could had better might should will would rather	+ infinitive

5.2 Verb + infinitive with *to* or verb+*ing* 5B 5 p50

- Some verbs have a different meaning when they are followed by verb+*ing* or verb + infinitive with *to*.

1 a) *forget* + verb+*ing* = looks back to memories of the past: *I'll never* ***forget losing*** *them.*
b) *forget* + infinitive with *to* = refers to now or in the future: *Don't* ***forget to*** *have a good time, too.*

2 a) *go on* + verb+*ing* = continue an action: *Neymar* ***went on playing*** *for Santos FC throughout his teens.*
b) *go on* + infinitive with *to* = begin a new action: *Making beats* ***went on to become*** *my life.*

3 a) *mean* + verb+*ing* = involve/necessitate: *… it* ***means coordinating*** *really well.*
b) *mean* + infinitive with *to* = intend: *Riding was just* ***meant to make*** *physiotherapy fun.*

4 a) *regret* + verb+*ing* = 'I'm sorry for what's already happened': *He never* ***regretted*** *making that decision.*
b) *regret* + infinitive with *to* is a formal way of saying 'I'm sorry about what I'm just about to say': *I* ***regret to say*** *that at school I was trouble.*

TIP

- Verbs of the senses (*see*, *notice*, etc.) can be followed by:

a) object + *ing* form when describing a repeated action/action in progress: *He* ***noticed me playing***.
b) an object + infinitive when describing a single action or a completed action: *I* ***saw him get*** *into the car.*

5.3 Verb–noun collocations 5B 8 p52

come to* a decision
look into* different options
go on courses
do work experience*/courses
gain an insight* / a place at university
work out* what to do
apply for* a place at university / courses
take some time out* / courses

*__come to__ make a decision or reach a conclusion
*__look into__ examine the facts about a situation
*__work experience__ work in a place, usually unpaid, to gain experience
*__insight__ the ability to understand what something is really like
*__work out__ understand the reasons for something
*__apply for__ ask officially for something (often in writing)
*__time out__ time spent not working or studying

5.4 Work expressions 5C 1 p54

be stuck in a rut /rʌt/ be too fixed in one particular type of job, activity, method: *I've been stuck in a rut at work for over a year and it's time for a change.*
a dead-end job a job in which there is no chance of getting a promotion: *I don't want to end up in some dead-end job like my brother.*
take on too much work accept too much work: *The danger of working for yourself is taking on too much work.*
be snowed under have so much work that you have problems dealing with it all: *We need some more support before we get snowed under.*
talk shop talk about your job with those you work with when not at work: *I'm banning you and Stephanie from talking shop while we're at dinner together.*
a team player someone who is good at working closely with other people: *Ann has never been much of a team player and generally prefers working alone.*
be self-employed not working for an employer but finding work for yourself or having your own business: *I'm self-employed so I tend to work on Saturday mornings.*
a pittance /ˈpɪtəns/ a very small amount of money, especially money received as payment or income: *She works so hard for that company and she's paid a pittance.*
a fortune a large amount of money, goods, property, etc.: *Sara earns a fortune working for a Swiss bank.*
high-powered a very important job or a very successful person: *Isn't your brother a high-powered executive at a computer company?*
run-of-the-mill ordinary and not special or exciting in any way: *We just need someone to do run-of-the-mill office administration.*
be thrown in at the deep end start a new job or activity without enough preparation: *The new job is going to be challenging. I've really been thrown in at the deep end.*
a deadline a time by which something must be done: *The deadline for proposals is not until November.*
against the clock If you do something against the clock, you do it as fast as possible and try to finish it before a certain time: *We would be working against the clock if we accepted the order.*
be up to your eyes in sth be very busy doing something: *I'm up to my eyes in work at the moment.*
take it easy relax and not use too much energy: *I'm going to spend a few weeks at home taking it easy over the summer.*
(climb) the career /kəˈrɪə/ **ladder** the sequence of job positions through which a person progresses in an organisation: *Rob's been steadily climbing the career ladder since he joined the company a few years back.*

GRAMMAR

Preview

REFLEXIVE PRONOUNS

- We use reflexive pronouns (*myself*, *yourself*, etc.) when the subject and the object refer to the same person, thing, etc.: ***She**'s teaching **herself** to swim.* (She's not teaching anybody else to swim.)
- There is a difference between ***each other*** and ***themselves***. We use *each other* when we are talking about actions or feelings that involve two or more people together in the same way: *The children are allowed to read to **each other** before they go to bed.* (Each child is allowed to read a story to the other children.) We use *themselves* when we talk about actions that involve two or more people, but do not involve the people together: *The children are allowed to read to **themselves** before they go to bed.* (The children are allowed to read books individually.)
- We also use reflexive pronouns to emphasise that we do something instead of someone else doing it for us: *I think I'll redecorate the house **myself**.*
- We use *by myself*, *yourself*, etc. to mean 'alone': *Geoff went to the cinema **by himself**.*

5.1 Reflexive pronouns 5A 9 p49

- We can use reflexive pronouns:
  - a after *as well as*, *as* (*for*), *like* etc. instead of object pronouns, although these are possible. This use of the reflexive can show politeness: *Daniel, what makes people like **yourself** want to be an extra?*
  - b to make it clear that an object (after a preposition) refers to the same person/thing as the subject of the verb: *She read the script to **herself**.* (*She read the script to **her*** suggests she read it to a different person)
  - c to emphasise a noun, pronoun or noun phrase: *I like the job **itself**, but …*

  If it is obvious that the object following a preposition must refer to the subject, we use an object pronoun. *I always take a laptop with **me**.* not ~~*I always take a laptop with myself.*~~
- We do not usually use reflexive pronouns with these verbs: *concentrate*, *feel*, *meet*: *… unless I really concentrate* not … ~~*unless I really concentrate myself*~~. *There are times when you feel very tired.* not ~~*There are times when you feel yourself very tired*~~. *It's a great opportunity to meet and have a chat.* not ~~*It's a great opportunity to meet ourselves and have a chat*~~.

TIPS

- We can also use verbs *exert*, *pride* and *occupy* with reflexive pronouns: *Don't exert yourself, lifting heavy boxes. We pride ourselves on good service. I can occupy myself with a book for ages.*
- Some verbs, e.g. *dress*, *shave*, *wash*, are only reflexive if we want to emphasise that someone does the action themselves: *Kate can dress herself now. Do you prefer to shave yourself, or go to the barber's?*

WRITING

5.1 Spelling: *ie* or *ei* 3 p53

- When the letters 'i' and 'e' occur together in words they are sometimes spelled 'ie' and sometimes spelled 'ei'.
- If the sound of the two letters together in a word is /iː/, we often write *ie*: *rel**ie**ve*, *f**ie**ld*, *p**ie**ce* (except after *c*, *conc**ei**ted*, *rec**ei**ve*, *dec**ei**ve*). The exceptions to this rule include: *n**ei**ther*, *s**ei**ze*, *spec**ie**s*.
- If the sound of the two letters in a word is not /iː/, we usually write *ei*, e.g. ***ei**ght*, *th**ei**r*, *n**ei**ghbour*. The exceptions to this rule include: *fr**ie**nd*, *pat**ie**nce*.

5.2 Connecting words: time (2) 4 p53

We use:

- ***instantly***, ***straightaway*** or ***at once*** to mean 'immediately': *I started work **straightaway/at once/instantly**.*
- ***immediately*** to mean 'without waiting': *I **immediately** started work./I started work **immediately**.*
- ***at once*** also to mean 'at the same time': *They all started talking **at once**.*
- ***previously*** to mean 'before the time that is referred to'. We do not use a time adverbial after *previously*: *I hadn't done anything very useful **previously**./**Previously**, I hadn't done anything very useful.*
- ***before*** to talk about an event earlier in time. We can use a time adverbial (*yesterday*, *last week*, etc.) or reference word (*this*, *that*), or another clause (*I met her*, etc.) after *before* if the time is not clear: *I hadn't done anything very useful **before** this/this week./**Before this**, I hadn't done anything very useful.*
- ***after*** to mean 'following': *I was relieved to get a new job **after a few months**. **After** that day, we were inseparable all through the summer. The year **after**, we had to go back to college.*
- ***later*** to mean 'after that time': *A few months **later**.*
- ***eventually*** to mean 'after a long time or a lot of effort': *I'd **eventually** like to go on to become a tour guide./**Eventually**, I'd like to go on to become a tour guide. I'd like to go on to become a tour guide **eventually**.*
- ***in the end*** to mean 'eventually': ***In the end**, I hope to go on to become a tour guide./I hope to go on to become a tour guide **in the end**.*
- ***recently/lately*** to mean 'not long ago': ***Lately/Recently**, I've been working as a guide./I've been working as a guide **lately/recently**.* We can use *recently* with both the past simple and the present perfect: *I've seen/I saw Mark recently.* However, we can't use *lately* with the past simple: ~~*I saw Mark lately*~~.
- ***up until*** to mean 'up to the time that': ***Up until** then, I had never worked.*
- ***prior to*** in formal contexts to mean 'before a particular time or event': ***Prior to** this, I had never worked.*

REAL WORLD

5.1 Conversational strategies 5C 5 p55

INCLUDING SOMEONE IN THE CONVERSATION

You look dubious, (Liz).
You're very quiet, (Josh).

ADDING SOMETHING TO THE ARGUMENT

Not to mention …
And of course there's always …

STRESSING AN IMPORTANT POINT

That's exactly what I was trying to get at.
That's precisely what I mean.

ENCOURAGING SOMEONE TO CONTINUE

Carry on, (Liz). You were saying?
What were you about/going to say, (Tracey)?

JUSTIFYING WHAT YOU SAY

All I'm saying is …
What I'm trying to say is …

GETTING THE CONVERSATION BACK ON TRACK

Anyway, (assuming you do want promotion) …
To get back to what (I) was saying about (promotion) …

SAYING YOU AGREE WITH SOMEONE

I'm with (you) on that.
I'd go along with that.

CONCEDING SOMEONE IS RIGHT

You've got me there!
Well, I can't disagree with that.

DISAGREEING POLITELY

Oh, I don't know about (that).
Actually, I'm not sure you can say (that).

ASKING SOMEONE TO SAY MORE ABOUT A TOPIC

By (provision) you mean …?
What do you mean when you say (provision)?

Language Summary 6

VOCABULARY

6.1 Words with different but related meanings 6A 9 p59

- Sometimes one word can have completely different meanings: *I commute on the **train** to work every day. She wants to **train** to be a psychologist.*
- Sometimes one word can have different meanings but the meanings are related: *The weather's **fine** today. I'm feeling **fine** now.*
- **odd** generally means 'unusual or peculiar' and can specifically mean:
  - a 'not matching' (i.e. not having the same colour or pattern as something else): *She wanted to put on **odd** socks every day.*
  - b 'strange or unexpected': *It was **odd** that he didn't phone.*
- **sweet** describes people, animals or food and generally means 'pleasant'. It can specifically mean:
  - a 'charming, attractive': *His daughter is really **sweet**.*
  - b 'sugary': *Dark chocolate isn't **sweet** enough for me.*
- **top** can generally mean 'the highest point or part in distance or quality' and can specifically mean:
  - a 'the highest part': *the **top** of her sweater.*
  - b 'the most successful': *He's always **top** of the class.*
- The general meaning of the words in **bold** is:
  - a **branch**: a division or subdivision of something
  - b **flat**: horizontally level without variation
  - c **break**: interrupt the regularity, uniformity, or arrangement of something
  - d **plain**: without pattern or interesting features
  - e **heavy**: a great amount or weight of something

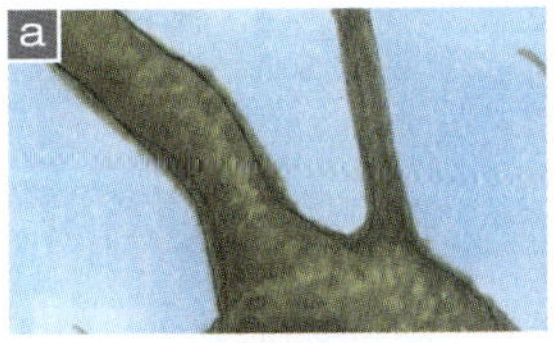

a **branch** of a tree

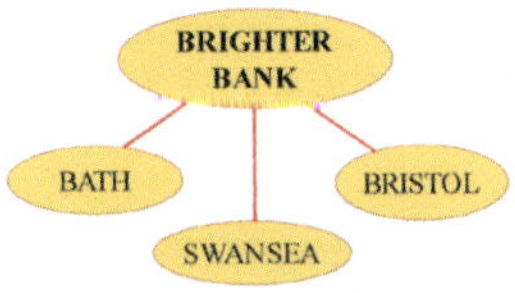

Brighter Bank has **branches** in Bath, Swansea and Bristol.

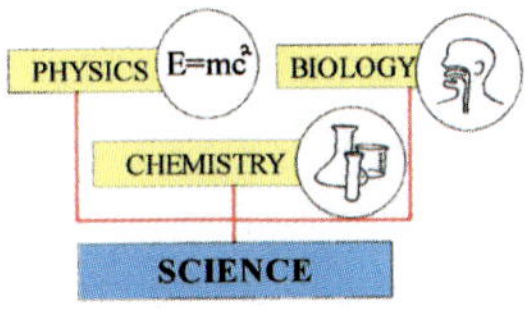

Biology is a **branch** of science.

Sally feels **flat**.

a **flat** piece of land

This lemonade is **flat**.

Tom had a **break** for coffee.

break a window

break the law

plain paper

plain food

a **plain** face

heavy traffic

a **heavy** coat

Martin is **heavy** sleeper.

6.2 Word pairs 6B 9 p62

take it or leave it said about something that you quite like but that you do not love or need badly: *I quite like coffee, but I can take it or leave it.*

on and off happening sometimes: *She's been working on and off for an advertising consultancy, but has never had a regular position with them.*

hit and miss if something is hit and miss you cannot depend on it to be of good quality, on time, accurate, etc: *Our recent marketing campaigns have been a bit hit and miss.*

over and over again happening or done many times: *I've watched this advert over and over again, but I still don't understand it.*

back and forth going from one thing to another, repeatedly: *I go back and forth between products.*

make or break make something a success or a failure: *This job is so big it could make or break the company.*

each and every every thing or person in a group or category: *Each and every student must register for the exam by tomorrow.*

part and parcel of (sth) be a necessary feature of a particular experience: *A quality website is part and parcel of most successful businesses nowadays.*

time after time repeatedly, again and again

in leaps /liːps/ **and bounds** /baʊndz/ changing or progressing very quickly: *Online marketing has come on in leaps and bounds over the last 10 years.*

GRAMMAR

Preview

WAYS OF COMPARING

- We can use different phrases with comparative adjectives to talk about big, small, or no differences.

a big difference	a great deal (more successful) considerably (better) far (smaller)	than
	nowhere near as (scary) twice as (hard) not nearly as (big)	as
a small difference	slightly (more/less willing)	than
	almost as (difficult) nearly as (beautiful) not quite as (clever)	as
no difference	just as (helpful)	as
	no (longer) not any (more expensive)	than

TIPS

- We use comparatives with *than*: *The paperwork is considerably more/less complicated than I thought it would be.*
- We use adjectives with *as … as*: *To me, interviews are nowhere near as scary as exams.*
- We can use ***twice/three times/four times***, etc. + **as …** ***(as)*** to compare two things: *However, it's twice as hard in the winter, when the weather is bad.*
- We can use ***the*** **+ comparative/*more* …,** ***the*** **+ comparative/*more*** to say that one thing depends on the other: *The more you work, the more you earn.*
- We can use ***just*** with **as … as** to add emphasis: *Mike is just as helpful as his brother.*

6.1 Formal and informal ways of comparing

6A 3 p57

- The formal words and phrases highlighted in the texts on pages 56 and 57 indicate a big or a small difference.

a big difference	a small difference
decidedly	somewhat
a good deal	barely (any)
significantly	marginally
distinctly	

- There are also some informal phrases which can modify comparative forms to indicate a big or small difference.

a big difference	a small difference
way	a tiny bit
loads	much the same
miles	pretty much the same
not half as … as	more or less the same
not anywhere near as … as	

Preview

ADVERBS

- We usually add *-ly* to adjectives to make **adverbs**: *surprising* → *surprisingly.*
- When an adjective ends in *-y*, the 'y' changes to 'i' before adding *-ly*: *unhappy* → *unhapp**ily***. There are some exceptions, e.g. *shy* → *sh**yly***.
- When an adjective ends in *-ble*, the 'e' changes to 'y': *incredi**ble*** → *incredib**ly***
- When an adjective ends in *-ic*, we add *-ally*: *scientif**ic*** → *scientific**ally***
- With some adjectives, we don't make the adverb with *-ly*: *late* → *late*, *hard* → *hard*, *high* (= *tall*) → *high*, *good* → *well*, *wrong* → *wrong*, *early* → *early*
- Some adverbs have two forms and there is a difference in meaning between them:
  - a *late* means 'not on time' and *lately* means 'recently': *He arrived late. I haven't seen him lately.*
  - b *hard* is the opposite of 'soft' and *hardly/barely* mean 'very little': *She hit him hard. I've hardly/barely spoken to you.*
  - c *high* means 'a long way up' and *highly* means 'to a large degree': *The cat climbed high into the trees. He had a really highly paid job but left to look after his children.*

6.2 Position of adverbials

6B 4 p60

- Adverbials of **place** describe where something happens/happened: *…* ***inside the bathrooms***.
- Adverbials of **time** describe when something happens/happened: ***These days*** *it's quite normal to …*
- Adverbials of **manner** describe how something is done: *… grabbing their attention* ***by force***.
- Adverbials of **indefinite frequency** describe how often something happens: *… it* ***sometimes*** *antagonises people.*
- Adverbials describing **level of certainty** say how likely it is that something happens: *Being intrusive is* ***probably*** *forgivable … .*
- Adverbials of **comment** are used to express/give an opinion on what we are saying: ***Interestingly***, …
- Adverbials of **definite frequency** describe how often something happens: *…* ***every day***.
- **In front position**, we put the adverb before the subject.

FRONT POSITION

comment	*surprisingly*	***Surprisingly****, it worked.*
level of certainty	*maybe, perhaps, surely*	***Maybe*** *the campaign will succeed.*

TIPS

- Adverbials of **time**, **definite frequency**, and adverbials of **indefinite frequency** are also very common in front position. In this position, the adverbials emphasise their meaning in contrast with information previously given: *The agency grew by 8% last year.* ***Next year****, we want to hit 10%.*
- When we put some negative adverbials of time in front position, we invert the subject and verb: ***Not once*** *have I asked you for money.*

- **In mid position** we put the adverbial between the subject and the verb or immediately after either *be* or an auxiliary verb.

MID POSITION

indefinite frequency	*always*	*She's **always** right.*
level of certainty	*probably, definitely*	*He'll **definitely** win.*

TIPS

• Adverbials of **degree** also usually go in mid position, e.g. *almost, hardly, quite, rather*: *I almost resigned.* Some adverbials of degree can go in mid or end position, e.g. *completely, enormously, entirely, slightly*: *I entirely agree.* = *I agree entirely.*

• Adverbials of **manner**, **place** and **time** can also go in mid position. This emphasises them more than any other position and is most common in formal written texts and newspaper reporting: *Pat **reluctantly** admitted defeat. The prime minister **yesterday** repeated that the economy was stable.*

- **In end position**, we put the adverb immediately after the verb or at the end of the clause: *We swim **every day** at our local pool. We swim at our local pool **every day**.*

END POSITION

manner	*hard*	*They work **hard**.*
place	*at the office*	*She's **at the office**.*
time	*a year ago*	*The advert came out **a year ago**.*
definite frequency	*every day*	*I try to exercise **every day**.*
indefinite frequency	*as a rule, from time to time, every so often*	*I work at home **every so often**.*

TIPS

• Where there are several adverbials at the end of the clause, the usual order is manner, place, time: *She sang **beautifully in the concert yesterday**.*

• We usually put adverbials in end position in sentences where there is a verb immediately followed by an object: *We explored the idea **briefly**.* not ~~*We explored briefly the idea*~~. However, if the object is long, then the adverbial can go in other positions: *We explored **briefly** the idea of starting the project in the summer.*

FOCUSING ADVERBIALS

- Focusing adverbials come before the word/phrase we want to stress.
- The position of focusing adverbials can affect the meaning of the sentence.

1a *Jan and I **only** worked on the Volkswagen advert.* (*only* in mid position modifies the verb to mean that Jan and I worked on the Volkwagen advert but we didn't work on anything else)

b ***Only** Jan and I worked on the Volkswagen advert.* (*only* in front position modifies the subject to mean that Jan and I, and nobody else, worked on the Volkswagen advert)

2a *Joe's been everywhere. He's **even** been to Tonga.* (*even* in mid position modifies the verb to mean that Joe's been to Tonga in addition to everywhere else he's been)

b *More and more people have been to Tonga. **Even** Joe's been there.* (*even* in front position modifies the subject to mean that you might not expect Joe to have been to Tonga but he has).

WRITING

6.1 Connecting words: purpose

2 p63

SO AS/IN ORDER (*FOR SOMETHING*) + INFINITIVE WITH *TO*

- We can use ***so as/in order*** (***for something***) + infinitive with *to* to talk about the purpose of an action. We put these phrases at the beginning of a clause: *The colours need to be bolder **so as to/in order to** make the design stand out. **In order for** the campaign **to be** a success, we must increase our budget.*
- In spoken and less formal written English we often simplify these two structures to an infinitive with *to*: *We have done research **to see** which adverts are the most popular.*

IN ORDER THAT/SO THAT/SO

- We use ***in order that***, ***so that*** and ***so*** to talk about the purpose of an action. We put these phrases at the beginning of a clause: ***So that** we can meet our deadlines, we'd appreciate your ideas by tomorrow. I'll send you some possible slogans **in order that** you can decide.*
- ***So (that)*** is less formal than ***in order that***: *I'd like to do a copywriting course **so that** I can go into advertising.*

TIPS

• If we use a **present** verb form in the clause with *in order that / so that*, we usually use a **present** verb form or modal verb in the main clause. The present verb form or modal verb has present or future meaning: *In order that the campaign **is** a success, we **must** increase our budget.*

• If we use a **past** verb form in the main clause, we usually use a **past** verb form or modal verb in the clause with *in order that/ so that*. This past verb form or modal verb has past meaning: *I **warned** you, in order that you **wouldn't** be disappointed.*

6.2 Punctuation: commas

3 p63

We use commas:

- after introductory clauses beginning with *after, although, as, because, if, since, when* and *while* that come before the main clause: *If the actors had admitted the truth, there would not have been a problem.*
- to separate three or more words, phrases, or clauses written in a series. We do <u>not</u> usually use a comma before the final 'and': *This approach might work in a number of industries, such as fashion, book sales and music.*
- after introductory words such as *surprisingly, however: Not surprisingly, some people disagree with this.*
- either side of non-defining relative clauses: *The campaign, which was the first of its kind, was very effective.* However, we do not use commas in defining relative clauses: *That's the man who I saw shoplifting.*
- after the verb and before the opening quotation marks in direct speech: *Tom Hicks, president of the company, said, "When people find out they have been fooled, they may feel angry."*
- before the end quotation marks in direct speech when the quote is followed by the speaker: *"You should set up a Neighbourhood Watch scheme," said the policeman.*
- In a list of adjectives, we use a comma when it can be replaced by the word 'and': *Buzz marketing requires a confident, creative approach.*

Language Summary 7

VOCABULARY

7.1 Phrases with *get* 7A 2 p66

get away with sth do wrong and not be punished: *The robbers got away with the jewel theft because there was not enough evidence to convict them.*
get away from sth leave behind: *It's hard for ex-offenders to get away from their criminal record when looking for work.*
get into sth become involved in: *My son has really got into crime novels recently.*
get out of sth avoid doing something you should: *Women are more likely to get out of a prison sentence if they have children.*
get round to sth do something that you have intended to do for a long time: *I lost my credit card a few days ago but I haven't got round to reporting it yet.*
get round sth find a way of dealing with a problem: *The government is trying to get round the problem of overcrowded prisons by releasing some prisoners early.*
get (my, your, our, their, etc.) own back (on sb) take revenge: *After her husband had left her, the woman got her own back by destroying his favourite shirts.*
get back to return to: *It's difficult for prisoners to get back to the life they had before they went to jail.*
get through sth finish something: *It can be more difficult for close relatives to get through a prison sentence than for the criminals themselves.*
get through to sb communicate successfully: *My work involves trying to get through to young offenders who think that crime is their only option.*

7.2 Phrasal nouns 7B 7 p72

- Phrasal nouns are compound nouns formed from verbs and a particle (a preposition or adverb).

break + up → *a break-up*   *out + cry* → *an outcry*
set + back → *a setback*   *on + set* → *an onset*

TIPS

- When phrasal nouns begin with a particle, they have no hyphen (*outlook*, *downpour*, *input*, *onset*, *outcry*). When phrasal nouns begin with a verb, they may or may not have a hyphen, e.g. *kick-off*, *breakdown*, *get-together*.
- Not all phrasal verbs can be made into phrasal nouns: *They pulled down two houses.* not ~~*There was a pulldown of two houses*~~.
- Some phrasal nouns are made up of the same words as phrasal verbs but have different meanings: *The* ***intake*** (= enrolment) *on the course was over 100. He spoke so fast I couldn't* ***take it in*** (= understand and remember).
- Some phrasal nouns are made up of the same words as a phrasal verb but reverse the order of the verb and the particle: *set on* → *onset*, *cry out* → *outcry*.
- Some phrasal nouns are countable and the plural is made by adding 's' to the verb or particle at the end of the phrasal noun: *break-up* → *break-ups*, *outcry* → *outcries*, *setback* → setbacks
- Not all phrasal nouns can be made into phrasal verbs, e.g. *update*, *upshot*, *overkill*, *downtime*.

7.3 Metaphors 7C 1 p74

- A metaphor is a way of describing something by referring to it as something else which has similar qualities. Metaphors use a non-literal meaning of words.

The police **grilled** him for hours.

I **grilled** the meat for five minutes.

grill 1 (non-literal) to ask somebody a lot of questions often over a long time: *The police grilled him for hours about what he'd done that night.* **2** (literal) cook something by direct heat: *I grilled the meat for five minutes.*
warm 1 (non-literal) friendly and affectionate: *We got a warm welcome from my cousin.* **2** (literal) having a comfortably high temperature, although not hot: *The pizza wasn't warm enough so I put it in the microwave.*
storm 1 (non-literal) attack: *The police stormed the building and rescued the hostages.* **2** (literal) an extreme weather condition with strong winds, heavy rain and often thunder and lightning: *The forecast warns a severe storm is on its way.*
flood /flʌd/ **1** (non-literal) fill or enter a place in large numbers or amounts: *The market is flooded with cheap, plastic goods.* **2** (literal) cause to become covered with water: *If it rains any more, the roads will soon be flooded.*
bright 1 (non-literal) clever and quick to learn: *He's a really bright lad – I can't believe he'd turn to crime.* **2** (literal) full of light: *It was such a bright day, I needed my sunglasses.*
dawn /dɔːn/ **1** (non-literal) begin to be understood by somebody: *It suddenly dawned on the inspector who the criminal might be.* **2** (literal) the first light of daybreak: *I have to get up at dawn to drive to work.*
freeze 1 (non-literal) stop moving and become completely still: *When I saw the burglar, I froze and couldn't move.* **2** (literal) lower the temperature of something below 0°C causing it to become very cold and often hard: *It was so cold that the lake froze.*
fly 1 (non-literal) pass very quickly: *The crime novel was so exciting, the time flew.* **2** (literal) travel through the air by plane, etc.: *My parents flew to Brazil last week.*
crack 1 (non-literal) become very stressed because of work pressure etc.: *Vicky is a good choice for the job because she doesn't crack under pressure.* **2** (literal) a very narrow space between parts of something: *I suddenly noticed the large crack in the ceiling.*

GRAMMAR

Preview

CONDITIONALS: BASIC FORMS

Zero conditional

- The zero conditional talks about an event/situation that is a general truth/fact: *If you do more than 50km/h along this road, you get caught by speed cameras.*
- We make the zero conditional with: *if* + subject + Present Simple, subject + Present Simple.

TIP

• *If* and *when* have the same meaning in the zero conditional: *If/When I look after plants, they die.*

First conditional

- The first conditional talks about a possible or likely future result.
- The *if* clause talks about things that are possible but not certain: *If you get any more points for speeding,* … (maybe you'll get more points for speeding). The main clause says what we think the result will be in this situation: *you'll be banned from driving.*
- We make the first conditional with: *if* + subject + Present Simple, subject + *will/won't* + infinitive.
- We can use *might* instead of *will* in the main clause to mean 'will perhaps'.

Second conditional

- We use the second conditional to talk about an unlikely or imaginary situation in the present or future. We often use it to talk about the opposite of what is true or real: *If you lost your licence, you'd probably lose your job.* (but you haven't lost your licence).
- We make the second conditional with: *if* + subject + Past Simple, subject + *'d* (= *would*)/*wouldn't* + infinitive.
- We can use *could* or *might* instead of *would* in the main clause. *Might* means 'would perhaps'. *Could* means 'would be possible': *If I won the lottery, I could/might go travelling.*

Third conditional

- We use the third conditional to talk about imaginary situations in the past. They are often the opposite of what really happened: *If you'd hadn't gone through that red light, the police wouldn't have stopped you* (you did go through that red light so the police stopped you).
- We make the third conditional with: *if* + subject + Past Perfect, subject + *'d* (= *would*)/*wouldn't* + *have* + past participle.
- We can use *could* and *might* in the main clause. *Might* means 'would perhaps'. *Could* means 'would be possible': *If I had gone to college, I might/could have studied maths.*

7.1 Conditionals 7A 5 p68

CONDITIONALS: NON-BASIC FORMS

- We can use a variety of verb forms in conditional sentences, not only those used in the four 'basic' conditionals.
  - a A **modal** is used instead of a present form: *If a person doesn't want to leave forensic evidence, they* ***should*** *just slide through a window.* (variation of zero conditional; a general truth)
  - b The **future** with ***going to*** is used to show future intention: *If you****'re going to*** *commit a burglary, you'll have to be careful what you wear.* (variation of first conditional; a possible future event)
  - c A **continuous form** is used instead of a simple form to emphasise an action in progress: *If I* ***were committing*** *a burglary, I'd be better off wearing gloves.* (variation of second conditional; an imaginary present/future event) *One burglar would have got away with it completely if he* ***hadn't been sweating***. (variation of third conditional; an imaginary past event)

TIP

• We can make variations of all of the four 'basic' conditional forms with these future, continuous and modal forms. *If I'm going to be late, I always ring home.* (future used instead of the present as a variation of a zero conditional)

MIXED CONDITIONALS

- In mixed conditionals, the main clause and the *if* clause sometimes refer to a different time period. The most common combinations are second and third conditionals. Compare:
  1 *If the kidnapper* ***hadn't licked*** *that envelope, he* ***wouldn't be*** *in prison now.* (mixed conditional)
  2 *If the kidnapper* ***hadn't licked*** *that envelope, he* ***wouldn't have gone*** *to prison.* (third conditional)

  In both conditionals we are referring to imaginary situations.
  1 The first sentence is a 'mixed' conditional because the *if* clause refers to a situation in the past and the main clause refers to a condition in the present (he is in prison now). In the *if* clause, we use a standard construction for the third conditional and in the main clause we use the construction of the second conditional (*would* + infinitive).
  2 In the second sentence, the *if* clause and the main clause refer to the past (he licked the envelope and went to prison) and we use a standard construction for a third conditional.
- Compare:
  1 *If they* ***weren't*** *such good actors, most of them* ***would have been found out*** *much earlier.* (mixed conditional)
  2 *If they* ***hadn't been*** *such good actors, most of them* ***would have been found out*** *much earlier.* (third conditional)

  In both conditionals we are referring to imaginary situations.
  1 The first sentence is a 'mixed' conditional because the *if* clause refers to a situation in the present (they are good actors) and the main clause refers to a condition in the past. In the *if* clause, we use a standard construction for the second conditional (Past Simple) and in the main clause we use the construction of the third conditional (*would* + *have* + past participle).
  2 In the second sentence the *if* clause and the main clause refer to a situation in the past (they were good actors and they weren't found out) and we use a standard construction for a third conditional.

TIP

• In conditionals that refer to unreal situations, we can use other combinations of verb forms if the time in the *if* clause is not the same as the time in the main clause. For example:

a *If **I hadn't lost** my bag, **I'd be leaving** tomorrow.* (*if* clause refers to the past and the main clause refers to the future)

b *If he **didn't have to** go back next week, I **would have invited** him to come.* (*if* clause refers to the future and the main clause refers to the past)

c *If we **have to pay** them next week, we **would need** to get the money now.* (*if* clause refers to the future and the main clause refers to the present)

d *If they **arrest** him now, they **would have** to charge him by tomorrow.* (*if* clause refers to the present and the main clause refers to the future)

FORMAL CONDITIONALS

- We use ***should*** in the *if* clause in the first conditional if we want to suggest that something is very unlikely. *If it should rain, we won't go out.* We can use ***happen to*** in a similar way or combine them (*should happen to*): *… if anyone **happens to** come across a body … .*
- We can use inversion in unreal conditional sentences when the first verb in the *if* clause is *were*, *had* or *should*. In these sentences, we can leave out *if* and we put the verb at the start of the clause:

  a ***Were they to find out** the truth, we would be in serious trouble.* (= *If they were to find out the truth …*)

  b ***Had she not tried** to sell the car, they would never have caught her.* (= *If she hadn't tried to sell the car, …*)

  c ***Should you see** the man again, please call us immediately.* (= *If you should see the man again, …*)

If a person doesn't want to leave forensic evidence, they should just slide through a window.

Preview

PASSIVE FORMS

- In a passive sentence, the focus is on what happens to someone/something rather than on who or what does the action.
- We often use the passive when we don't know who or what does the action.

passive verb form	be	past participle
Present Simple	*am/are/is*	*sent*
Present Continuous	*am/are/is being*	*blamed*
Past Simple	*was/were*	*written*
Past Continuous	*was/were being*	*encouraged*
Present Perfect Simple	*has/have been*	*stolen*
Past Perfect Simple	*had been*	*left*
be going to	*am/are/is going to be*	*announced*
modal	*should, could,* etc. + *be*	*told*
modal + *have* + past participle	*could, should,* etc. + *have* + *been*	*invited*

7.2 Impersonal report structures 7B 3 p71

- We use impersonal report structures when we want to distance ourselves from information which is not necessarily our opinion. They are commonly found in reports and newspaper articles.

REPORTING WITH THE PASSIVE

- To make impersonal report structures we can use:

  a *it* + passive + *that* clause: ***It is claimed that** even your financial records can be accessed.* Other verbs which are commonly used with this structure are: *accept, agree, allege, believe, consider, expect, feel, know, predict, say, suggest, think, understand.*

  b subject + passive + infinitive with *to*: ***Cameras are known to operate** in more and more buildings.* Other verbs which are commonly used with this structure are: *believe, consider, find, say, think.*

  c *there* + passive + infinitive with *to*: ***There are now estimated to be** more mobile phones than people in many countries.* Other verbs which are commonly used with this structure are: *allege, believe, claim, expect, find, say, think.*

TIPS

• We use a variety of infinitive forms with impersonal report structures: *She is known **to have spent** five years in India. He is rumoured **to be resigning** next month.*

• We often use these verbs to report with the passive: *claim, allege, estimate, believe, think, fear, expect, report, understand.*

REPORTING WITH *SEEM* AND *APPEAR*

- The verbs *seem* and *appear* can also be used to distance yourself from events you are reporting; *seem* and *appear* are **not** used in the passive. ***It seems that** they will soon become the norm … . **Opinion appears to be** divided. **There also appear to be** many hospitals using them.*
- We can use a *that*-clause after *It seems*/*It appears*: *It seems **that no one knew** about the problem.*
- We can use an infinitive with *to* after *seem*/*appear*: *The government appears **to be** obsessed with the idea of watching people.*

TIP

• We can also talk about an apparent fact using either *It* + *seem/appear* + *that* clause: *It appeared that people were unaware they were being watched.* or subject (e.g. *people*) + *seem/appear* + infinitive with *to*: *In the main, people seem to support the use of CCTV.*

WRITING

7.1 Connecting words: condition 2 p73

- We can use ***unless*** in conditionals to mean 'if not': ***Unless*** *ex-prisoners are given help, they are likely to re-offend.*
- We can use ***in case*** to talk about something we do in order to be ready for possible future situations. If the clause refers to the future, *in case* is followed by a verb form in the present: *Take a sandwich* ***in case*** *you get hungry later.*
- We can use ***otherwise*** when we talk about an undesirable situation which would happen if something else did not happen. We usually put ***otherwise*** at the beginning of a clause: *We must act now,* ***otherwise*** *the prison population will double.*
- We often use ***provided/providing***, ***as long as*** and ***assuming*** instead of *if* in conditionals: *Ex-prisoners should be helped financially,* ***as long as*** *there is enough money.*
- ***Provided/providing*** and ***as long as*** mean 'only if (this happens)': *Prisoners can become responsible citizens,* ***providing*** *we allow them to.*
- We can use ***whether*** in conditionals when you are mentioning two or more alternatives. We put ***whether*** in front of the first alternative and ***or*** in front of the second alternative: ***Whether*** *the governor is right* ***or*** *wrong, there are many who disagree.*
- ***Imagine*** and ***suppose/supposing*** have the same meaning (= form a picture in your mind about what something could be like): ***Imagine/Suppose/Supposing*** *the prisoners aren't well enough to work, what happens then?*
- We can use ***imagine*** and ***suppose/supposing*** as an alternative for *if* in questions: ***Imagine/Suppose/Supposing*** *there was no crime, what kind of world would we live in?*

7.2 Punctuation: colons and semi-colons

3 p73

We can use colons:

- to introduce lists or to indicate a subdivision of a topic: *There are three sections: the introduction, the main argument and the conclusion.*
- when the second clause explains the first: *The new traffic laws will be passed early next year: the current laws are no longer sufficient.*

We can use semi-colons:

- instead of full stops and commas to separate two main clauses which are connected in meaning: *Learning to drive is not easy; it takes time and a great deal of concentration. The conclusions in this paper are incomplete; further research needs to be done.*
- instead of full stops to end a clause before a conjunctive adverb (*however, nevertheless*, etc.): *After the operation, driving is prohibited for 48 hours; however, after that period, you can resume driving as normal.*

TIP

• We tend to use full stops and commas instead of semi-colons in modern written English.

REAL WORLD

7.1 Functions and intonation of questions 7C 5 p74

- Intonation patterns in English are varied and complicated. However, the following guidelines may be helpful.
- We often ask questions to find out new information (N) or check if our information is correct (C).

  What does? (N)

  Isn't this about the time George usually goes out? (C)

  How much? (C)

  So, you went out on your own, did you? (C)

  How come? (N)
- We often use:
  1. a **falling** tone when asking questions to find out new information.
  2. a **rising** tone when checking information we think is right.
  3. a **falling** tone in question tags when we expect the listener to confirm that we are right.
- We sometimes have different reasons for asking questions, other than requesting 'new' or checking 'old' information. Sometimes no reply is expected and a **falling** intonation is used. For example:

  a Giving instructions:

  Could we just go over this one more time?

  b Aggressive/defensive response to a question:

  How should I know? / So what?

  c Making a sarcastic comment:

  Isn't that a coincidence?

  d A rhetorical question (expecting agreement):

  He never stays in on a Friday evening, does he?

TIP

• We use a rising tone in question tags when we are finding out new information:

She'll be back later, won't she?

Language Summary 8

VOCABULARY

8.1 Phrases with *time* 8A 1 p76

have time to kill have nothing to do for a particular period of time: *If you've got time to kill, you could do some washing up.*
in plenty of time earlier than an arranged time or deadline: *If I take the motorway, we'll arrive in plenty of time.*
take (my/your/etc.) time said to mean that someone can spend as much time as they need in doing something: *There's no hurry for the report. Take your time.*
have time to spare have an excess of time to do an activity: *We arrived at the airport with time to spare so we did a bit of shopping before checking in.*
for the time being said to describe a situation that will be like that for a limited period of time but may change later: *For the time being, I'm going to stay in London.*
it's only a matter of time used to say something is certain to happen but you do not know when: *It's only a matter of time before we will experience an environmental catastrophe.*
there's no time like the present said to encourage someone to take action immediately instead of waiting: *Why don't you call him now? There's no time like the present.*
have (got) no time for sb/sth disapprove of somebody/something and not want to be involved with them: *I've got no time for people moaning about the smoking ban.*
make time for sb/sth fit somebody/something into a busy schedule: *We must make time for a meeting before starting the new project.*
give sb a hard time make things difficult for someone: *My wife gives me a hard time about buying bottled water.*

8.2 Word building (2): suffixes 8B 5 p81

NOUNS

- Some nouns and verbs have the same form, e.g. *a sound/sound*, *a change/change*, *a challenge/challenge*, *a plan/plan*, *a test/test*.
- We can make **nouns** by adding these suffixes to **verbs**: *-ance*, *-y*, *-er*, *-sion*, *-al*, *-ment*, *-ure*.

  disturb → *disturb**ance***

  recover → *recover**y***

  ride → *ride**r***

  divide → *divi**sion***

  survive → *surviv**al***

  excite → *excite**ment***

  fail → *fail**ure***

- We can make **nouns** by adding these suffixes to **adjectives**: *-ness*, *-ity*. If an adjective ends in *-y*, we usually change the 'y' to an 'i' before adding the suffix.

  happy → *happi**ness***

  possible → *possibil**ity***

VERBS, ADJECTIVES, ADVERBS

- To make **adjectives** from **nouns** we can use *-ly*, *-y*, *-ous*, *-al*, *-ic*, *-ed*: *coward/coward**ly***, *mood/mood**y***, *courage/courage**ous***, *culture/cultur**al***, *sympathy/sympathet**ic***, *talent/talent**ed***
- To make **adverbs** from **adjectives** we can use *-ly*: *recent/recent**ly***, *confident/confident**ly***, *final/final**ly***
- To make **adjectives** from **verbs** we can use *-ive*, *-ent/-ant*, *-able/-ible*: *create/creat**ive***, *depend/depend**ent***, *remark/remark**able***
- To make **verbs** from **adjectives** we can use *-ise*, *-en*, *-ify*: *rational/rational**ise***, *wide/wid**en***, *clear/clar**ify***

TIPS

- Sometimes we change the spelling of the word before we add a suffix: *clear* → *clarify*, *create* → *creative*
- Sometimes verbs and adjectives have the same form, e.g. *dry*, *warm*, *calm*: *Calm down! He's always quite calm.*
- We can make abstract nouns by adding these suffixes to concrete nouns: *-hood*, *-ship*, e.g. *childhood*, *friendship*.
- The American spelling of *-ise* is *-ize*: *criticize*, *realize*, etc.

GRAMMAR

Preview

WISH, IF ONLY

- We often use ***I wish …*** or ***If only …*** to talk about imaginary situations. They are often used to talk about the opposite of what is true.
- We use ***wish/If only*** + Past Simple to make wishes about states or activities in the present: *If only I **knew** someone who could help. I wish Tom **was/were** here.*
- We use ***wish/If only*** + Past Continuous to make wishes about actions in progress: *I wish it **wasn't/weren't raining**.*
- We use ***wish/If only*** + Past Perfect to make wishes about past events, states, etc. These wishes are used to express regret and are often the opposite of what happened: *If only I **had known** you were coming.* (but I didn't know) *If only **we'd been taught** languages at school.* (but we weren't)
- We use ***wish/If only*** + *could* + infinitive to make wishes about abilities or possibilities: *I wish I **could** live here.*
- We use ***wish/If only*** + *would* + infinitive to make wishes about things other people, organisations, etc. do that we would like to change. This is often used to show annoyance or impatience about things that are outside our control: *I wish more young people **would** vote.* (but they refuse to do so) *If only Nancy **would** get her hair cut.* (But she refuses to do so).
- After constructions with **wish**, we often add a clause with *but* + subject + auxiliary verb: *I wish I could live here, **but I can't**.* (the situation now is that I can't live here). *I wish I hadn't broken up with him **but I did**.* (the situation is that I broke up with him in the past). *I wish I wasn't going to the dentist tomorrow, **but I am**.* (the situation is that I'm going to the dentist in the future)

TIPS

- We can say *I wish I/he/she/it was* … or *I wish I/he/she/it were* … : *I wish I **was/were** more organised.*
- We do not often say *I wish I would* … . e.g. *I wish I didn't smoke.* not ~~*I wish I wouldn't smoke*~~.

8.1 Past verb forms with present or future meaning 8A 6 p78

- Past verb forms do not always refer to past time.
- None of these sentences refer to past time. Instead, they all tell us what the speaker would like to happen.
  1 It's time to accept the fact that everyone can make a difference.
  2 It's time **we** all accepted the fact that everyone can make a difference.
  1 I'd sooner do one of the jobs.
  2 I'd sooner **someone else** was doing one of the jobs.
  1 I'd prefer to get directly involved.
  2 I'd prefer it if a lot more **people** got directly involved.
  1 I'd rather look at the small things I could do.
  2 I'd rather **people** looked at the small things they could do.
- The verbs above in blue are all infinitive forms (with or without *to*). When *it's time* and *would prefer* are followed by a verb we use an infinitive with *to*. When *would sooner* and *would rather* are followed by a verb, we use an infinitive.
- The verbs in pink are either Past Simple or Past Continuous verb forms. When *it's time*, *would sooner*, *would rather* and *would prefer it if* are followed by a subject + verb, we use a past verb form.

TIPS

• We can also say *It's about time* or *it's high time* + subject + past verb form to suggest something is urgent: *It's high time we **realised** we can't keep using up the earth's resources like this.*

• When we talk about past situations with *would sooner / would rather* + subject + verb, we use the Past Perfect or Past Perfect Continuous: *I'd rather you**'d told** me before.*

• When the preference is also in the past, we can use *would have preferred it if*: *We would have preferred it if you **had warned** us at the time.*

8.2 *wherever, whoever, whatever, etc.* 8B 9 p82

- When we add *ever* to question words (*wherever, whoever, whenever, whatever, whichever, however*) it usually has one of these meanings:
  1 It doesn't matter *where*, *who*, *when*, etc.; it can be any place, anyone, any time, etc.:
  ***Whoever** saw the photos identified the same emotions.* (it doesn't matter who saw the photos)
  ***Wherever** this experiment was carried out, the results were the same.* (it doesn't matter where the experiment was done)
  ***Whenever** you do this in private …* (it doesn't matter when you do this)
  2 An unknown place, person, time, etc.
  ***Whoever** said that is wrong.* (I don't know who the person was)

TIPS

• *Whenever* can also mean 'every time': ***Whenever** she calls, I'm out.* (= Every time she calls, I'm out.) *Whoever, whichever* and *whatever* can be the subject or the object of the verb: ***Whoever** saw you …*, (subject) ***Whoever** you saw …*, (object)

• *However* can be followed by an adverb: *However hard she tries, she can't please her teacher.* (It doesn't matter how hard she tries.)

• *Whichever* is often followed by *of*: ***Whichever of** you is last out of the house, lock the door.*

• We can use *wherever, whoever, however, whatever, whenever* and *whichever* to show surprise or to emphasise something:
a *What's the matter?* (you look sad)
b ***Whatever's** the matter?* (emphasises the question, for example because the person is crying)

• We can use *wherever, whoever, however/whatever*, etc. in informal conversation as an answer to a question, to indicate that we really don't mind. *Whatever* is the most common of these expressions: **A** *What do you want to eat?* **B** *Whatever.* This use of 'whatever' can also suggest that the speaker really doesn't care and therefore might seem impolite.

WRITING

8.1 Spelling: commonly misspelled words 3 p83

These words are commonly misspelled: *receipt, accommodation, colleague, acquaint/acquaintance, business, address, medicine, exaggerate, admitted, beginning.*
Other words include: *necessary, occurs, government, (un)hygienic, neighbour/neighbourhood, gradually.*

8.2 Connecting words and expressions: cause and effect 4 p83

leads to/results in (verb + prep) causes sth: *This leads to traffic jams on major roads, which results in severe delays and frayed tempers.*
due to/ owing to caused by sth; because of sth: *Most cities suffer from increased pollution due to / owing to the constant traffic on our roads. Many people suffer from allergies due to / owing to the poor quality of the air.*
so (that) used to show the purpose of sth: *It is time we dealt with the traffic situation so (that) we can improve the quality of life for those who live in cities.*
in order to/to with the purpose of doing or achieving something: *It is necessary for the public to take action in order to persuade the government to intervene. It's high time something was done to improve the cleanliness of our streets.*

TIPS

• In formal, written English, we don't usually use **owing to** after the verb **be**. *The road accidents were **due to** bad weather.* not ~~*The road accidents were **owing to** bad weather.*~~

• *so (that)* is followed by: subject + verb
*Please sign our petition and pass it on to your contacts **so that** as many people as possible can support this cause.*

• *in order to* is followed by an infinitive verb without *to*.
*It is necessary to take action **in order to** persuade the government to intervene.*

Language Summary 9

VOCABULARY

9.1 *Price and cost* 9A 1 p86

- *Price* and *cost* have similar meanings but are used in different ways.
- *Price* (noun) means 'the amount of money for which something is sold': *The **price** of oil has risen sharply. Price* (verb) is often used in the passive to say what the price of something is: *The television was **priced** at £1,400.*
- *Cost* means 'the amount of money needed to buy, do or make something': *Is the cost of dental treatment high?* (noun) *How much does this **cost**?* (verb)
- We can use *price* and *cost* to make words/phrases such as:

reasonably priced*	cost-effective*
half price*	cost of living*
priceless*	cost a fortune*
price tag*	
overpriced*	
at any price*	

PRICE

***reasonably** /ˈriːznəbli/ **priced** not expensive: *Do you think basic commodities are reasonably priced?*
***half price** half the usual price: *The big department stores have all got sales on and everything is half price.*
***priceless** describes an object which has such a high economic or sentimental value, the price of it cannot be calculated: *Do you have anything that you would consider priceless?*
***a price tag** a piece of paper with a price on, which is fixed to a product: *When you shop for clothes, do you always check the price tag before you buy them?*
***overpriced** costing too much: *Have you bought anything recently that you thought was overpriced?*
***at any price** however much something cost: *I love my coat so much; I would have bought it at any price.*

COST

***cost-effective** If an activity is cost-effective, it is good value for the amount of money paid: *Travelling by train in Britain is not cost-effective.*
***cost of living** the amount of money that a person needs to live on: *Has the cost of living risen much over the last year?*
***cost a fortune** be very expensive: *Have you ever bought something that cost a fortune and then regretted it?*

TIP

- When we ask about the price or cost of something, we usually say *How much does this cost?* not ~~*How much is this priced?*~~. However, we can say *What is the price of this?*

9.2 Word building (3): productive suffixes 9B 3 p90

Suffixes usually change the class of a word, e.g. *govern* (verb), a *govern<u>ment</u>* (noun). However, productive suffixes: *-led*, *-minded*, *-free*, *-worthy*, *-able*, *-proof*, *-ish*, *-conscious*, *-related* have meaning and can be used to create new words.

We use:

- *-led* with **nouns** and **nationalities** to form adjectives which mean 'controlled by', e.g. *community-led* describes something that is controlled by a community: *There were many community-led campaigns. The record-breaking walk will be attempted by an English-led team.*
- *-minded* with **adjectives**, **nouns** or **adverbs** to form adjectives which describe people with a particular character or interest, e.g. ***money-minded*** describes someone who is interested in money issues: *The two men, who weren't particularly money-minded, anyway, set off … .*
- *-free* with **nouns** to form adjectives and means *without*, e.g. ***stress-free*** describes something that has no stress: *Their 8.000-mile walk certainly wasn't entirely stress-free. The flight was fantastic – completely stress-free.*
- *-worthy* with **nouns** to form adjectives which say something is suitable or deserving to receive a particular thing: *… and it's **noteworthy** that apart from crossing the English Channel and the Atlantic by boat … Don't worry about leaving Tom to lock up. He's completely **trustworthy**.*
- *-able* with **verbs** to form adjectives which mean 'can be': *Is that jacket **washable**? Their journey was totally **unpredictable**.*
- *-proof* with **nouns** to form adjectives which mean 'resistant to', e.g. ***waterproof*** means something can resist water from passing through it: *It was raining, but they didn't have waterproof clothing.*
- *-ish* with **adjectives** to form adjectives which mean 'to some degree or partly', e.g. ***reddish*** = quite red, ***sixish*** = about 6 o'clock: *They started walking around sixish every morning.*
- *-conscious* with **nouns** to form adjectives which mean 'thinking about or very concerned about something', e.g. ***health-conscious*** describes someone who is particularly careful about their health and what they eat: *They were very health-conscious and only ate vegetarian food.*

TIPS

- We can also use:
- *-ish* with **nouns** to form adjectives which describe what something or somebody is like, e.g. *childish* describes an adult who behaves like a child or something that is typical of a child: *You're being so childish about this. I find cartoons too childish.*
- *-related* with **nouns** to form adjectives that say one thing is connected with another, e.g. *stress-related* describes something connected with stress: *He's off work for stress-related reasons.*
- *Self-conscious* means 'uncomfortably or unnaturally aware of yourself and your actions': *She's very self-conscious about her height.*

9.3 World issues and economics 9C 1 p94

economic growth an increase in a country's capacity to produce goods and services over a period of time: *Governments can control economic growth by raising or lowering interest rates and taxation.*

economic decline a decrease in a country's capacity to produce goods and services over a period of time: *Our company has beaten the general economic decline to grow by 10% this year.*

economic recession /rəˈseʃən/ a period of economic decline often accompanied by high unemployment: *The country is likely to stay in economic recession for the rest of the year.*

mass-produced describes goods made cheaply and in large numbers, often using machines in a factory: *These days almost all children's toys are mass-produced in countries like China.*

overseas aid the help, mostly economic, which is provided to countries abroad: *Last week the Prime Minister promised to increase overseas aid by £1.5 billion.*

developing countries countries with a relatively low level of income per person and little industrialisation: *We're running a scheme to donate books to people in developing countries.*

renewable /rɪˈnjuːəbl/ **energy** a form of energy, e.g. solar or wind energy, which can be produced as quickly as it is used: *Power from flowing water, or hydropower, is the largest source of renewable energy.*

housing market describing the supply and demand of property in a town, region or country: *The housing market tends to slow down when interest rates go up.*

an economic /ˈiːkənɒmɪk/ **superpower** a country which has very great economic power: *Newly discovered oil fields in Brazil could soon make it into an economic superpower.*

record levels higher levels than ever achieved before: *In the early 1980s some towns had record levels of unemployment of over 25%.*

nuclear /ˈnjuːklɪə/ **power** a type of power that is produced by dividing the nucleus of an atom: *Nuclear power has long been the most controversial method of energy production due to the danger of the materials involved.*

gender discrimination /dɪskrɪmɪˈneɪʃən/ different treatment of people because they are either male or female: *The company has been accused of gender discrimination for paying its male and female staff on different scales.*

GRAMMAR

Preview

SIMPLE V CONTINUOUS

- We usually use **simple** verb forms to talk about things that are repeated, permanent or completed.
  Present Simple: *I **don't** often **meet up** with old school friends.* (repeated) not ~~*I'm not often meeting up with old school friends*~~.
  Present Perfect Simple: *I've read six of his books lately.* (completed recently) not ~~*I've been reading six of his books recently*~~.
  Past Simple: *He **died** on 20 March, 1997.* (completed) not ~~*He was dying on 20 March, 1997*~~; *I **lived** there for six years.* (completed) not ~~*I was living there for six years*~~.; *I was just leaving when Jim **turned** up.* (completed) not ~~*I was just leaving*~~ *when Jim **was turning up**.*
- We usually use **continuous** verb forms to describe a process and to talk about things that are in progress, temporary or unfinished.
  Present Continuous: *I think **I'm becoming** less materialistic.* (a process); *What are you doing? **I'm looking** for my contact lens.* (in progress); ***I'm living** in rented accommodation at the moment.* (temporary but we can also say ***I live*** *in rented accommodation at the moment.*)
  Past Continuous: *I **was** just **leaving** when Jim turned up.* (in progress)
  Present Perfect Continuous: *I've **been living** here for a long time.* (unfinished)

ACTIVITY AND STATE VERBS

- Verbs that describe states, feelings or opinions are not normally used in the continuous form. *I **believe** you.* not ~~*I'm believing you*~~. Examples of state verbs include: *hate, prefer, understand, know, recognise, want, suppose, agree, mean, seem, contain, consist, belong, own.*
- Verbs that describe activities can be used in both the simple and continuous form. *I **live** in Cornwall.* = ***I'm living*** *in Cornwall.* Examples of activity verbs include: *work, plan, play, do, walk, listen, study, talk, take, give.*

9.1 Simple v continuous: verbs with different meanings 9A 4 p88

- Some verbs can describe states and activities but their meanings change. Look at the tables (blue = state, pink = activity).

verb used to describe state/activity	meaning
have more money	possess
be having a better time	experience
many of us can think of times when	remember
if you are thinking of applying	consider
not in the way you would expect	believe will happen
when you're expecting (sth)	wait for

sentences	meaning of verb describing state/activity
His clothes fit me perfectly.	be the correct size
They're fitting new brakes in my car.	put in place
He appears to be fast asleep.	seem
She's appearing in a play on TV.	perform
It looks expensive.	seem
He's looking at a new car today.	go to see
She comes from London.	originate
She's coming from London.	travel
He's difficult.	have a permanent characteristic
He's being difficult.	temporarily behave in a particular way
I imagine she really likes Canada.	believe something is probably true
There's nobody there. You're imagining things!	think something exists although in fact it is not real or true
I now see why she found it difficult.	understand
I'm seeing Joe tonight.	meet

Preview

A/AN, *THE* OR NO ARTICLE

- We use ***a*** or ***an***:
  - a to talk about a person or thing for the first time: *… have **a method** for checking the identity of **a VIP guest**.*
  - b when we don't know, or it isn't important, which one: *They send **an entry pass** …*
  - c with jobs: *This is scanned by **a doorman**.*
- We use ***the***:
  - a to talk about the same person or thing for the second/third/fourth, etc. time: *a barcode to **the VIP's** mobile phone.*
  - b when there is only one (or only one in a particular place): *At a recent night at **The Ministry of Sound** in London …*
  - c with countries that are groups of islands or states: *Clubs in **the USA** …*
  - d with superlatives: *Some of **the hottest** nightclubs*
- We don't use an article:
  - a for most towns, cities, countries and continents: *At a recent night at The Ministry of Sound in **London** …*
  - b to talk about people or things in general: *… students were offered discounts if they used **mobile phones** to buy **electronic tickets**.*
  - c for some public places (*school, hospital, university/college, prison*, etc.) when we talk about what they are used for in general: *I went to **college** in London.*
  - d with superlatives and pronouns: *I'm **her biggest** fan.*

TIP

• We use *the* with public places when we talk about the building: *I went to **the college** at lunchtime.*

9.2 *a/an* v *one*; *few*, *a few*, *quite a few* 9B 8 p92

A/AN V *ONE*

- *A/an* and *one* both refer to one thing and can be used with singular countable nouns. However, we usually use *one*:
  - a if we want to emphasise the number. Compare these examples:
    *It takes just **a** tenth of a second to complete most transactions.*
    *It takes just **one** tenth of a second to complete most transactions.* (= not two or three tenths)
  - b when we are thinking of one particular day (in the future or the past), but we don't say exactly which day:
    *We paid that bill **one** day last month.* not … ~~***a** day last month*~~. *We can see the bank manager **one** day next week.* not … ~~***a** day next week*~~.
  - c in phrases with *one … other/another/the next*:
    *Many of us move from **one** means of payment to **another** …* not ~~*Many of us move from a means of payment to **another** …*~~

TIP

• We use *a* with singular countable nouns in exclamations, e.g. *What a big mistake! What a lovely day!*

FEW, *A FEW*, *QUITE A FEW*

- *Quite a few* means 'a considerable number': *However, **quite a few** American bankers are optimistic.*
- *A few* means 'some, but a small number': *If payments for **a few** coffees, a train ticket and a newspaper are made every day … .*
- *Few* means 'not enough' (not as many as you would expect): ***Few** financial experts would dispute the fact that some of these methods of payment will soon become a thing of the past.*

TIPS

• *Few* is often used in more formal situations: *She has few friends.* (formal) *She doesn't have many friends.* (informal).

• *little / a little* is used with uncountable nouns in the same way as *few / a few* is used with countable nouns. *He spends **little** time with his children* (= not much, not enough) *He spends a little time with his children* (= some time, but a small amount)

• We can make comparatives with *fewer (than)*. We use *fewer* with countable nouns: *There are **fewer reasons** these days to carry cash than ever before.* We use *less* with uncountable nouns: *People carry **less cash** than they did in the past.*

WRITING

9.1 Spelling: *-ible* or *-able* 3 p93

- The adjective suffixes *-ible* and *-able* are often confused.
- We usually use:

  a ***-ible*** if the root (= the word to which the suffix is added) is not a complete word, e.g. *ed + -ible = **ed**ible, **vis**ible, **destruct**ible, **incred**ible*. Exceptions include: *contemptible, digestible, flexible, responsible, sensible*

  b ***-able*** if the root is a complete word, e.g. *accept + able = acceptable, do + able = do**able**: **understand**able, **notice**able, **believ**able*.

TIP

- If a root word ends in *-e*, we usually replace the *-e* with the suffix, e.g. *believe* → *believable*. However, there are many exceptions to this rule: *love* → *loveable, notice* → *noticeable*. Sometimes both spellings are possible.

9.2 Connecting words: cause and effect (2) 4 p93

- We use *because/because of* to give the reason for something. They go at the beginning of a clause of reason.

  *He's successful **because he's determined**.*

  reason clause

- *because of* is followed by a noun phrase:

  1 ***Because of poor visibility**, there were several road accidents*. not ~~*Because of visibility was poor*~~, …

  2 ***Because of terrible floods**, they lost all their crops*. not ~~*Because of there were terrible floods*~~ …

- We use *due to* at the beginning of a phrase to introduce the result of a situation. If an event ***is due to*** something, it happens as a result of it. *Due to* is followed by a noun phrase. *His success is due to his determination*. not ~~*His success is due to he's very determined*~~.

  ***Due to** the bad weather yesterday, I didn't go climbing.*

- We use *so, as a result, therefore, accordingly* and *consequently* to introduce the result of a situation. *Three people were ill **so** the meeting was cancelled*. We usually use *as a result, therefore* and *consequently* at the beginning of a sentence.

  *My Spanish is really bad. **As a result**, he didn't understand me.*

- *Accordingly, as a result, therefore* and *consequently* are mainly used in formal contexts. *There were terrible floods. **Therefore**, they lost all their crops. Visibility was poor. **Consequently**, there were several road accidents. Three people were ill. **Accordingly**, the meeting was cancelled.*

- We use *as/since* to mean *because*: ***Since/As** you don't want to help, I'll do it myself.*

TIPS

- We use 'cos' /kəz/ in informal speech to mean 'because'.
- If we put a verb after phrases like *as a result of, due to* or *because of*, we use a verb+*ing* after the subject. This type of structure is more common in formal contexts: *As a result of my Spanish **being** really bad, he didn't understand me. Because of the visibility **being** poor, there were several road accidents.*

REAL WORLD

9.1 Presenting information 9C 5 p94

We usually use these phrases towards the beginning of a talk to tell our audience what we will be speaking about and to give them an idea of the structure of the talk.

I'm going to divide the talk into (three sections). First of all, (how economics is related to real life). Then I'll go on to (the intellectual challenge). And finally I'll (discuss future careers).

TO MAKE THE FIRST POINT
First of all …
Let's start with/by …
TO REFER TO A POINT MADE EARLIER
As I said before …
To go back to …
To return to something I mentioned earlier …
TO SIGNAL A NEW POINT
Now I'll talk about …
Let's move on to …
Leaving that aside for a moment …
TO SUMMARISE WHAT'S BEEN SAID SO FAR
So, to sum up …
Just to recap …
TO SIGNAL THE LAST POINT/BRING THE TALK TO AN END
In conclusion …
Last but not least …
And finally …

Language Summary 10

VOCABULARY

10.1 Adjective–noun collocations 10B 7 8 p100/101

A

- ≠ means 'is the opposite of'

  the toughest/most challenging/lowest* moment ≠ the sweetest/easiest moment

  a big/huge relief ≠ a slight relief

  an important/significant message ≠ a trivial message

  thin/light gloves ≠ thick gloves

  a cool*/calm guy ≠ a crazy guy

* *lowest* describes an unhappy emotional state: *My lowest moment was when I was robbed at knife-point. I really felt like coming home.*
* *cool* can be used as an adjective of opinion to comment positively about a person's attitude to life or style: *He's such a cool guy. I'd love to be like him.*

B

- Other common antonyms include:

a rough surface ≠ a smooth surface		a rough sea ≠ a calm sea
a light colour ≠ a dark colour		a light meal ≠ a heavy meal
a gentle wind ≠ a strong wind		a gentle person ≠ an aggressive person
an old person ≠ a young person	BUT	an old building ≠ a modern building
a tall building ≠ a low building		a tall person ≠ a short person
a dry wine ≠ a sweet wine		a dry day ≠ a wet day
plain food ≠ rich food		a plain shirt ≠ a patterned shirt
a strong coffee ≠ a weak coffee		a strong possibility ≠ a faint possibility

GRAMMAR

10.1 Subject/verb agreement 10A 4 p97

- A verb usually 'agrees' with its subject (i.e. a singular subject has a singular verb and a plural subject has a plural verb):
  ***Horses**, too, **have** powered the information superhighway for thousands of years.*
  *Further north, **mail was** being delivered to the icy corners of the world by huskies.*
- We use a **singular** verb:
  - a if the subject of the verb is a clause: *Having cats **is** now a thing of the past.*
  - b with nouns which end in *-s* but are not plural: *News **comes** via email these days.*
  - c with expressions of quantity, measurement, etc.: *2,000 miles **is** a long way to travel.*
  - d after words such as *everyone*, *anything*, etc.: *The information that everyone **was** waiting for.*
- We use a **plural** verb:
  - a for nouns which don't end in *-s* but which are not singular: *The police **were** using a pigeon service.*
  - b after words such as *both of*, *all of*, *plenty of*, *a number of*, *a couple*: *Only a couple **were** recruited.*
- Some collective nouns and names can take either a **singular** or a **plural** form:
  - a When focusing on countries which are a group of states, an institution or organisation as a whole, the verb is usually **singular**: *The USA **has** 50 states; The British army **was** also dependent on pigeons; the team **was** a financial failure.*
  - b When focusing on a collection of individuals, the verb is usually **plural**: *The public **were** fascinated by the Pony Express.*

TIPS

- When the subject is two or more nouns linked by *and/or*, we use a plural form: *A letter **and** a parcel **were forwarded** to our new address.*
- In clauses with *what* as subject, if the following noun is plural, the verb is either plural (in more formal contexts) or singular (in more informal contexts). *What surprised me **was/were the sheer numbers** of pigeons used in the war.*
- In complex sentences, the verb agrees with the main noun: *During the four-month siege, **more than a million letters were delivered** to the citizens of Paris.*
- We use a singular verb with ***the** number of* (but a plural verb with ***a** number of*): ***The** number of applicants always **exceeds** the number of places.*

Preview

FUNCTIONS OF MODAL VERBS

- We talk about ability using *can* and *could*: *Unfortunately she **can't** touch-type. My brother **could** surf when he was eight.*
- We ask or give permission using *can*, *may* and *could*: *You **can** use my phone. **May** I use your phone? **Could** I leave early today, please?*
- We talk about obligation using *must* and *have (got) to*: *Ben had an eye test and he**'s got to** wear glasses. You **must** get your brakes fixed, they're dangerous.*
- We give advice using *should* and *ought to*: *You **should** return this as it doesn't work. He **ought to** change his accountant.*
- We talk about repeated/typical behaviour using *will* and *would*. We often use *always* or *often* with *would*: *She**'ll** come home and immediately turn on the TV. He**'d always** stop for lunch at noon.*
- We refuse using *won't* and *wouldn't*: *I **won't** let her use my car. She **wouldn't** give me a lift last night.*
- We criticise people's past behaviour using *ought to have/should have* + past participle: *They **ought to have told** you. She **should have gone** to university.*
- We talk about prohibition using *can't*: *You **can't** smoke on any public transport.*

SEMI-MODALS

BE ALLOWED TO

- We use ***be allowed to*** to say we have permission to do something: *We **were allowed to** wear whatever we wanted at school.*

MANAGE TO

- We use ***manage to*** to say that we succeed in doing something, often after some difficulty: *I lost my key but I **managed to** climb in through the window.*

BE ABLE TO

- We use ***be able to*** to talk about ability or possibility. We also use *can* to talk about ability and possibility but *can* only has two forms: *can* and *could*. Therefore, we sometimes need *be able to*: *I might be able to come.* not ~~*I might can come*~~.
- If we say someone ***was able to*** do something, then we usually mean they had the ability to do something and they did it. We cannot use *could* for this meaning. If we are talking about a single achievement rather than a general ability in the past, we usually use *be able to/managed to* instead of *could*: *I **was able to** meet him last Friday.* not ~~***I could** meet him last Friday*~~. However, we can use ***couldn't*** to talk about a specific situation in the past: *I tried to start the car but I **couldn't**.* We can use *could* with verbs such as *see, hear, feel*, etc. to talk about specific situations when we were able to do something: *I could see it in the distance.*

NEEDN'T/DON'T NEED TO

- We use *need to* to talk about things that are necessary for us to do. In positive sentences we use *need* + infinitive with *to*: *I need to buy some stamps.*
- In negative sentences we say *don't need to* and *needn't* with no change in meaning. *I don't need to/needn't go yet.*

DIDN'T NEED TO/NEEDN'T HAVE

- In negative sentences referring to the past, we can say *didn't need to/needn't have.*
- However, these two structures have a difference in meaning: *I **didn't need to** change planes, because there was a direct flight.* (= it was not necessary for me to change planes so I didn't.) *I **needn't have** changed planes; there was a direct flight.* (= It was not necessary for me to change planes, but I did.)

10.2 Modal verbs: levels of certainty about the past, present and future 10B 3 p99

We use:

- *will, won't, can't, must, would(n't)* when something is definite:
  1. *… I'm sure he'**ll be working**.* (present)
  2. *He's certain he'**ll find** a buyer for his next film.* (future)
  3. *Janine Jansen, for example, you just know it **won't have been** an easy life for her.* (past)
  4. *… It **can't be** easy having Martin as your partner.* (present)
  5. *My father says it's obvious that I **can't have wanted** it badly enough …* (past)
  6. *Clearly, he **must enjoy** what he does; why else would he work so hard?* (present)
  7. *She **must have devoted** most of her life to practising.* (past)
  8. *My father says it's obvious that I can't have wanted it badly enough or I **wouldn't have given** up.* (past)
- *should* when we think something is probable: *People are just starting to notice his work, so it **shouldn't be** long before he gets the recognition he deserves.* (future)
- *may, might, could* when we think something is possible:
  1. *I **may have had** some natural talent, who knows?* (past)
  2. *He **might be creating** a new animation character …* (present)
  3. *… or he **could be working on** his next short film.* (present)
- When modal verbs refer to the present we often use: modal verb + infinitive or modal verb + *be* + verb+*ing*: *He **must enjoy** what he does. It is Saturday night and I'm sure he'**ll be working**. It **can't be** easy having Martin as your partner.*
- When modal verbs refer to the future we often use: modal verb + infinitive. *… **shouldn't be** long before he gets the recognition he deserves. He's certain he'**ll find** a buyer … .*
- When modal verbs refer to past certainty we use: modal verb + *have* + past participle: *Janine Jansen, for example, you just know it **won't have been** an easy life for her. She **must have devoted** most of her life to practising. I **may have had** some natural talent, who knows? My father says it's obvious that I **can't have wanted** it badly enough or I **wouldn't have given up**.*

TIPS

- ***Ought to** / **ought not to*** have the same meaning as *should/shouldn't*, but can sound more formal: *She shouldn't be too much longer. She ought not to be too much longer.*
- We don't use **can** to talk about levels of certainty. We use **may**, **might**, **could** instead: *He could be at home now.* not ~~*He can be at home now*~~.
- We use **couldn't** or **can't have** + past participle to mean certainty about the past: *It couldn't/can't have been easy.*
- We don't use **can** or **mustn't** when we speculate. We use **can't**, **could**, **might**, **may** or **must**: *He can't have known about it.* not ~~*He mustn't have known about it*~~. *He could have been at home at that time.* not ~~*He can have been at home at that time*~~.

It **can't be** easy living with him.

Audio Scripts

CD1 1

AMY So, Ann, why did you suggest this book?

ANN Well, I've bought quite a few self-help books over the past few months and I suggested this one for the book club because my brother's been telling me to read it for ages. **Apparently, it's sold over 16 million copies** and it's still selling well, which surprised me because it's pretty basic stuff, really. I mean, you know, smile at people – that's a bit obvious, isn't it? Or, make the other person feel important. That's pretty obvious, too. But as my brother said, if what Carnegie's saying is that self-evident, then why don't people do it? And he's got a point.

SY Yeah, I agree with your brother there. And OK, even if some of the points he makes in the book seem basic, I mean, I still find it fascinating. **Actually, I think people are getting fed up with me talking about it!** I've told at least ten people about it at work this week. **To be honest, it's the first time I've read a book like this**, and even though I haven't quite finished it yet – I mean, I've, I've read about 150 pages so far – I totally agree with what he's saying. I mean, the bit where it says "as a rule we aren't good listeners," I mean, that's so true. I mean we're usually just waiting to speak. If someone's talking about something that's happening to them, or happened to them, then most people are just waiting to butt in, aren't they, with, you know, "Same thing happened to me," and off they go, you know, wittering on about themselves. I mean, I think Carnegie's right when he says that if you want people to like you, you've got to learn to really pay attention to what they're saying. Yeah, I mean, actually encourage the other person to talk about themselves, by asking questions, I mean, showing that you're interested in them. Anyway, I've been trying to be a more attentive listener and not interrupt, but it, I tell you, it takes some self-discipline, I can … Soon as you've [I've] finished reading it, I mean, I'm going to give it to my brother, because he's got no social skills whatsoever! I mean, it's true! What about you, Dean. Did you like it?

DEAN Yeah, I did, and to be honest, I wasn't expecting to. Like Sy, I agree with a lot of what it says, like the bit about how important it is to remember people's names. Never thought about that before, but a friend of mine, John, he's brilliant at that. And it works, especially when he's chatting up girls. For instance, last night we went for a pizza. I went to the loo. I hadn't been gone for more than a minute, but by the time I got back to the table, he'd introduced himself to the three girls at the table next to ours and learnt their names. There he was, saying stuff like "So, Clare, how are you enjoying London?" You could see Clare was thinking "What a nice guy." And I'm sure it was just because he'd called her by her first name. Actually, since Ann suggested this one I've read a couple of his other books.

ANN Yeah, I bought one of his other books recently, too.

AMY Well, during the last couple of weeks I've actually been trying out some of Carnegie's suggestions, as well, you know, like the one where he goes on about how powerful a smile is.

ANN Yeah, but that's true, though, isn't it? I mean, most people walk around with a scowl on their face. So, that when someone actually does smile at you, it really makes an impression.

AMY It does! You know he suggested smiling at everyone you come into contact with for a week and note what happens. Well, I did and it really does make a difference. Like, I've been going to the same train station for years and up until now, I've never really had any contact with the guy in the ticket office other than, "Return to Richmond, please." So, I started with him. You know, a smile and a bit of eye contact and it was amazing! He's been really chatty ever since. Much nicer way to start the day. And remember the bit where Carnegie says, even if you don't feel like smiling, force yourself to, 'cos smiling actually brings on a nice feeling. Well, I've been trying to do that too, and it works!

ANN Yeah, it's a different mindset, isn't it? And I loved that quote – that, the Chinese proverb, "A man without a smiling face must not open a shop!" I know a few shop assistants who could learn from that, especially …

CD1 3

DAVE I do go out and see friends on a fairly regular basis. It's usually based around squash, or playing sports or something, and we'll end up with a drink and talk afterwards. What we talk about isn't deep and meaningful, though – far from it! It's usually about current affairs, something like that, and it usually degenerates into a list of five best cars, or old films, or whatever. I think the whole issue of friendship between men isn't, sort of, based around the emotional bit, it's much more to do with common interests, and the fact that someone is sort of into something that you are. I think if it was something serious, something close and emotional you'd tend to go with and talk to older friends – people that you were at college with, someone that you think you could unload everything on to. The problem with men is that they don't do that – what usually happens is we sort of bottle things up, and don't use friends as well as women do.

HELEN Well, if something major happened, it would probably be my parents I'd talk to first – they'd be the first people to know. But, I do confide in my friends a lot on a day-to-day basis. We tend to meet about once a week – and we we meet in a café. We always meet in the same place, actually, and the reason we meet there is that they put up with all our noise. We try to snatch about half an hour, but – that's what we say – but it usually goes on. We just relax and giggle and I always end up saying much more than I'd intended to. So, yeah, friends are a really big part of my life and they have to put up with a lot from me, but I hope I'm able to give them a little bit back, but most importantly we do manage to have a really good laugh about things.

ANDREA OK, a person who I tend to confide in is my hairdresser, funnily enough. I think the reason I confide in him is precisely because I don't want to unburden all my worries on my family, so the hairdresser's is a neutral ground if you like, where I can just go and talk and I know what I say won't go any further 'cos it's of no interest to my hairdresser. We've got a set routine, I suppose. We sit down and he's focusing on, on my hair, and we have a quick "how are you?" and he tells me very briefly, and then I launch onto, onto what I've got to talk about. It was great, but it wasn't until he broke up with his girlfriend that my hairdresser started to confide in me, which really changed the dynamic of our relationship. Suddenly, he became this person who had needs and who wanted to unburden himself onto me. I mean, if it wasn't for the fact that he gave me such a good haircut, I'd definitely think about moving to another hairdresser.

ALEX I mainly talk to my friends, usually on MSN or by text, because they're my age group and they're the most interesting people to talk to, and we talk about a lot, like what's happened at school, and the latest sports results, and a lot of things like that. If there was a problem, I'd talk to my friends because they'd be more likely to understand what I was going through, or maybe my sister, because she's also young and she'd know. I probably wouldn't talk to my parents, because my mum would get in a flap, and I don't think they'd really understand.

CD1 4

CLAUDIA Well, my favourite saying is "Let's cross that bridge when we come to it". It's probably not very exciting for British people, but for me as a non-native speaker I thought it was really, really nice. It basically means that you can't always plan ahead and you can't control everything. Well, to put it simply you can't really worry about things that are way in the future. The first time I heard it was from my then boyfriend, Ben, and nothing has influenced my life more than that saying actually.

CHRIS My favourite expression is "You pay peanuts, you get monkeys," which kind of basically means that the less money you pay the worse the service. It's an expression I've always wanted to tell my boss but never really had the courage to do that.

CLAIRE One of my favourite sayings is "If you fly with the crows, you'll get shot with the crows". I can remember my grandmother saying it to me when I was growing up in Scotland. And, what it means is that if you hang about with the wrong crowd, and what she was saying to me is, at school, that if people who be, behave badly you'll get punished with them, even if you were [weren't] wrong. I've not heard the expression in years, but recently I've heard it quite a lot in the news and political contexts.

LYNN Well, my favourite saying is something I, I picked up from my mum and I use it because I'm not a very practical person. The saying is "Why have a dog and bark yourself?" And this basically means there's no need to bother doing something difficult if someone around you can do it better than you. So, for example my boyfriend's a fantastic cook, and when people say to me "Do you cook?" I can say "Why have a dog and bark yourself?" because, because there's really no need for me to bother.

PETE Well, I grew up in a horsy family and everyone in my family rode horses, except for me. And as a result of that, I picked up quite a few expressions involving horses. One of my favourites is "Horses for courses". Basically, different horses are involved in different kinds of races, and the horses are suited to its [their] particular course. So, in real life every person is suited to a particular job, every machine to a particular job and "Horses for courses" basically sums up that connection between the thing and the job it should do.

CD1 5

COMPERE OK, Peter will you please tell us the definition of the Australian expression 'She'll be apples'?

PETER Lovely expression, isn't it, 'She'll be apples'? Or should I say 'She'll be apples'? Well, what this basically means is someone is going to be really pleased, or surprised, or really thrilled with something. For example, if you show me a present that you've bought for your mother and I say "She'll be apples" – this simply means I think she'll love it.

C Naomi, your definition is?

NAOMI Peter's pronunciation is very good, but of course that's not the real definition of 'She'll be apples'. Let me explain the real meaning to you. As you know, apples are nice, they're sweet, they're good. So if a person is frightened or worried about something, then Australians try to comfort that person by saying, "Ah, she'll be apples". In other words, everything's going to be fine so, don't worry – she'll be apples.

C And finally Ralph.

RALPH Actually, neither of those definitions is true. 'She'll be apples' basically means you think someone is perfect for a particular job – if at an interview, let's say, the person applying for the position is fantastically well-qualified and the best applicant, then you'd say 'she'll be apples'. Or to put it another way, you have a lot of confidence in the person.

C OK, Shirley's team. Which do you think is the true definition of 'She'll be apples'? Does it mean someone is going to be really pleased, or surprised, or is it a way of saying 'don't worry everything will be fine', or does it mean someone is perfect for a particular job?

CD1 6

COMPERE OK, Shirley's team. Which do you think is the true definition of 'She'll be apples'?

SHIRLEY Well, they're all convincing. But we think Ralph's definition is true. We can imagine after a job interview, the interviewers choosing someone saying, 'He'll' or 'She'll be apples', meaning they'll be the best person for the job.

C Ralph?

RALPH Sorry. Wrong!

C And the true definition is?

NAOMI It means 'don't worry, everything will be alright'.

C So Peter's team is in the lead with two points to one.

CD1 7 CD1 8 CD1 9

PRESENTER Walking into Tommy McHugh's semidetached home, you're overwhelmed by a cornucopia of shape and colour. Everywhere you look – on every wall and ceiling – there is a mass of abstract designs, animals and faces. Until he hit his 50s – only six years ago – Tommy was a Liverpool builder, with a bit of a rough past as a street fighter, and no apparent interest in art. Nowadays though, he's a man with a passion – full of emotion, driven to create. He describes his mind as a volcano exploding with bubbles, each of which contains a million other bubbles full of unstoppable creative ideas. He spends his days – and most of his nights – painting, sculpting and carving.

TOMMY When you walk into my house, you walk into my brain. I've got that much going on in me brain, I have to let it all out or it overloads. I can't switch it off.

P The transformation in Tommy has been quite // remarkable. // So, // what happened six years ago // to bring it about? // The extraordinary answer // is // a brain haemorrhage. // One day Tommy was in the bathroom, // when he remembers something // "popping in his head". By the time he reached hospital, his eyes had turned bright red and he was in agonising pain. Two arteries in his head were leaking blood, and a delicate life-saving operation followed. Tommy's ex-wife describes what happened next.

JAN A few days later, // he was sent home with a bag full of tablets. // I didn't know what to do // he couldn't walk, // or feed himself, // or do anything really. // Sometimes // he didn't even know where he was. // It was awful. // He was totally frustrated, // angry, // and in pain. So, he took it out on me because I was the only one there. We didn't have any aftercare whatsoever.

P Jan was desperate to find anything that might give her husband an outlet. She'd always painted as a hobby, so she handed him a pen and a piece of paper and suggested he tried drawing. When she turned back from cooking the tea only a minute or two later, he'd filled the whole page with tiny faces – all different. Not surprisingly, Jan was unnerved, but this was only the beginning of it all. As soon as he was fit enough, Tommy started on the walls and also began to melt candles to sculpt heads of wax. At this stage, he didn't enjoy his manic creativity and wrote cries for help to doctors around the world. Most ignored him but two letters hit home, including one to the artist Marion Kalmus, who recognised in him an extreme version of what many artists feel.

MARION I told him I couldn't stop the bubbles exploding in his head, but I did know a lot of people who felt like that. It's called being an artist.

P This was a turning point for McHugh – it gave him a new name and a new identity and he began to enjoy his work. The other letter, meanwhile, had reached Alice Flaherty, a neurologist from the US, who has a special interest in this field. Flaherty has corresponded with McHugh for several years and recently came to the UK to meet him. Cases such as his, she says, are rare, but not unknown.

ALICE Tommy's manic creativity is extremely likely to be down to changes in his temporal lobe, the part of the brain responsible for understanding meaning. Van Gogh almost certainly had temporal lobe epilepsy, and at times of great creative output, he not only painted but would write constantly, which is not uncommon. Tommy does it, too.

P Flaherty strongly believes that the increased creative output may be partly because the brain is becoming less self-critical, and stresses that creativity is not necessarily a guarantee of quality. Indeed, McHugh's early paintings are nothing to write home about, but some of his recent work, now that he's had some practice, is wonderful – in particular his stone carvings. And even though there is no way of knowing how much longer Tommy will survive, he's not in the least bit depressed any more. His life has become an adventure, and he loves every minute of it.

CD1 10

BRUCE One of the places I remember most are the Galápagos Islands.

PAT Oh, yes.

B This group of islands about 600 miles out from Ecuador.

P I've heard of them, yes.

B Yeah, fantastic place. We went to see some friends in Ecuador and then they organised this boat trip for us which lasted about a week.

P And were they exotic, sun-kissed tropical islands as the brochures would have you believe?

B Not at all, actually. They were quite grey, I just remember greyness, sort of volcanic rock, bit of vegetation, very cold, forbidding sea and a lot of, yeah a lot of cloud. Even though we went in August, it was quite cloudy.

P Oh, did you get to see a lot of animals and birds?

B Oh yeah, it's brilliant for that. Absolutely brilliant, you know. I was really excited – they have these giant land tortoises, you know the famous tortoises. They've got albatrosses, which are unique to the island, marine iguanas, blue-footed boobies.

P What are they?

B Oh, they, they're great. They're sort of rather stupid-looking clumsy birds with blue feet and long necks and they're about the size of a goose and do really strange, flappy dances.

P And are they tame?

B Yeah, all the animals are absolutely tame. You can walk right up to them, you can walk through them they, they don't run away at all, they're absolutely fantastic.

P Oh, incredible.

CD1 11

MELISSA I'm not sure I've told you about my trip to Ireland, have I?

BRENDAN No, no, you haven't.

M No, well this was last summer. I haven't seen you for a while. We were expecting, sort of two weeks on sandy, beautiful, sandy beaches …

B OK.

M … and we were expecting the lush, green hills of Ireland. I mean, I'm American so you know, all the clichés of Ireland apply to me and, we all love to go there. Anyway, we were expecting a beautiful lodge that, that we'd rented from some friends of friends. After we got there, there was sort of 18 hours travelling in this driving, pounding rain – we stopped off, our first stop, when we got near to the house, was to buy the toughest waterproof gear that we could find.

B Right.

M We then arrived very late at night at the house which turns out to be not a beautiful lodge but a very stark, modern …

B Right, OK.

M … log cabin.

B No rustic charm then.

M Primitive …

B Oh, OK.

M … is, more than rustic I think, the word there. And the thing that we decided to do the next day was get up and explore our surroundings. Instead of a sandy beach, what we had was a very thin strip of gravel.

B Oh, dear.

M And the owner had forgotten to tell us that the beach was actually half an hour, sail away in a very small dinghy.

B Which is something that you don't want to be doing in bad weather.

M Not really, in the choppy seas that we were surrounded by. So, I have to say it wasn't our best holiday.

CD1 12

INTERVIEWER Can you tell us how many overseas visitors come to China each year?

CHENG Oh a lot. Last year, over 66 million visitors came to China, with more than a third of those staying overnight. People come from all over the world. It's a very popular choice for tourists nowadays!

INTERVIEWER And where do they head when they get here?

CHENG Overwhelmingly, they go to Beijing and Shanghai. They are by far our most popular destinations. And of course they are fantastic cities to visit, but it's a shame that most people don't venture far from these cities, because China has much, much more to offer. It is a very diverse country.

CD1 13

INTERVIEWER So, where would you suggest people go to find this diversity?

CHENG Well, it depends what you want to do really. We like to think we've got something for everybody. Most overseas visitors probably [wouldn't] think of China as the obvious place for a beach holiday, but if you go to Hainan Island off the south coast, you'll find a tropical island paradise with incredibly beautiful beaches. And if you enjoy experiencing local culture, there are several festivals there in the spring, including the coconut festival and the 'love festival' where the young people seek love. Visitors can watch the traditional Li wedding ceremonies on that day, which is very popular, especially for newly married couples! And if you're [you] enjoy stunning scenery, from Hainan you can cross to the mainland and visit Guilin in the south, which is definitely worth seeing. The area around Guilin is dotted with spectacular caves and strangely shaped hills or 'karsts' that appears [appear] to spring up straight from the ground. They look like elephants, camels, lotus plants and bamboo shoots! In addition, Guilin has many waterways. In fact, the Li River boat trip is one of our planet's most stunningly beautiful journeys. It is also an important culture [cultural] city with a history of more than 2,000 years.

I And of course, China is steeped in history.

C Yes. If it's history you're after, then you're spoilt for choice. One of the most popular attractions for tourists is the Forbidden City in Beijing, but if you really want to experiencing [experience] something special in Beijing you should head into the *hutong*, which are these narrow winding lanes all around the Forbidden City. Actually, everywhere there is a lane, there is a story. The narrowest *hutong* is Qian Shi (which means 'money market') where the narrowest part is only 40 cms wide, so when two people meet, they have to turn sideways to pass each other! But besides Beijing, I would recommend Xi'an. It's one of the oldest cities in China – much older than Beijing – and it's one of the birthplaces of the ancient Chinese civilisation in the Yellow River Basin. In ancient times it was called Chang'an (meaning the 'eternal city') and it was the beginning and end of the Silk Road – the famous trade route which brought the city material wealth – as well as being home to the terracotta warriors, of course.

CD1 14

CHENG If you're into nightlife, then, again, China's big cities offer something for everyone. But the most vibrant and colourful nightlife in China takes place in Shanghai, which has some of the most sophisticated and exciting nightspots in Asia. And karaoke is also still very popular wherever you go in China.

INTERVIEWER And what about local cuisine?

C Well, although Chinese food has become so well known and loved all over the world, visitors are often surprised when they experience real Chinese food.

I Yes, why is that?

C Well, it's the Cantonese style of Chinese food that is the most popular in restaurants around the world, for example Cantonese 'dim sum'; but in Europe especially, it tends to be adapted to Western tastes. Cantonese food comes from the Guangdong province in southern China, where there is a saying that anything that walks, swims, crawls or flies is edible! Cantonese chefs take a real pride in their cooking, which is characterised by its fresh ingredients and very mild spices. But there are many different styles of cuisine in China, besides Cantonese, including the Beijing style, the Shanghai style and the Szechuan style. So in Beijing you can enjoy the delicious Peking duck. In Shanghai, you must try the Shanghai pork bun, and in Szechuan province you will find that the food tends to be hot and spicy. Because the climate is so different depending on where you are in China, the cuisine is very diverse.

CD1 15

PRESENTER Have you heard of 'impostor syndrome'? No, it's not someone trying to steal your identity. It's the nagging feeling that even though, to everyone else you are supremely successful and capable, inwardly you are convinced that you are just bluffing your way through and that at any moment now you'll be found out. Sound familiar? We interviewed people about the latest syndrome to hit the psychiatrist's couch …

CD1 16

INTERVIEWER Valerie, had you heard of impostor syndrome before?

VALERIE Yes, I had actually, it's interesting 'cos you read a few, sort of bi, biographies of famous people and they start, a lot of them all start talking about it, but I didn't actually put those words to it, but I understand what, what it's about and I feel that, perhaps I am a bit of a sufferer.

I And your profession is?

V I am a garden designer. But I've come late to that, I used to be a teacher. And I think having come late to something you begin, you're kind of feel a bit more of an impostor because you've lived so long as a teacher. You can't possibly be a real garden designer. Because, I think the more you learn about something, the more you know that you don't know, so of course, you know, your confidence begins, you're sort of not totally confident.

I So, do you think that your clients are going to, sort of, rumble to the fact that, you sense this within yourself or?

V Well, I don't think they do because I think years of teaching have taught me that you, I can overcome that, but I do feel it inside.

I And, did you have it when you were a teacher?

V Yes, I think I'm the sort of person, doesn't matter what I do, I'll always feel I don't know it all, and I will be, you know, somebody's going to catch me out one day.

I Richard, had you heard of the term 'impostor syndrome' before?

RICHARD No, I hadn't, not until you explained it to me.

I And you do think you've personally had experience of it?

R Why, no. I don't want to sound arrogant but, but it's not something I recognise.

I And what in fact do you do for a living?

R I'm a cameraman. I work in television.

I So, you have all these directors and producers expecting rather wonderful images from you, and in general you feel quite self-assured that you can give them what they need?

R Well, I'm not saying I'm perfect, but I, I think I'm good enough that most of the time when I make a mistake, only I realise I've made one.

I I see. And, in the media in general do you think there, there are people out there who have this sort of nagging self doubt?

R No, I don't think so. The media is famously full of probably overly self-confident people. No, nobody, nobody likes to show any doubt in the media.

I Miranda, had you heard of 'impostor syndrome' before?

MIRANDA Well, well, I hadn't and then I kind of put the idea of 'impostor' and 'syndrome' and, and, and then I read about it and thought well, actually, I feel a little bit like an impostor because I've been incredibly lucky. I've had an enormous amount of good fortune in, in, in being given this privilege of, of being, of having a place at this wonderful university and a fully funded PhD, which is not only fully funded for all my fees, but I'm also being paid to travel the world to go and collect my data. So, how could this happen? How could this happen to me? And when I go and see my supervisor, I keep thinking that he's going to say, "I'm sorry Miranda but actually, that, it was all a trick, it really wasn't what you thought it was and we've found out that you're not who you say you are."

CD1 17

1 Naomi and Rachael

NAOMI What do you do then Rachael, to cheer yourself up?

RACHAEL Well, when I'm feeling really down about things and maybe feeling a little bit lonely, or anything especially when you've just moved to a new place, I've got, I've kept all the letters that people have sent me over the years and photographs and, just odd loose photographs and tickets from plays and, concerts that I've been to, in lots of shoeboxes marked with the year when I did those things, and sometimes I'll open one of those and go through things and it kind of reminds me that, the friends that I've had, and the good times I've had, and that there will be some more to come.

N That's lovely. That's really nice.

R What about you?

N Well to be honest, sometimes I do that as well. I have some lovely photos of when I've travelled. And it's lovely to look at them, but then it always makes me think I haven't seen these people for ages I want to see them, and then I start planning something sociable to do, or something fun, so actually it really does take you out of your, your down moment, doesn't it?

R Yeah, because sometimes you get too stuck in the moment that you're actually in, and you forget you, you lose perspective. So, I think that gives me a bit more perspective.

2 Helen and Alex

HELEN So, what's your preferred pick me up then, Alex?

ALEX Oh, it's always been perfume ever since my grandmother let me play with her beautiful art deco glass and silver atomiser that she had, it smelt of violets, it was wonderful. And I've always found that perfume seems to go straight into my brain, and lifts my mood, and I can choose perfume to suit the occasion, and of course I can, I can do it anytime I like. What about you, what do you do?

H Well, I need some kind of physical release really. I really like going for a really fast bike ride at top speed with the wind whistling in my ears. It's impossible to feel stressed when you're zipping around like that.

A I suppose that's true.

3 Fran and Ian

FRAN So, Ian how you do cope when you're feeling a bit down?

IAN Well, I have a couple of tricks really; if I just need cheering up, I like to go kite flying because it's, it's just great fun and it's colourful and it's quiet and peaceful, and I'm on my own, but if something is threatening to get a little bit too serious, that it's perhaps bothering more, me more than it really should, then I try to be cynical about it to get it in context.

F Oh, right!

I And I think about what I do when I'm cynical, and when I'm cynical about something, I raise one eyebrow so I, find that if I just raise an eyebrow and thinking about something it, it brings out the cynicism and it all goes away.

CD1 18

IAN How about you?

FRAN Well, generally if I, um, if I'm not feeling, um, too happy then, um, I need something to work towards, so, um, I try and make contact with friends that I don't really see very often and, um, and I find that if I'm, I'm with them then I kind of forget about what's going on at the time and just remember the things I, you know, used to do with them, and, um, they just kind of, er, accept my personality so I don't have to, you know, that, that trivial thing that's usually making me not very happy. Doesn't really mean very much to them so …

I Yeah, good memories always help.

F Exactly.

CD1 19

1

BOSS Oh, hi Al. I've been looking for you everywhere! Listen, would you and Lisa like to come round tomorrow evening for a bite to eat?

a)

AL Well, actually, we were planning to go to the cinema tomorrow, so … But yes, we must all get together some time.

b)

AL We can't tomorrow. We're going out.

2

MARY Do these look OK?

a)

LIZ I don't like bright colours on you. And they're too tight round the hips.

b)

LIZ Well, I think darker colours suit you better. I'd go for black instead if I were you. And they could do with being a bit looser around the hips.

3

GREG That was great, wasn't it? Did you enjoy it?

a)

KAREN No, I didn't. Most of it was really slow and the woman who played the main role was rubbish.

b)

KAREN Well, it was sort of interesting in parts. But quite honestly, I've seen better performances.

4

WAITER Did you enjoy your meal, sir?

a)

MAX It could have been a bit hotter. And unfortunately, the steak was on the tough side, too.

b)

MAX It was stone cold and the steak was tough.

CD1 20

We were planning to go to the cinema tomorrow.
I'd go for black instead if I were you.
We must all get together some time.
I think darker colours suit you better.
Quite honestly, I've seen better performances.

CD1 21

DAN So, what were you watching on telly last night, Sue?

SUE Oh, *Big Brother*, you know, you know I like that.

D Oh, reality TV. It's just everywhere you look on the television, reality TV, it's rubbish.

S It's just relaxation, sometimes you just want to put your feet up and let it wash over you.

D It's not. It's intellectually bankrupt and it's just rubbish.

S Well, I think it's fun and actually, sometimes you need to keep in touch with the youth of today, don't you, and they like this sort of thing, so reality TV is fine by me.

D Well, it's a sad indictment on society, frankly.

S Well, it's fun to see people outside their normal environment testing themselves.

D But they're not though, are they? They're not.

S Why not?

D It's aw, it's a tired template that's been used, that's provocative, it's there to create conflict, it's to see the worst in people. It's actually, it's poking fun at people, at their misery.

S Well they know what they are letting themselves in for, what's the problem?

D Well, more fool them frankly. Most of them are trying to get fame a shortcut way.

S What would you rather watch then?

D Well, I'd like to watch more sport and more comedy, frankly.

S There's enough sport on TV as it is. It's on all the time. What about some costume drama?

D Oh, that's a bit dull though isn't it, that's a bit heavy.

S Well, you say you want to be intellectually stimulated by the television, that's exactly what you want.

D No, actually, what I want is some good comedy for me to relax. And laugh.

S See, relaxing, just like reality TV.

D No, no, no, no, something that involves, you know, creativity. Something that's in, innovative, something that makes you laugh. That's not reality TV. Reality TV, as I said, it's poking fun.

S Well, each to their own.

CD1 23

PRESENTER 1 *Star Trek* was first shown in the 1960s, and then again in the 1980s, as a TV science-fiction show. The series was not only extremely popular but appears to have been the inspiration for a range of products which first appeared in the show as imaginative props.

PRESENTER 2 Was *Star Trek* the inspiration for cell phones? Apparently so. Dr Martin Cooper is considered the inventor of the first portable handset and the first person to make a call on a portable phone, in April 1973, much to the bewilderment of passers-by in a road in New York. The first call he made was to his rival, Joel Engel, who was the head of research at Bell Labs. Cooper was later to reveal that watching Captain Kirk talking into his communicator on the TV show *Star Trek* had inspired him to research the cell phone. The first phones weighed over a kilo compared to most modern phones that weigh a hundred grams or less.

Did *Star Trek* inspire Voyager 1 and 2 which were launched in 1977? Well, Dr Marc Raymon was five years old when he first watched *Star Trek* and became fascinated by the idea of space travel. He wanted to know how far into space we could go and he dreamed of being a science officer on the *Starship Enterprise*. Instead, he would become a senior science officer for NASA and was involved in the Voyager probes. Voyager 1 is now at the edge of the solar system and heading for interstellar space. Interestingly, following a letter campaign, NASA agreed to name its prototype space shuttle after the *Starship Enterprise*.

And was *Star Trek* the inspiration for MRI and CT scans? It probably was. Dr John Adler, professor at the Stanford University Medical Center, acknowledges that the non-invasive diagnostic technology used by *Star Trek's* medical officer, Dr McCoy, helped inspire a medical revolution. Medicine in the 1960s and 1970s was a world away from *Star Trek*. It involved messy, dangerous, exploratory surgery where surgeons would cut through tissue to discover what the problem was. The idea that diagnosis could be done the way Dr McCoy did it, quickly, painlessly and without a surgeon's knife, was something to strive for. In fact, Dr Adler has invented the 'CyberKnife' which can destroy cancerous cells by passing hundreds of beams of radiation through them.

Was *Star Trek* the inspiration behind the iPod? Well, *Star Trek* certainly inspired Steve Perlman who, back in the late '80s, was an employee at Apple Computer, Inc. While watching an episode of *Star Trek: The Next Generation* he saw something that fired his imagination. The robotic character, Data, was able to call up any music he wanted from his computer. Steve would later be part of a team that invented QuickTime technology which can select, store and play movies and audio files. It was this software that helped pave the way for the iPod.

CD1 24

Answers 1 were going to be 2 would go on 3 were to find out 4 were about to be 5 was just supposed to offer

CD1 25

INTERVIEWER Could you tell us, Andrew, is there still a difference between the tabloid newspapers and the so-called quality press in Britain?

ANDREW Oh yeah, there's a huge difference. I mean, traditionally you could see the difference straightaway because a tabloid paper was smaller, while the so-called quality press always tended to be bigger. However, nowadays, with so many people reading the news online, the physical difference is often irrelevant. But whether you read the news in a paper or online the tone of the tabloids and quality press hasn't changed. The quality press, for example *The Times*, still uses more serious language, they still use smaller headlines, they still present the news in a more sober kind of fashion. Whereas, a tabloid tends to shout at you a bit more, tends to attract attention using huge pictures, huge headlines – it tells you what to think and how to react. Also, the tabloids tend to have a a much bigger circulation – they have millions of readers whereas the quality press has hundreds of thousands, and that's, well, that's a sort of reflection of the kind of, the way society breaks up, you know – of the way society is constructed. The more intellectual news sources appeal to a lot fewer people than the more downmarket sources.

I And what kind of stories really sell news?

A Well, it depends what news source you're talking about, the, well you have to – as a journalist – think about who's reading your news when you're deciding how to prioritise your stories. The quality press tends to focus on the more serious stories – political stories especially are a great favourite for them to lead on. If you go right to the other end of the market with the downmarket, so-called red-top tabloids, they like TV stories, they like stories about film stars, they like stories about royals, they like crime stories, something with a much, sort of brasher, instant appeal. Our newspaper, the paper I work for, is somewhere in the middle of the market, so sometimes we'll 'splash' – the splash is the main story on the front page, it's a term that journalists use – sometimes we'll decide that the splash should be a political story, sometimes a crime story. We like family stories, we like stories that relate to the kind of people that are buying our paper, the middle-class families that we think are at the heart of our audience.

CD1 26

INTERVIEWER Clearly, the stories in different news sources are written in different ways. Could you explain to us how the journalists know what kind of language to use?

ANDREW As I mentioned earlier, the pictures are bigger, and the headlines are bigger in more downmarket news sources. But what you find when you get to read the actual story is that the language in a tabloid tends to be snappier, shorter words, shorter crisper sentences, what we call a sort of 'crash bang wallop' style, a sort of straight to the point without any elaboration, without any flamboyant sentences, without words that are too long. Most paragraphs – if you, if you look at a tabloid – most paragraphs are about 20 words, very few paragraphs are longer than 30, and some are as short as about 10. It means the story is easier to read, it has a faster pace, it's, it's more in tune with the kind of audience, with the kind of readership that a tabloid has. And if you see, if you read a story in the quality press, the paragraphs will be much longer and much harder work to get through. So, that's a, that's a really discernible difference.

CD1 27

INTERVIEWER Could you describe for us the process of deciding on which story to headline?

ANDREW Yes, I mean, this is probably the most exciting part of the job, deciding what the best story of the day is and how to present it. Every reporter wants to get his or her story to be headline news, you know, to be on the front page, so they'll be trying their hardest to convince the news editor that theirs is the best story and that's where it should go. So, reporters are trying their best to get the, well, to get everything they can out of a story to write it in the most exciting and accessible way so that they can get the support of the news editor.

I Thank you very much Andrew.

CD2 1 CD2 2 CD2 3

INTERVIEWER When you go to the cinema or watch telly and see all the people in crowd scenes, the chances are you never give them a second's thought. And yet for many people this is their job – they're extras, like Daniel and Kate, who are with us today. Good morning.

DANIEL Hi!

KATE Hi.

I Daniel, what makes people like yourself want to be an extra?

D Good question. Well, I guess I've always been keen on amateur dramatics and so, I suppose it's a way of keeping in contact with the acting world. Luckily, the working hours for my normal job are quite flexible, otherwise, I wouldn't be able to do it. You never know when you'll be needed on set.

I I suppose there's a lot of hanging around?

D Yeah, they're long hours, but I have no problems amusing myself. I'm a writer, so I always take my laptop with me and, well, just get on with my work.

I Now, you've appeared in some big films, haven't you? What's it like seeing yourself on the big screen?

D Well, half the time, I can't even spot myself, unless I really concentrate, but I'm usually in crowd scenes as a wedding guest, or a person in the street – you know, that kind of thing.

I Are there ever jobs when you are more than just a face in a crowd?

D I get given short scenes from time to time, when I'm a postman or a taxi driver, or whatever. Sometimes, I have to react to what someone says. I mean, you often find out that you've been edited out later, which can be disappointing, but it makes a change and you get paid more, so that's always welcome. The money's not bad at all really, for what you actually do.

I Do you have any hope you'll break into film acting yourself?

D No chance. It would be like being given wings and asked to fly.

I Kate, how did you end up being an extra?

K Well, I kind of fell into it. I once knew somebody who'd done it and I thought it would be a way of supplementing my income and enjoying myself at the same time.

I You do mostly TV work, don't you?

K Yes, you know, lots of soap operas, period dramas, that sort of thing.

I And what kind of people become extras?

K Oh, all sorts, from young drama students to solicitors on their day off, bored housewives, whoever. We do all share a common interest so it's a great opportunity for us all to meet and have a chat and a good laugh.

I Do you ever get the chance to meet the principal actors?

K Well, we're actually actively encouraged not to interact with them – they have a job to do. But we sometimes bump into them on set. The stars themselves are quite friendly on the whole – it's the minor actors who tend to be a bit standoffish.

I And are you treated well in general?

K Mostly. I think the money is reasonable. There's a lot of standing around, though, and there are times when you feel very tired.

I Is there a lot of stress on the set?

K If there are delays, nerves do get frayed as there's a sense that time and money is draining away. We aren't really affected though – we're not important enough!

I Are there any other rules about how you treat the actors?

K Not really, other than it's understood you let the crew and principals help themselves first in the canteen at lunchtme. But that's fair enough – it's common sense – they need to get back to work.

I Right. And do you enjoy it?

K I like the job itself, although the unpredictable hours can be a bit of a pain.

I What do you like about it?

K It's good being able to dip in and out of different worlds, like last week I was in a fire on an 18th-century ship.

CD2 5

INTERVIEWER Good morning. With us in the studio today are three young people about to leave sixth-form college. We talk to them about the difficult choices they have to make as they decide which university course to follow, or which job to go into. So, Claire, do you know what you want to do when you leave college?

CLAIRE Not really – it's something that I've struggled with for a long time, what I want to do with my life. The problem is there's so many possibilities out there, so many different options, and I think it's quite hard for people to decide, and to find out what the real world the, the real working world is like.

I So how are you trying to come to a decision?

C Well, recently, I've been trying to do lots of work experience in lots of different fields and talk to people in those different areas to try and gain an insight. I've looked into different options like teaching, publishing, I've done some charity work, so just basically trying to gain some experience.

I Is this working?

C Yes and no, I've certainly found some things that I don't want to do. And I've really enjoyed doing some work experience in a small publishing firm, so I'm thinking about that.

I So, Will, you're taking a gap year before going to university. Was that an easy decision to make?

WILL Not really – when I finished secondary school I didn't really know what I wanted to do at sixth form college let alone at university.

So, I kind of chose, I chose four subjects that I enjoyed for A Level and then chose to have a gap year because I thought that would give me an extra year to work out what I wanted to do. And I just wanted to have a gap year for a bit of time out really because things have been, well, there's been a lot of pressure for a lot of years, so I wanted to take some time out to work out completely what I wanted to do.

I And do you think you'll be using this year to look into your options?

W Absolutely, I've, I've now found a place at university to do sports science so I'm really glad I've got it sorted in the end.

I So, Charlie, do you know what you want to do when you leave college?

CHARLIE I do now. I, I want to do law at university and I've applied and, luckily got a place, but I made that decision after a lot of difficulty because I wanted to do English originally, but it was a much bigger step up from the English I'd been doing than I thought it would be, and I felt a little bit out of my depth, and I looked round universities thinking of doing English and it didn't click, it didn't feel right, and that's when I thought law is what I wanna do.

I And you're confident in your choice now?

CHARLIE Yeah, it feels, it feels a lot better and more right with me than, than English did. I've done a lot of research into it and I've gone to places like the Old Bailey in London and looked at law cases, and I found it very interesting. I've gone on law courses and, yeah it, well, it's a bit daunting but it, it definitely feels right.

CD2 6

1

JOSH It's totally ludicrous, isn't it really, I mean, the salaries these company directors and corporate lawyers and financial people in the City get paid, don't you think? I mean it's completely out of proportion to what they actually do, for one thing.

TRACEY Yeah. Not to mention the astronomical sum that footballers and film stars and so on get, too. I suppose it's all about market forces but it does seem very unfair.

J Well, it is, you know, when you consider that someone like a nurse or an ambulance driver gets paid a pittance – relatively – you know, for what they do and, I mean, how could we get along without them? And what about all these jobs nobody wants to do, but have to be done?

T Can you imagine having to clean the streets, or collect the rubbish or …

J That's exactly what I was trying to get at. I mean, they're horrible jobs, so … what I think is that anyone who has really, you know, a hard job should expect to get paid well for it. You look dubious, Liz.

LIZ Well, it's a difficult one, because well, historically people expect to get paid less if they've got no qualifications.

J But how come, though? Is it their fault if they're no good at exams, or financially they couldn't afford higher education, or if, you know, …

L Yeah, no of course not, but I don't understand how would it work in practice …

2

T Does what job you have matter that much anyway? I mean, there's a whole world out there beyond work. It's only a means to an end, so you can eat and stuff.

J For you, maybe. But for some people it's the be all and end all to earn a lot and get on.

T Yeah, but surely it's an interesting job that's the main thing, not …

J Well, yeah, I'm with you on that, but all I'm saying is many other people – for them, their job is the main thing in their life, it's how they define themselves.

T Well, they're saddos, if you ask me. They should get a life – find some interests. Well, that's why people get so stressed out and have to take so much time off work – because they work too hard and get things out of proportion.

L But, for some people they love their work and anyway, when you're young if you want to get on, you know, you have to put …

T Climb the career ladder, whoopee!

J Hang on. Carry on, Liz. You were saying?

L … well, you have to work long hours and put a lot in, or people think that you – well, you know, they, they won't give you promotion.

T Well so what?!

J You say that now, but wait until you want a nice house or a flash car or …

T Er, excuse me? It was you saying that what mattered was interest.

L Anyway, assuming you do want promotion, you usually have to …

3

L What I do feel strongly about is that employers make provision for working mothers.

J By 'provision' you mean … ?

L Well, for example so they can have flexibility, so if they have to, have to drop kids off at school or if one of them is ill they can work at home or if they …

T And allow more women to work part-time or, or job share.

J … or men of course!

L Yeah, right. How many men do you know who work part-time so that they can look after the kids?

J Ah. You've got me there! Well, perhaps they would if it was more accepted.

L That's just what I was going to say. It's a kind of chicken and egg situation. Until employers offer people more flexible hours, parents – well, mothers really – are stuck because they feel guilty working full-time but need to work for whatever reason and often, they have no choice anyway – they need the money.

T The problem is, people with no kids might turn round and say "Well, why should we cover for you? It's your choice to have children," and they might resent it if working mothers …

L Or fathers.

T … or fathers have special treatment.

J Oh, I don't know about that. I mean, after all, as a society we're all responsible for the future generation, aren't we? But it'd certainly be a hassle for employers to organise.

L Which is why it would have to be law that they did it. After all …

CD2 10

Listening Test (see Teacher's Book)

CD2 11

PETE I have a friend called Martina and she owns two rabbits. Not so strange in itself but she's got a habit of taking them everywhere she goes. So, a typical afternoon round a friend's house will consist of people crawling around in a neighbour's hedges looking for them. And then there's the chicken wire over her bookcases to stop the rabbits eating her books. And the thing that I'll never forget is the first time I met her. She came to the pub, dressed very glamorously – long coat and high heels, opened her coat and there hopping out of the top of her sweater were the two rabbits.

NATALIE Really! Blimey. I commute on the train to work every day and, on the way back home, there's a guy that gets on the train and he starts at one end of the platform. He, he hops on the train at the back end, and he patrols all the way up the carriages, through to the, the front of the train and then patrols back again until he finds the perfect seat. I think, I guess that's what he's looking for, I mean, I've been travelling for two years now. And, I've sort of…

KEITH He's not a ticket inspector then?

NATALIE No, no he's not a ticket inspector …

ALEX Undercover.

N … he's, you know, he does the same thing, day in day out and the only thing that I can put it down to is that he's just trying to find the best seat on the train. I thought that was quite bizarre.

A That is very bizarre. I used, I used to commute to Liverpool Street for ten years and you've just reminded me actually, there was a couple, who used to get on at King's Lynn and go all the way down to Liverpool Street, and she – the woman – had extraordinary eyebrows that were painted on with very, very heavy eyebrow pencil. But they used to have a, a bag of toy animals. Stuffed, you know, children's toys …

N Oh, OK.

A And they used to get them out and line them up. I've only just remembered this.

K How very strange.

A Yeah, and they used to line them up, so that the, the toys could look out of the window.

N That is very, very bizarre.

A It was extraordinary.

K Very odd behaviour.

A We all used to sit there just, ignoring them and nobody, you know, nobody, 'cos we're British, nobody would say anything.

N No.

A Like, why are you lining up all these toys? You're a grown-up couple.

N Gosh.

K My daughter does that but she's six, so I think it's more understandable.

A Yeah, quite.

K But she does, she does strange things, I mean she can, she, she collects pebbles which really winds us up, 'cos we've, she's just got her this really nice coat and she always like, she comes home from school and she's always got pockets and pockets full of pebbles. Grubby pebbles that just, make holes in the pockets and so on, you, you take, you know help her off with her coat and it's so heavy … We empty them every day we've got this great heap of pebbles in the garden. She collects them with her friends.

A You can get her to make a path one day.

K She collects with her friends, I think, and sort of compare them. And the other thing actually, recently, she went for a week and she insisted on putting on odd socks every morning.

N Really?

K Yeah, she wanted to put on different colour socks. It's obviously the height of fashion …

N Oh, wow.

A It's sweet though isn't it?

K … in her class at school.

CD2 13

GRAHAM Well, I've worked in advertising and marketing for about 20, 25 years, mostly on the copy-writing side. So, when we've come to plan campaigns, it's the words that make or break a campaign for me. And I was particularly impressed, it's a few years back now, but particularly impressed with the Coca-Cola campaign, which focused on the words 'It's the real thing'. At the time when it came out, I wondered how this would work but they used that phrase across TV advertising, billboards, on commercial radio, and I was particularly impressed, as I say, by the campaign because of the words 'It's the real thing'. The word 'it's' just implies that's part of everyday life. Coca-Cola, you don't have to use the name, in the actual slogan or the strapline they're using. Then you have 'the real thing'. The 'real' implying, well it's genuine, it's the real article, it's not, of course, their main opposition Pepsi Cola, it's, maybe it, it even suggests it's healthy and good for you. So 'the real thing' and then 'the thing', well, an everyday item, something that's part of your life. I just felt this worked so well, and people would say 'it's the real thing' and you just thought of Coca-Cola and you didn't need to say "Coca-Cola, the real thing", you just thought of the product when you saw the strapline or the phrase because you'd seen it over and over again. And that did work for a number of years, and I think there's still a lot of people around, if you say to them, "It's the real thing" they will think 'Coca-Cola' and they won't think about anything else. Even though that's a phrase, of course used generally in society and in language, in an everyday kind of way.

CD2 14

LINDSAY A successful advertising campaign that springs to my mind is the iPod campaign that was around a few years ago now – you know, the ones where there's a dark silhouette of a young, probably attractive, really trendy, urban person who's listening to some great funky music? And they're throwing themselves around, really enjoying themselves and it's, it's set against a really vivid background, kind of bright purple, bright blue, almost neon. And they've got the iPod in their hands with the white earphones going into their ears. And the, I think that the thing with the iPod is that it's really a design icon. It's such a simple design, but it's something that people recognise, almost instantly if you see their, well, someone wearing the earphones walking around the street then you know what product they have. And I think the adverts really really complement this because they, they show a lifestyle they; don't actually give any information about the product itself. It's more an image that people want. They want the product, they want this lifestyle and, you know, I love my iPod and for me, I may not be that young anymore but, you know, I want that kind of fashionable lifestyle and this wonderful fashion accessory. Erm, some of their more current ad campaigns have been a bit hit and miss in my opinion, but I think this was a really good, simple, effective advert that people remember and I'm pretty sure that advertising people since have probably been influenced by it in designing campaigns for their own products.

CD2 15

JOHN A good story has to have several standard components – it's got to have a beginning, it's got to have a middle, and it's got to have an end. And the way that works is you have something that sets the story in its situation and context, and you can call that the premise, and the character is speaking, or the narrator is telling you about the character, and then someone else maybe comes in and the situation gets complicated. This is known as the development, and whatever then happens makes the story even more interesting, that's a complication and then something gets sorted out and you have the ending – the resolution. And these elements can be mixed up in any length and shape, and a joke can be a story, or a narrative can be a story, or just someone telling something that happened to them that morning can be a story. Anything can be a story, but if you're putting it on the radio it needs to hook the listener in straight away. So, you've got to have something to catch their attention, and that is where the interest is struck up and you've got to maintain the interest, build up the tension until somewhere along the line, the reader is ready for the story to come to an ending – positive, negative, happy ending, sad ending or even a laugh – because a joke is a story as well.

CD2 16

"Are you Steve?" asked the man, who was about a foot taller than me. I looked up at him, and nodded uncertainly.
"Julie said you'd be coming." he muttered, and offered me his hand. A big, strong hand. I shook it. "Carlos," he said, then turned his back and went inside the restaurant. "Come in."

I followed him inside the restaurant. It was all very elegant, with tables prepared, and soft lighting. Only two things were missing: people eating, and Julie.
"Where's your guitar?" said Carlos.
"Pardon?" I replied.
"The guitar. Julie said you were a guitar player."
"Am I? Did she?" I stammered back. Carlos loomed over me like a giant.
"You haven't brought your guitar?" He folded his arms and looked at me like I'd ruined his day. He sighed bitterly and stormed off into a back room. I was left standing in the deserted restaurant.

I wondered if I should quickly escape now before anything else happened. What was Carlos going to do next? Was I in the wrong restaurant? Before I could formulate an effective plan, the front door opened and Julie ran in, out of breath. She looked just as lovely as the night before. I wanted to say something charming and friendly, but all I could manage was "Uh, hi."

"Steve!" she exclaimed. "You're here! Great! Where's your guitar?"

I still wasn't precisely sure why people kept on asking me this question. But once again, my thought processes were disturbed when Carlos marched back into the room, brandishing a battered old guitar. It had seen better days.
"It's not perfect, but you'll have to use this," he muttered, brandishing the guitar at me.

To add to my confusion, Julie went to Carlos and hugged him, kissed him on the cheek, and held his arm. They stood next to each other, looking at me expectantly. I meekly took the guitar and looked at it like I'd never seen one before.

After what seemed like hours, Julie asked, "Well, Steve? What do you think?" To be honest, the only thought in my head was that Julie and Carlos were clearly a couple. So what was I doing here?

"You said you wanted to stay longer on the island," said Julie, as if she'd read my mind. "And you're a brilliant guitarist," she reminded me. Oh yes, I might accidentally have exaggerated my musical skills last night. I didn't realise I was going to be tested on it the next day. "So, we thought we'd offer you a job! We need something to draw the customers in. Live music. That's what we thought, isn't it, Carlos?" Julie looked up adoringly at Carlos, who in turn looked at me like a stray dog had just walked into his fantastic restaurant.

Well, needless to say, the evening started off quite badly, and quickly got worse. Some customers did appear that evening – two elderly tourists – and I thought I played my only two tunes very well. And when I finished, I played them again. The couple clapped politely. And quickly left. I made up a story that the guitar was so old that I couldn't play all my other tunes.

At the end of the evening, I handed the guitar back to Carlos, and he offered me a free dinner for all my 'hard work'. But I made my excuses, and left the restaurant as quickly as I could, without properly saying goodbye to Julie.

The next evening, I was back in the club with my friends. There was still something missing but my dancing was better than ever.

CD2 17

JOHN When you're telling a story on the radio, the first and most important thing is to get the listener involved. Get the listener listening, and you do that with various tricks and techniques and pauses and rhythm and stress. And you've got a range of words: adverbs, adjectives, even the verbs, to keep the story moving, to keep it lively. The livelier your choice of words, the more interested the listener is going to be and you've got to vary the pace, you've got to vary the stress, you've got to build up the tension, perhaps make it scary, or perhaps hold something back to surprise the listener with a twist in the tail if the story is going to go in that direction. The tone of the story is going to be judged by the listener from your tone of voice as you tell the story. So, is it going to be gripping and exciting, or is it going to be light and frivolous? Is it going to be serious, is it going to be scary? What kind of atmosphere do you want to create with your voice and with the range of vocabulary that you are offering in your telling of this story? You've got to make it sound as if it has the elements we mentioned earlier – the beginning, the middle, the end – but you also have to give it a flow to make sure the listener is carried along with your telling of the story, and make sure that the listener enjoys it.

CD2 18

INTERVIEWER Good morning! In the studio with us today we have Zoë Powell, a freelance science journalist. Zoë has recently been working on a TV documentary in which potential criminals try to outwit a forensic scientist and get away with it. Zoë, I'm sure our listeners would find it very useful to hear how they did it!

ZOË Interesting, rather than useful, I hope! Well, at one time, if someone committed a crime, you didn't have as much to go on. These days, of course, techniques are much more sophisticated. Recently, for example, there was the famous case when a kidnapping was solved 20 years later, after the seal of an envelope was re-examined and the tiniest trace of dried saliva found there.

I So, if the kidnapper hadn't licked the envelope … ?

Z He wouldn't be in prison now, exactly. You have to be so careful not to leave any trace of yourself at all.

I Which is easier said than done, presumably, since our DNA is in virtually every cell in our body.

Z Indeed. If a person doesn't want to leave forensic evidence, they should just slide through a window because any broken glass, or other damage for that matter – scratched paint, for example – comes in very handy to forensic scientists. One burglar, who was found recently through his DNA, would have got away with it completely if he hadn't been sweating at the time.

I And if I were committing a burglary, I'd be better off wearing gloves, of course, so as not to leave fingerprints.

Z Yes, providing you didn't leave fibres behind as these can also be traced fairly easily. It's the same with socks.

I So, best to go barefoot, then?

Z Ah, but even the tiniest fragment of skin is enough to match you, so you'd actually be better off covering up as much as possible!

I But can't you can get round the problem by wearing smooth clothes like silk?

Z Absolutely!

I No woolly gloves and socks, then.

Z And needless to say, if you're going to burgle a house, you'll obviously try not to draw attention to yourself. Don't stagger out with a huge television, or whatever. Do it quietly. And avoid the temptation to rush out and sell whatever you've stolen right away!

CD2 19

INTERVIEWER And what does a would-be murderer have to bear in mind?

ZOË Well, what's similar about most killers is they are cool, detached sort of people. They seem to be able to carry on as if nothing's happened, behaving perfectly normally. In fact, if they weren't such good actors most of them would probably have been found out much earlier.

I So, a lot of it comes down to personality?

Z Yes, and you obviously need a water-tight alibi, too. And having a few maggots to hand to confuse the scientists might help.

I Maggots?

Z Yes, forensic scientists use creepy crawlies to help them work out the time and place of death. By counting how many maggots are on a body, and how mature they are, you can have a pretty good idea of when someone died. Unless the murderer has put them there themselves, of course!

I You're joking!

Z It has been known. And flies are useful, too. The kind of place you're in will attract different kinds of flies, so if you found a body in the countryside with urban flies on it, the murder would probably have been committed in the city.

I That's incredible!

Z Then obviously, you also have to destroy your weapon, or at least get rid of any distinguishing marks.

I If you'd used poison, there wouldn't be a weapon as such, would there?

Z Yes, but the thing with poison is it's actually quite easy to find out where it was obtained and trace it back to the suspect. Actually, the ideal weapon is one which destroys its own evidence.

I Such as?

Z Well, for example, you could use an icicle, which of course will then melt.

I So, if anyone happens to come across a body next to a small puddle of water, you'll know what's happened!

Z Thankfully, violent crimes are still relatively rare. But should any of your listeners be considering committing a crime, be careful – scientific advances are making the likelihood of detection more and more probable every day!

I Indeed. Anyway, if you tune in to our programme …

CD2 21

INTERVIEWER In your opinion, how much state intervention should there be in people's everyday lives?

STEFANO I think that, basically, if the state intervenes, for example, to ban smoking from enclosed public places, that's, that's a good idea. It's been proved that passive smoking is harmful for people and so, it's important that the government prevents this. People are free to smoke outside. And, so, there's no [not] an excessive limit in their liberties. I do agree when smoking is banned from enclosed places, but of course, I wouldn't agree if the government ruled that people are not allowed to, for example, to smoke in a public park – that would be definitely too drastic.

HILTRUD In the case of rubbish, there clearly has to be more state intervention because, rubbish is piling up and landfill sites are running out. So, we need to do something and, charging for rubbish seems to me a good idea. It is fairer because people pay for what they throw away, and it is also effective.

JUSTYNA I also agree with a certain degree of state intervention in areas like health or environmental issues. However, when it comes to the state intervening in people's lifestyles, for example, promoting marriage over other types of partnership, I think it is highly unfair and, for example, in England, there is a debate going on about tax exemptions for married people, which I think is a terrible example of bias against other partnerships and relationships. This basically means that people who want to benefit from tax exemptions will have to forsake their, their choice of lifestyle, and for example, get married. I think this is a state intervention gone too far.

CD2 22

POLICEMAN Right, Mike, could we just go over this one more time?

MIKE When are you going to realise it's useless to keep grilling me about this? I've told you everything I know. I went round to a friend's. I got back home late. There'd been a break-in and police were swarming all over the flat. End of!

PM You see, it all strikes me as very odd.

M What does?

PM Well, that it's on that particular night you suddenly take it into your head to go and visit your ex-girlfriend.

M So what? Can't people stay friends?

POLICEWOMAN A convenient alibi, though, isn't it? Her living just opposite, right on the doorstep, and all.

M If you say so.

PW Anyway, you say you went out at about 7.30. Isn't this about the time George usually goes out? He never stays in on a Friday evening, does he?

M How should I know? We're not joined at the hip, you know.

PW Well, that's not what we've heard. We've heard you're always out together. Anyway, just by chance that's the night you decided not to go out with him. Isn't that a coincidence? Wouldn't have had anything to do with the £2,000 in cash he'd been paid that day for a building job, by any chance?

M How much?

PM Oh, come on, Mike. We weren't born yesterday! You knew he'd stashed it away somewhere. And who else would have known his secret hiding place under the stairs?

M You tell me, since you obviously know all the answers.

PM Anyway, you're still saying that you stayed at Emma's the evening the money was stolen?

M Apart from when I nipped out to get a pizza.

PW I? Right, so you went out on your own, did you?

M Is that a crime? Emma had already eaten.

PW How come? You said she was expecting you.

M Dunno. Ask her.

PM And when was it you went out, exactly?

M Around eight – give or take five minutes.

PM Took the opportunity to go back to your flat, did you?

M Are you serious? Why would I want to do that?

PM Well, that's what we'd like to know. But your neighbour swears she saw you going in around 8.20. Her dog was barking, so she looked to see what was going on.

M She would! She's a nosy old bag, and as blind as a bat at the best of times.

PM So, you're saying you didn't go back?

M That's right.

PW So, it's just a coincidence that we found most of a pizza in the bin at your flat, is it?

M Must be.

PM And, when you got back to Emma's, what did you do then?

M Watched the end of that new soap opera *Hospitals*.

PM Oh yeah? I saw a bit of that. But I missed the end. What happened?

M Er, well, E, Emma was going on about something so I lost track of what was happening.

PW Stayed late at Emma's, did you?

M Quite late. Time flies when you're having fun.

PW Mmm. Expensive phone you've got there.

M It was a present from my mum.

PW No fun, is it – being unemployed? Especially for a bright kid like you. Must have hit you hard, losing your job. Must be tempting to get money when you can.

M Look, you've got nothing on me and you know it! Why don't you just leave me alone?

CD2 23

1
POLICEMAN You see, it all strikes me as very odd.
MIKE What does?

2
POLICEWOMAN Anyway, you say you went out at about 7.30. Isn't this about the time George usually goes out? He never stays in on a Friday evening, does he?

3
POLICEWOMAN Well, that's not what we've heard. We've heard you're always out together. Anyway, just by chance that's the night you decided *not* to go out with him. Isn't that a coincidence? Wouldn't have had anything to do with the £2,000 in cash he'd been paid that day for a building job, by any chance?
MIKE *How* much?

4
MIKE Apart from when I nipped out to get a pizza.
POLICEWOMAN I? Right, so you went out on your own, did you?

5
MIKE Is that a crime? Emma had already eaten.
POLICEWOMAN How come? You said she was expecting you.

CD2 24

1
POLICEMAN Right, Mike, could we just go over this one more time?

2
POLICEWOMAN Anyway, you say you went out at about 7.30. Isn't this about the time George usually goes out? He never stays in on a Friday evening, does he?
MIKE How should I know? We're not joined at the hip, you know.
POLICEMAN Well, that it's on that particular night you suddenly take it into your head to go and visit your ex-girlfriend.
MIKE So what? Can't people stay friends?

3
POLICEWOMAN Well, that's not what we've heard. We've heard you're always out together. Anyway, just by chance that's the night you decided *not* to go out with him. Isn't that a coincidence? Wouldn't have had anything to do with the £2,000 in cash he'd been paid that day for a building job, by any chance?

4
POLICEWOMAN Anyway, you say you went out at about 7.30. Isn't this about the time George usually goes out? He never stays in on a Friday evening, does he?

CD2 25

1
A I haven't got any money on me!
B Isn't that a surprise?

2
A So we're meeting at nine, are we?
B Yes. Sorry, I've forgotten already. Where are we meeting?

3
A Could you put everything in the dishwasher, please?
B Why should I always do it?

4
A Thank goodness it's arrived at last!
B What has?

5
A I heard from Terri last night.
B Oh, so she finally decided to phone, did she?

6
A I believe 200 people are coming to the wedding.
B Are you sure?

7
A I need some money.
B Oh you do, do you?

CD3 1 **CD3 2**

EDDY CANFOR-DUMAS One person that I think is very inspirational, is a woman called Hazel Henderson and the reason her story has struck me so strongly is because she was an ordinary person who did something extraordinary. She was born before the Second World War and she had a very typical upbringing for a, a young girl. She went to school and hated school – couldn't wait to leave. She left as soon as she could without any qualifications and she got a job in a local dress shop – she was born in Bristol and brought up in Bristol. And she enjoyed that for a time, but then started to think that the world held other possibilities. So, she took a job in a hotel as a receptionist, enjoyed that, and then realised that because hotels are around the world she could get a job elsewhere. So, she applied for and got a job in New York and enjoyed that very much and met an American man, fell in love, married had a family. And one day she noticed that her, her young child who would play everyday in a, in a local park in New York was covered in soot and in fact it was quite typical that she would come home very dirty, and she'd have to put her in a bath and scrub her to, to get this dirt off her. So, she went to investigate where the soot was coming from and saw that all of the equipment in the, the playground was covered in soot. And the reason for this was because the, the quality of the air in New York was so poor from the pollution of the cars and also there were lots and lots of incinerators that burnt rubbish. So, she started to talk to some of the other mothers whose children played in the park and they also saw this was a, a problem. But she did some investigating and discovered that the, the, the town hall in, in New York used to measure, every day, the quality of the air. She'd written to the, the mayor of New York about pollution in New York and he said actually the pollution wasn't pollution it was mist rolling in from the sea, but she didn't take this for the answer. So she did this investigation and she found that, that the, the air was measured and she asked that this information be made public as part of the, the daily weather forecast. But she then did some more research and found that there was a federal law about information, that you know, about public health and so on. So, she used this to persuade ABC, one of the, the networks to, to take this. Eventually, they, they agreed 'cos they saw that there was a, a need. And very soon every media outlet in New York City was carrying this information. And of course once it started in New York it travelled across the country to all sorts of other cities, and eventually it travelled around the world. So the, the daily pollution in, index that you have in, in weather forecasts all comes about because of one woman. The great thing about Hazel Henderson is that she didn't stop there. She's an advisor to governments and organisations in 30 countries around the world, and her articles appear regularly in 400 newspapers around the world. So again, this all comes about through one ordinary woman deciding that she wasn't going to put up with what her daughter was experiencing in the local park and taking it on, and deciding to make a, a real difference.

CD3 3

ANNOUNCER And now, *Science Today*, introduced by Simon Grey.
PRESENTER Today we are looking at emotions and with me in the studio are our resident scientists Dr Aaron Palmer and Dr Marion Bates. First Aaron, we hear people refer to basic emotions. What are they exactly?
AARON Well in the 1970s a Dr Ekman from the University of California devised a list of six basic emotions, which are: anger, disgust, fear, joy, sadness and surprise.
P And are these emotions common to all human beings?
A I think it's fair to say most members of the scientific community agree that, yes, basic emotions are universal.
P But men don't experience the same emotions as women, do they?
A Whoever said that is wrong. All human beings experience the same basic emotions. They may choose to express their emotions differently.
P OK, so can you explain how Ekman arrived at this list?
A Well, initially he based his theory on cross-cultural research done on a tribe in Papua New Guinea. It was a completely isolated tribe; they still used stone to make tools and weapons. And Ekman found that the people from this tribe could reliably identify six facial expressions of emotion. To do this he used photographs of people from around the world. And they could identify all the basic emotions from the photographs, even though they'd had absolutely no contact with any other culture before.
MARION Yes, in fact, wherever this experiment was carried out, the results were the same. Whoever saw the photos identified the same emotions. Ekman's discovery showed that the facial expressions associated with these basic emotions are universal. He therefore concluded that humans are born with the ability to recognise them in others.
A Of course, our ancestors relied on these basic emotions to stay alive. The survival value of emotions like fear, disgust and joy are still obvious. Whenever you come across something that frightens you, run away from it; whenever you come across something that disgusts you, don't eat it; whatever gives you pleasure, do more of it, etc. But beyond these basic emotions there are others which are referred to as 'higher emotions'.

P And they are?

A Well, these are not as well defined as the basic ones but they include such things as guilt, embarrassment, shame, pride, sympathy. These are emotions which are thought to be confined to, if not humans alone, then to a subset of large-brained mammals, several of whom are related to humans.

P So, what do these 'higher emotions' have in common?

M Well, with these emotions it isn't just what the person experiencing the emotion actually feels. For example, in the case of fear, the person's body reacts, the heart starts pumping faster, you might start sweating, etc. Higher emotions, on the other hand, are triggered by what other people might be thinking about you.

P Can you give an example?

M OK. Well, let's take embarrassment and, let's take a situation like, say, spilling coffee all over yourself. Now, whenever you do this in private, say, in your own kitchen, and however many times you do it, it's unlikely to cause embarrassment. But if you spilt coffee all over yourself in a very public place, you might well feel embarrassed.

P So, you're saying there isn't embarrassment in the act itself, but in what others might think of you?

M Yes, exactly, and that's the difference between higher and basic emotions.

P OK, I can see that with embarrassment, but is it the same with guilt or pride? Do we only feel guilty or proud when someone else witnesses the act and … ?

CD3 5

INTERVIEWER Do you think that being a man or a woman has ever stopped you from doing something you wanted to do? And if you could live your life again as a man or a woman, which would you choose and why?

BANA Well, actually, I faced this situation quite recently when I wanted to travel. To go abroad to study for several years. For a few girls in my country – in Saudi Arabia – you are part of a circle of people, of girls, and you cannot break that circle. So that's how it was for me. So, if you want to travel with your friends, there are several conditions for doing that if you are a girl. Like, if my brother wants to travel with his friends, that's OK, but if I want to travel with my friends, a parent or another adult should be with us to protect us, because we are not as strong as boys. But in fact, I *did* travel alone. I came here alone. And I survived! It's been a good experience, actually. If I could live my life again, I would choose to be a woman because I like being a woman! When I mix with men I notice a lot of differences. And we're kind and warm-hearted and we care about people, you know … yes, it's nice being a woman!

BOB I've never really thought about it. Everything I've sort of wanted to do has always been from a male perspective. So, I don't know any other way of behaving other than being a man. No, all the things like sport and work and that, I've never had any problems with – it's all flowed probably from being, well, a man, I guess, so no, I don't think it's hindered me at all. Definitely, I'm happy staying a man, I real, you know, I really enjoy it. But if for a day or two I could come back as a woman, just to gain, gain a greater understanding or empathy, then I could probably do that. As long as I could revert back to being a man … at will.

MICK Well, yeah funnily enough the one thing that I cannot do and probably will never be able to do unless science progresses far beyond I imagine it will, is give birth. It's something that biologically, obviously I can't do. And it is something I do think about. I have lots of female friends that have got babies and have given birth and have said that it's the hardest thing but it's also the most rewarding thing they have ever done in their life. And like I say, it's something that I will never ever be able to do. In some aspects I wish I was a seahorse, 'cos seahorses are the only mammal where the male gives birth. But having said all that, if I were to come back, I think I probably still would be a man.

KAY Well, when I think about my childhood I was at a huge disadvantage being a girl 'cos I was brought up in a house of brothers and I desperately wanted to join in with the football. And I think I would have been really rather good at it, but I wasn't allowed. They wouldn't, they wouldn't let me join in ever and I ended up doing ballet, which of course I wasn't good enough at. But I think I would have been a, a pretty good footballer one way and another. And, and I love the game; I really enjoy it. So that's, that would have been a, a good reason to be a fella. And if I was to live my life again, I think, I think I probably would try it as a male. One reason being that you wouldn't have to queue up in the toilets. And they only have to, they only have to think of one thing at a time – men.

JOEY It hasn't ever stopped me from doing anything I've wanted to do, but being a woman makes life harder and more complicated in that you're trying to do a job and you're also having to look after your family. And I have definitely seen with women that I work with, trying to juggle those two things can be quite difficult and it can hold up their careers or make them feel that they're not successful at doing both things at once. I'd quite like to be a man to see what it's like, but I think I'd choose to be a woman because I think women are better communicators and they have richer lives with their friends. And they can have it all really if they, they work at it.

LEO OK, so, actually, in my case, being a man has never stopped me doing anything I wanted to do because I have always liked things like karate, judo, tennis, rugby … really male sports, or hobbies like the guitar, but the electric guitar, or the piano, but jazz piano, so I didn't have those kind of problems. But actually, I have a friend who wanted to do ballet – dancing – so he suffered a lot because of his father who, er, didn't want his teenage son doing ballet dancing. If I were to live my life again, I think I would like to be a man, because, er, I come from a Sicilian family and we have some values, which are not macho, but that the man is responsible and has to take care of the family. And I like responsibilities. Actually, I think nowadays there's not much difference between men and women. Not like there was before. So, I don't think it's better to be a man or a woman, it's just that I feel comfortable as a man, and I like making other people feel comfortable.

CD3 6

CATE 'Money can't buy you happiness' is actually a statement I think I would have to agree with. I recog, I mean, I recognise that we need money, we do need money for our basic needs, but money is not the route to happiness. I think there are, there are other factors that play far more important roles.

MAUREEN I know a lot of people say that, Cate, but then they're thinking of possessions and things, and sure possessions can't ultimately buy you happiness. But maybe it's the opportunities that, that having money give you that makes me think money *can* buy you happiness. You know, it can buy you time to do the things you want to do: travel, learn something new, spend time helping people, whatever. So, in that way, I think money really *can* buy you happiness. I'm not saying it always does.

C You mean, if you don't have to worry about money, that in itself allows you to do some of the things that might contribute towards your happiness. Is that what you're saying, Maureen?

M Sure. I think, yeah, you know, you could really become whatever you wanted to be if you have plenty of money. You know if, if rich people aren't happy then I don't have any sympathy for them 'cos they haven't used the opportunity they have to find what it is that *would* make them happy.

PETE Well, what about things that don't necessarily take a lot of money but still make you happy? One of the happiest moments in my life was when the football team I play for, we, we won a cup in an amateur tournament.

C And I expect you had a brilliant time.

P Yeah, that happened a few years ago, it was one of the happiest times I've ever had, and I shared it with 12 other people. *And* it didn't cost us a penny. It doesn't matter how wealthy you are, you can't buy that kind of feelgood factor. I mean, it's like what you say, Cate, I know a guy who worked in the City, you know, in the money markets and he worked all hours, and I mean all hours just to be able to buy some amazing home-entertainment system. That's all he dreamed of. And finally he got it, and he wasn't any happier.

M Yeah, but I wasn't saying that. That's back to possessions – I was saying money can let you do what you want to do and that could include, you know, giving it away like Bill Gates – you could become a better person, if you like.

C As I said earlier, I think we need *some* money. I would agree with that. Yeah. And not having money can really make you miserable, but …

P Yeah, I've been there, worrying about where the next penny comes from. It's no joke. So yes, money can free you from worries, but the question was, can it buy you happiness? I mean that's different.

M For me it isn't. And it's like when they say money can't buy you health – well, that's not true, either. You just have to look at how long people live in poor countries. I can't remember where it was, but I recently read about a place where the average life expectancy is 40-something.

P Yeah, I'm with you on that one.

M And when they say money can't buy you love? Again I think it can sometimes.

C Oh, I don't know about that!

P Well, I'd like to have loads of money just to check all this out.

M You mean, do some research?

C Yeah. Hear, hear!

CD3 9

ANNOUNCER And now *Spotlight* introduced by Kate Conrad. The subject of today's programme is Satish Kumar.

PRESENTER Back in the early 1960s in Europe, the UK and the US, there were many community-led campaigns against nuclear weapons, and Satish Kumar wanted to be part of this peace movement. So he and a friend planned to leave their native home of India and walk round the world for peace, visiting the heads of state in Moscow, Paris, London and Washington. Before they left India, one of Satish's teachers told them not to take any money with them on their journey. His reason was this: at the end of each day after they had walked 20 or 30 miles Satish and his friend would be exhausted, and if they had money, they'd look for a restaurant and a bed for the night. If they did this, the teacher said, they wouldn't meet anyone and they wouldn't pass on their message. However, if they had nothing at all, they would be forced to rely on the kindness of strangers, who were bound to ask them why they were making this journey. So the two men, who weren't particularly money-minded anyway, set off without any means of paying for anything whatsoever, which meant their journey was totally unpredictable.

CD3 10

PRESENTER And, as we might imagine, their 8,000 mile walk certainly wasn't entirely stress-free. It took Satish and his companion through deserts, mountains, storms, snow and blazing heat. They were thrown into jail in France, they faced a gun in the US, but nothing put them off their mission for peace. In fact, their determination was made even stronger when, on their way to Moscow, they met two women who worked in a tea factory. After Satish explained why they were doing the walk, one of the women gave them four small packets of tea, one to be delivered to each of the leaders of the four nuclear powers with this message: "When you think you need to press the nuclear button, stop for a minute and have a fresh cup of tea." Satish and his friend did eventually deliver 'peace tea' to the leaders of the four nuclear powers and their journey is chronicled in Satish's book, *No Destination*. They began their journey at the grave of Gandhi in India and the journey ended at the grave of John F Kennedy in the US. And it's noteworthy that apart from crossing the English Channel and the Atlantic by boat, they really did walk all the way.

CD3 11

PRESENTER That journey taught Satish a great deal. In particular, he said he learned that if he travels as an Indian with an Indian flag he'll meet a Pakistani, or a Russian, or a US citizen carrying their flags. If he goes as a socialist, he'll meet a capitalist. If he goes as a brown man, he'll meet a white man or a black man, but if he travels through life as a human being, he'll meet only human beings. So, Satish concluded that if people could forget boundaries of country, religion, language and culture, then they could begin to understand that basically, we are the same, and as such we can learn to live with one another in peace.

CD3 12

TEACHER OK, so, why should anyone want to study economics? After all, it has been referred to as 'the gloomy science,' but believe me it isn't. Perhaps you think it relates only to finance and the business world. If so, it might surprise you to find out that economics is actually at the heart of everything we do. So, if you have an understanding of economics, you can use that information to really understand what's happening in our lives and around the world. So, on that note, I hope I can convince you –in three minutes – that rather than being gloomy, a knowledge of economics is in fact optimistic – it throws light on your world.
So, **I'm going to divide the talk into** three sections. **First of all**, how economics is related to real life. **Then I'll go on to** the intellectual challenge. **And finally**, I'll discuss future careers.

CD3 13

TEACHER Let's start with world issues. How many of you would like to make the world a better place? Let's take poverty. The continuing rise in world food prices is likely to lead to serious outbreaks of famine in less-developed countries which rely on rice and wheat. We hear a lot about this from politicians, yet its roots and consequences are economic. In fact, most of the world's problems can be understood in terms of economics. Obviously, it won't provide easy answers to these problems but it does clarify the issues. For example, we exploit the earth's resources – trees, oil, etc., – in order to create economic wealth, but we don't realise the real cost of doing so. What do we make plastic from? Oil, right? So, what is the real cost of, let's say, using a plastic bag? It isn't just the cost of producing it; you have to think about the cost of disposing of it when you throw it away. Economists can do that, they can analyse the full *social* costs of our actions, so we can make better choices like, should we have more airports or more railways? Should we use *nuclear* power or *renewable* energy? What are the real costs and benefits of each?
As I said before, economics won't provide *all* the answers but it will help you form balanced and informed opinions and with those, you may find solutions. **So, to sum up** this first section, if you have a wish to really understand and analyse the background to world issues and not just have an emotional response to them, then economics is absolutely essential.
Let's move on to the intellectual challenge involved in economics. It's a subject that suits people who are logical thinkers and who enjoy serious debate. It's for those who like creating and testing theories. I'm not saying it's easy. It does need a good understanding of mathematics and you do have to be able to communicate clearly in writing. But if you have these skills, then economics might just put them to the best use. And even if you aren't interested in the business world as such, because economics is related to most other subjects it will give you a deeper understanding of anything you want to study from politics to rocket science to fashion.
And finally, there's the small matter of how you're going to earn a living. Well, careers in business, finance and management obviously all have economics at their heart. However, careers in architecture or engineering also need an understanding of what we call opportunity cost, the building block of economics. Perhaps you're interested in agriculture, overseas aid, politics or journalism? Whatever your ambition, the study of economics provides a good grounding for these and many other careers.
So, in conclusion, if you want to study an interesting and interdisciplinary subject, which provides relevant knowledge and skills for your future career, go for economics. It's not gloomy at all. It is, in fact, a lively and exciting science; challenging and deeply satisfying. Right, does anyone have any questions?

CD3 14

PRESENTER Everything has to start somewhere, and some things which are a matter of course in our everyday lives have some interesting, not to say very strange origins.

MAN The first idea for ice cream, for example, can be traced back to the 1st century AD, when the Roman Emperor, Nero, ordered buckets of snow to be sent from the mountains in the north down to Rome, where it was mixed with red wine and honey and served at banquets. It's probably the Chinese, though, at around the same time, who invented the first form of the half-frozen fruit-flavoured ice cream we know today. When Marco Polo returned from the Far East in the 13th century he was a mine of information about how to make ice cream from snow, fruit juice and fruit pulp. As a result, it became popular in Europe, although it wasn't until the end of the 19th century that ice cream became a treat for ordinary people.

WOMAN Turning to drinks, tea is something we'd find very difficult to do without in Britain, and this has an even stranger origin. According to ancient myth, in 2737 BC, a handful of dried leaves from a bush blew into a pot of boiling water, into which the Chinese Emperor was staring. There is no record as to why the water was boiling, why the leaves were dried, or why the Emperor was staring into the pot, but the resulting brew was to be known henceforth as 'tchai'. Is there an element of truth in this story? Nobody really knows, but what we do know is that it was to become China's national drink during the 1st century AD.

M And how many of us realise that coffee was originally eaten, not drunk? Before 1000 AD, it appears that a tribe in Ethiopia began to eat ground coffee beans mixed with animal fat for extra energy. Rumour has it that a goatherd, Kaldi, had noticed his goats jumping around with more energy after chewing berries from wild coffee bushes, so he tried them and found the same happened to him. Whether this rumour is true or not is a matter of opinion but what we do know is that news of Kaldi's magic beans spread rapidly and coffee consumption became a national habit, later spreading throughout the world as a popular drink.

W Moving away from food and drink, skyscrapers are very common these days, and yet it wasn't until 1885 that the first one became the centre of attention in its home town of Chicago. Nowadays, the term 'skyscraper' is only applied to over 40 storeys. The Home Insurance Building in Chicago, with its ten storeys was to revolutionise urban life. Its construction set off a train of events, because higher buildings led to larger numbers of people living and working in the same areas.

M The first escalator actually started off as a

ride in an amusement park near New York in 1891. Jesse Reno pioneered a kind of moving ramp built at an angle of 25 degrees, which was a novelty for the 75,000 people who rode on it during the two weeks it was at the park. Another American inventor then developed a moving stairway with wooden steps and both were displayed at an international exhibition in Paris in 1900, where the word 'escalator' was coined. Ultimately, the two designs merged, a stroke of genius which created the escalator that is commonly used today.

P So, as you can see every invention tells a story! More on this can …

CD3 15

ADELA My brother Martin's a good example of someone who sticks with it. He's amazing. He's really bright. He actually studied Latin and Greek at Oxford University, but his real love is animation. Ever since he was a kid, he's always drawn funny little characters. And now that's his job. He's naturally talented, but he still puts hours and hours into every little animation film he does. Like, here it is Saturday night and I'm sure he'll be working. He might be creating a new character, or he could be working on his next short film. Clearly, he must enjoy what he does, why else would he work so hard? But I feel sorry for his girlfriend, it can't be easy having Martin as your partner. She has to be so patient. I mean, like for example, whenever they are about to go out, he always says, "Just need to finish this bit. It shouldn't take me long," and of course it always does. But when I see Martin giving his all to a project, it makes me realise if you want to be really good at something, then you've just got to work at it. People are just starting to notice his work so it shouldn't be long before he gets the recognition he deserves. Another thing, he's always so positive; like he's certain he'll find a buyer for his next animation film. So yes, being positive and sticking with it are important.

LOUIE Some famous golfer said this, I can't remember who. Anyway, when whoever it was was asked if he thought luck came into the game he said, yes, but he noticed that the harder he practised the luckier he became. I like that. And it's obvious, isn't it? Take world-class performers: Janine Jansen, for example, a famous violinist. I mean, you just know it won't have been an easy life for her. She must have devoted most of her life to practising. And though I'm no Janine Jansen, I've got some idea of what her life must have been like because I went to a school for gifted kids and I remember practising for hours every day. I may have had some natural talent, but who knows? But, I did practise six hours a day – at least – sometimes more. We all did at that school. I remember hearing a programme about gifted people once, it said that 'the gift' seemed to be they just didn't mind spending hours practising. And what really marks them out is that they don't ever give up. You know, there are points in life when most of us stop practising because we want to go out with our mates or spend more time with our children or whatever. Like me. I mean, I'm afraid I didn't stick with it – well, not enough to earn a living as a soloist. My father says I can't have wanted it badly enough or I wouldn't have given up. And I guess he's right.

CD3 16

MARIA PIA I think I had different strategies for different levels, really. At a very low level, I started off by memorising a lot of vocabulary and only after that I actually started looking into how the sentences [were] built – so the grammar side of things – that was clearly supplemented with an awful lot of grammar exercise, which is always very important. But, it's quite interesting 'cos it wasn't, the memorising's always worked for me, and not only in learning English but also learning other languages – Russian, for example. But at a higher level, I think things change quite a lot. The thing, the things I've always done are, for example, reading the papers. I think that's very, very important – it just not only helps you to learn new words, especially if you start reading the big, the big newspapers, but you can also keep up with what's going on in the country, you know, where the language you're learning is spoken. But, in addition to normal newspapers, I think it's quite important to remember that language is changing at all times. So, for example, you know, reading the classics has always been one of my passions, which is absolutely, you know, it's absolutely brilliant and you can learn so much from those books, but you have to remember that you run the risk of using words which are terribly out-of-date, and you end up speaking like Jane Austen, which I almost did at some point in my language learning! So, just reading magazines, for example, is a perfect way to keep up-to-date with the current language and new terminology, and so is using the Internet. I found the Internet very, very useful at a higher level. Also, the other thing is, to be honest, watch television and listen to the radio. In England, there's so many local and regional accents, and so you just learn to hear the different ways of pronouncing words. And the other thing when you learn new words, I've always tried to use them and in conversations always bring them up, and for me it was a very easy way to remember new words. I used to have – I don't do this any more – but I used to have a little, like little notebook, with an alphabetical order, it was like one of those booklets you buy for telephone numbers, and every time I came across a new word, **I would just jot it down in my little book**, and just maybe writing it would help me memorise it … a little bit, a little bit quicker, little bit faster so at the end of this, my period of studies, I actually ended up with my own little dictionary. But I suppose the main thing is, just try and speak as much as you can. You can do a lot of grammar work, you can do a lot of lang, take a lot of language lessons but I think it's very important to try and put into practice what you've learned from [on] the books and maybe just depends, it's just the kind of person I am, but **I'm a very gregarious learner** I think, so going out, meeting people, even, you know, find myself an English husband, you know, just try and interact with other people as much as possible and, the more you speak, the better the language skills will be, I think.

CD3 17

BRUCE Yes, I, I've tried to learn various languages at different points of my life, including French, Italian, Mandarin and Arabic, all with rather different levels of success. I think when starting out, I found the classroom experience very helpful. I enjoy the sort of, the sociable nature of learning in a group, and being instructed by, by you know, a professional. However, as I move up into, sort of, intermediate, good intermediate level, I prefer to work more independently. What's been really useful for me is, is reading – **anything from trashy magazines to crime novels** to love stories, even actually things in, in translation have been quite good, because translators tend to simplify the original language, also reading newspapers. Because I think in this way, you, you acquire language a bit like a sponge acquires water, so you absorb new vocabulary, you consolidate your knowledge of grammar, you just get a feel for the right word in the right place.

I also like to listen a lot, so I buy CDs occasionally or download stuff to my iPod so I can listen in the car, or when out for a walk. I go and see foreign films when, when possible – I *hate* anything that's dubbed, you know, I really think that spoils it. But it all takes effort and I think people tend to underestimate the amount of time it takes to, to learn a language. Yeah, having said that, you know, I do feel I ought to do more grammar exercises 'cos **I'm still a bit woolly about some of the grammar.** I do like to learn new vocabulary and I often put a, I look up words in a dictionary and I put a tick next to the word when I look it up so if I have to look it up *again* and I already see a tick, I know I really have to have to learn it because it's a high-frequency word. And, you know, you just have to go for it. I think people are actually quite tolerant of you, when you try to speak their language. They don't mind you making mistakes, so yeah, just go out and be creative with the language, even. There was a great Irish writer called Samuel Beckett and **he used to write in English, and then he switched to French** as he found it gave him more freedom to express himself away from the, the constraints of the English language. Now how amazing is that?!

I think once you've got to an advanced level, you need to leave the classroom behind, really. I mean, language learning doesn't stop there, there's a whole load of things to learn, but you have to go out and do it by yourself and interact with people and do all these things like reading and listening by yourself.

CD3 18

Listening Test (see Teacher's Book)